THE **HACKED** WORLD ORDER

THE **HACKED** WORLD ORDER

HOW NATIONS FIGHT, TRADE, MANEUVER,
AND MANIPULATE IN THE DIGITAL AGE

ADAM SEGAL

A COUNCIL ON FOREIGN RELATIONS BOOK

PUBLICAFFAIRS
NEW YORK

PublicAffairs books are available at special discounts for bulk purchases in the U.S. by corporations, institutions, and other organizations. For more information, please contact the Special Markets Department at the Perseus Books Group, 2300 Chestnut Street, Suite 200, Philadelphia, PA 19103, call (800) 810-4145, ext. 5000, or e-mail special.markets@perseus books.com.

Book design by Jack Lenzo

Library of Congress Cataloging-in-Publication Data
Names: Segal, Adam, 1968– author.
Title: The hacked world order : how nations fight, trade, maneuver, and
    manipulate in the digital age / Adam Segal.
Description: New York : PublicAffairs, 2016. | Includes bibliographical
    references and index.
Identifiers: LCCN 2015030885| ISBN 9781610394154 (hardback) | ISBN
    9781610394161 (ebook)
Subjects: LCSH: Internet and international relations. | Technology and
    international relations. | Internet in espionage. | Cyberterrorism. |
    Cyberspace—Political aspects. | Hacking—Political aspects. | BISAC:
    POLITICAL SCIENCE / International Relations / General. | POLITICAL SCIENCE
    / Political Freedom & Security / International Security. | COMPUTERS /
    Internet / Security.
Classification: LCC JZ1254 .S44 2016 | DDC 327.10285/4678—dc23 LC record available at
http://lccn.loc.gov/2015030885

First Edition
10 9 8 7 6 5 4 3 2 1

For my children, Lily and Noah Segal

CONTENTS

· ·

Chapter 1

THE HACKED
WORLD ORDER

· ·

J ust as historians consider 1947 as the year that two clear sides in the Cold War emerged, we will look back at the year that stretches roughly from June 2012 to June 2013 as Year Zero in the battle over cyberspace. It was by no means the first year to witness an important cyberattack or massive data breach; those had arguably happened several times before. In the 1990s the United States used cyber weapons against Serbia, and in 2007 hackers stole credit and debit card information from at least 45 million shoppers at T.J.Maxx and Marshalls. In 2008 hackers, suspected to be working with the Russian intelligence services, breached the Pentagon's classified networks. But it was in 2012 that nation-states around the world visibly reasserted their control over the flow of data and information in search of power, wealth, and influence, finally laying to rest the already battered myth of cyberspace as a digital utopia, free of conventional geopolitics. The assault on this vision was comprehensive, global, and persistent.

The conflict in cyberspace will only become more belligerent, the stakes more consequential. An estimated 75 percent of the world's population now has access to a mobile phone, and the Internet connects 40 percent of the planet's population, roughly 2.7 billion people. Information and communications networks are embedded in our political, economic, and social lives. Individuals and civil society now participate in global politics in new ways, but sovereign states can do astonishing and terrifying things that no collection of citizens or subjects can carry

1

out. We will all be caught in the fallout as the great powers, and many of the lesser ones, attack, surveil, influence, steal from, and trade with each other.

YEAR ZERO: A TIMELINE

Year Zero began with a newspaper article. In June 2012, US officials leaked details of a computer attack on Iran's nuclear program, code-named "Olympic Games," that had begun under President George W. Bush. For years, the United States had been trying to stop Iran from building a bomb through diplomatic pressure and financial sanctions. Someone, probably the Mossad, Israel's intelligence agency, had also been assassinating Iranian scientists: a remote-controlled bomb attached to a motorcycle killed Masoud Alimohammadi, a physics professor, just as he stepped outside his home in the north of Tehran. Cyberattacks formed a quieter, much less deadly component of this campaign.

The malware (malicious software) known as Stuxnet, allegedly developed by the United States in cooperation with Israel and first detected in 2010, surreptitiously slowed down and sped up the motors in Iranian centrifuges being used to enrich uranium and opened and closed valves that connected six cascades of centrifuges. Eventually the motors tore themselves apart, and Iran had to replace 1,000 damaged machines. As it was doing its damage, Stuxnet provided false feedback to operators so that they had no idea what was going on. The goal was to make the changes so imperceptible that the Iranians would think the destruction stemmed from bad parts, faulty engineering, incompetence, or all three. Ralph Langner, a German cybersecurity expert who was among the first to decode bits of Stuxnet, estimated that 50 percent of the malware's development costs went into efforts to hide the attack. One US government official told the *New York Times* that Stuxnet aimed "to mess with Iran's best scientific minds" and "make them feel they were stupid."[1]

Although the Iranians admitted some infections of their computer systems, the ultimate strategic effect of the malware on their nuclear program remains unclear. Reza Taghipour, an official in Iran's Ministry of Communications and Information Technology, downplayed the new weapon: "The effect and damage of this spy worm in government systems is not serious." Some US government officials claimed that it set Iran's nuclear program back eighteen months to two years; other technical experts said the attack did little to slow down Iranian efforts and in fact may have sped them up. As the Iranian scientists worked to get the centrifuges running properly, they made improvements in their performance and design that resulted in greater output.[2]

The time gained from the attacks may have been an important factor in bringing Iran back to the negotiating table and reaching a deal on its nuclear program in July 2015. The delay, even if only amounting to two years, gave the economic sanctions on the country more time to bite. The poisonous code was also useful in persuading Israel not to conduct airstrikes against Iranian facilities. In 2008, Israel reportedly asked the Bush administration for bunker-busting bombs it hoped to use against production and research sites hidden in mountainsides and buried underground. In rejecting the request, President Bush assuaged the Israelis by telling them that he had authorized the Olympic Games mission to sabotage Iran's nuclear infrastructure.[3]

Whatever the impact on Iran's nuclear program, Stuxnet was notable on two fronts. First, it was extremely sophisticated, "unprecedentedly masterful and malicious" in the words of one technical journal. The malware used five "zero days"—that is, unknown software vulnerabilities that allow an attacker to access a computer, router, or server; never having detected these flaws before, developers have zero days to fix or patch them. Zero days are valuable to both attackers and defenders. They can fetch six-figure prices on the black market, and so even an advanced attack deployed by a nation-state will usually use one, maybe two.

In addition, the computers that controlled the centrifuges were not connected to the Internet. Stuxnet had to jump this "air gap" and be delivered into the system, perhaps via a thumb drive or other portable device. In addition, Stuxnet was configured to work only on a specific system. Although the malware spread widely—the total number of infections surpassed 300,000 in more than one hundred countries, including Australia, Brazil, Brunei, China, India, Indonesia, the Netherlands, and even the United States—it would activate only when it saw a configuration of a specific line of Siemens programmable logic controllers, and it would destroy centrifuges only when it saw it was on a computer at Natanz, Iran's primary enrichment facility.[4]

Stuxnet was only one of the sophisticated tools at the United States' and Israel's disposal. Two other programs, Flame and Duqu, appear to have been part of Operation Olympic Games, designed to gather intelligence on computer networks in Iran and other Middle Eastern countries. Flame, for example, searched a computer for keywords on top-secret PDF files, then made and transmitted a summary of the document, all without being detected.

Stuxnet's complexity put it out of the reach of individual hackers and pointed to the involvement of a nation-state intending to do physical damage to a target. This parentage is Stuxnet's second noteworthy characteristic, and it represented a strategic sea change. As Michael V. Hayden, former chief of the Central Intelligence Agency (CIA) put it, "Somebody crossed the Rubicon." Before Stuxnet, computer code had served primarily to steal or destroy data on other computers; now it was causing equipment to malfunction. It was creating physical outcomes. Yet, unlike with conventional or even nuclear weapons, the effects and rules of cyber weapons were largely unknown. There was no understanding of the consequences Stuxnet might unleash, though there was fear that the same type of weapons might eventually target the United States. "If you are in the glass house, you should not be the one initiating throwing rocks at each other," Gregory Rattray, now an information security specialist at JPMorgan Chase, said at a 2012 conference. "We will have rocks come back at us."[5]

Stuxnet made it clear that the United States was committed to developing offensive capabilities. At a time when the rest of the defense budget faced severe cuts, Pentagon officials announced increased funding for the development of cyber capabilities, along with drones and special operations. Ashton Carter, then deputy secretary of defense, told a gathering of cybersecurity experts in San Francisco in February 2012, "No moment in all those [budget] deliberations was it even considered to make cuts in our cyber expenditures . . . ships, planes, ground forces, lots of other things on the cutting room floor; not cyber." The number of cyber warriors assigned to US Cyber Command, the command center for the Pentagon's cyber operations, was quintupled from 900 to 4,900 troops. And in late 2012, the Pentagon unveiled Plan X, an effort to build on programs like Stuxnet and develop the offensive capabilities needed to "dominate the cyber battlespace." Regina Dugan, head of the Defense Advanced Research Projects Agency, laid out a roadmap: "In the coming years we will focus an increasing portion of our cyber research on the investigation of offensive capabilities to address military-specific needs."[6]

Iran did not simply sit back—it hit back with its own cyberattacks. Between September 2012 and June 2013, an activist group called Izz ad-Din al-Qassam Cyber Fighters took credit for roughly two hundred distributed denial-of-service (DDoS) attacks on almost fifty financial institutions, including SunTrust, JPMorgan Chase, CitiGroup, Wells Fargo, U.S. Bancorp, Capital One, PNC, and HSBC. Compared to Stuxnet, DDoS attacks are unsophisticated: they are like protestors blocking access to a government office. Stuxnet was analogous to a Tomahawk cruise missile launched from 1,000 miles away blowing that office up. In a DDoS attack, hackers use thousands of computers or servers to flood a website with so much data that it can no longer respond. Security researcher Graham Cluley put it more colorfully: "It's a bit like 15 fat men trying to get through a revolving door at the same time—nothing can move."[7]

Over time the attacks grew more complex. The amount of data flooding websites grew massively. It cost one bank close to $10 million to get back online. Izz ad-Din al-Qassam claimed it was acting independently and in retaliation for "Innocence of Muslims," an anti-Islam video made by a California resident and uploaded on YouTube, but behind the scenes US government officials and outside experts blamed Iran.

In August 2012, the Shamoon malware struck Saudi Aramco, Riyadh's state oil giant. This was a qualitatively different type of attack, involving the destruction of data. Shamoon corrupted tens of thousands of hard drives and shut down employee e-mail; the company had to replace 30,000 computers in order to rid its networks of the malware. Saudi Aramco supplies about a tenth of the world's oil, but the malware only damaged office computers and did not affect systems involved with technical operations. "All our core operations continued smoothly," CEO Khalid Al-Falih told Saudi government and business officials. The company managed to put its networks back online almost two weeks after the attack. A subsequent attack damaged Rasgas, a joint venture between Qatar Petroleum and ExxonMobil and the second-biggest producer of liquefied natural gas in the world. Again, data was destroyed, but production continued.[8]

As with the attacks on the banks, a proxy was involved. A group calling itself the Cutting Sword of Justice claimed responsibility, but US officials believed Iran was behind the attacks. Not only was there motive, but Iran had a few years earlier announced its intent to develop cyber forces. Hossein Mousavian, a former Iranian diplomat, told an audience at Fordham Law School, "The U.S., or Israel, or the Europeans, or all of them together, started war against Iran. . . . Iran decided to have . . . to establish a cyberarmy, and today, after four or five years, Iran has one of the most powerful cyberarmies in the world."[9]

The Shamoon attack on Saudi Arabia seriously spooked the US government. Secretary of Defense Leon Panetta called it "a significant escalation of the cyber threat." In a speech in October 2012 at the Intrepid Sea, Air, and Space Museum, Panetta warned a group of business executives of a potential "cyber Pearl Harbor." Computer hackers could gain control of "critical switches," he cautioned, and "derail passenger trains, or even more dangerous, derail trains loaded with lethal chemicals. They could contaminate the water supply in major cities, or shut down the power grid across large parts of the country." President Barack Obama echoed this threat in his State of the Union address, stating, "Our enemies are . . . seeking the ability to sabotage our power grid, our financial institutions, and our air traffic control systems."[10]

Ironically, the Shamoon attack showed that Iran was learning from Israel and the United States. In April 2012, an aggressive piece of code, known as Wiper, had attacked the Iranian Oil Ministry and the National Iranian Oil Company and erased hard drives, removing any trace of itself. A year later, General Keith Alexander, director of the National Security Agency (NSA) and commander of US Cyber Command, left Fort Meade for a meeting with his counterpart in the United Kingdom's Government Communications Headquarters (GCHQ). Talking points, prepared for the meeting with Sir Iain Robert Lobban and leaked by former NSA employee Edward Snowden, claimed Iran had "demonstrated a clear ability to learn from the capabilities and actions of others." In other words, Shamoon had been possible in part because of Wiper.[11]

Even as Iran and the United States were trading blows in cyberspace, China-based hackers were continuing a massive cyber theft campaign against technology firms in the United States, Japan, and Europe. For years, Chinese hackers had raided defense contractors and the Pentagon, stealing secrets from dozens of weapons programs, including the Patriot missile system, the F-35 Joint Strike Fighter, and the US Navy's new littoral combat ship. They gradually expanded their attention to technology companies, financial institutions, law firms, think tanks, and the media. In July 2012 General Alexander called these and other economic espionage cyberattacks on American companies the "greatest transfer of wealth in history" and estimated that American companies had lost $250 billion in stolen information and another $114 billion in related expenses.[12]

During Year Zero, I probably received e-mails about twice a month that appeared to come from my boss, Richard Haass, president of the Council on Foreign Relations (CFR). The messages usually contained an attachment and a short message like, "I thought you might be interested in President Obama's schedule for his upcoming trip to Asia." I deleted them straightaway. Immediately erasing e-mails from your boss may not sound like the best way to get ahead professionally, but it was the safest thing to do. Glancing at the sender's e-mail address, I saw that it was something like Hass.Richard@yahoo.com or President CFR@gmail.com. Neither of these is Richard's e-mail address.

These e-mails, probably from China-based hackers, are known as spear-phishing attacks. E-mails are made to look like they come from someone you know (hackers may study job titles on your company's website or your social networks on Facebook, LinkedIn, or Twitter) and craft a subject line designed to be of interest to you. The e-mails often arrive in the morning, before you have had your first cup of coffee. Attackers may send one just before a long weekend, knowing the recipient will want to get any work out of the way before leaving the office. Opening an attachment or clicking on a link downloads software that allows attackers to gain control of your computer. They then gradually expand their access and move into different computers and networks, sending files back to computers in China or elsewhere. In some instances, the hackers use the computer's microphone and camera to record entire meetings.

Chinese hackers used this type of attack against the *New York Times* sometime at the end of 2012 as the paper's journalists were preparing a story on the massive wealth allegedly accumulated by the family of former prime minister Wen Jiabao. The hackers targeted reporters' passwords and accounts. Soon after, *Bloomberg*, which published a similar story on the wealth of the family of Xi Jinping, China's top leader, admitted that it also had been hacked. In February 2013, Mandiant, a private security company formed by former US Air Force officer Kevin Mandia, published a report naming Unit 61398 of the 3rd Department of the People's Liberation Army as responsible for the attacks on the *New York Times* and others. In attributing the digital assault, a private company had acted like a national intelligence agency.[13]

The hacking became a major irritant for Washington and Beijing. Not wearing ties and taking a more relaxed attitude toward protocol, Presidents Obama and Xi met for a two-day "shirt sleeve" summit in California in June 2013 in the hope of building a personal relationship and stemming the growing distrust that seemed inevitable between the world's superpower and a rising China. Despite all of the efforts at diplomatic bonhomie, President Obama told Charlie Rose that they had had "a very blunt conversation about cybersecurity" and that he had warned President Xi that hacking could "adversely affect the fundamentals of the US-China relationship." And so, in the twelve months between June 2012 and June 2013—the period between the first publicly admitted cyberattack by a nation-state and the summit between Obama and Xi—cyberattacks had gone from a discreet and veiled activity to a public strategy with the capacity to upend what many consider the most important bilateral relationship of the twenty-first century. The hacked world order was in full public view.[14]

Year Zero culminated with the revelations of former NSA contractor Edward Snowden. Two days before Presidents Obama and Xi met in Sunnylands, California, the British newspaper the *Guardian* published the first report on what would be a massive, years-long leak about the National Security Agency and allied surveillance programs. Despite numerous public assurances from officials that the government did not gather information on US citizens, the leaks would expose the collection of American users' cell phone metadata—what number is called, what time the call is made, and the duration of the call, but not the content. Through a program called PRISM, the NSA was able to demand access, under Section 702 of the Foreign Intelligence Surveillance Act (FISA) Amendments Act of 2008, to data of non-US citizens stored at most of the American technology giants, including Google, Apple, Facebook, and Microsoft. This gave the NSA the ability to collect and analyze the e-mails, texts, chats, phone calls, Facebook posts, tweets, and documents of people worldwide. Through a process the NSA calls upstream collection, it taps directly into the cables and networks passing through the United States. Huge amounts of data traveling across AT&T, Verizon, and other networks are copied, and then the data of non-US citizens are selected for analysis based on certain government criteria. But the process of targeting foreign communications results in the incidental collection of the data of ordinary users, which the NSA can store and analyze later.

NSA reportedly spied on adversaries and friends alike, tracking Somali terrorists and breaking into Chinese networks, but also hacking the European Union's offices in New York, Washington, DC, and Brussels, bugging the computer hard drives of the Indian embassies in Washington and New York, and listening to the calls of Brazilian president Dilma Rousseff, German chancellor Angela Merkel, and at least thirty other world leaders.

These leaks unsettled foreign relations and impacted the geopolitics of cyberspace. Tensions between Washington and Moscow grew when Russia granted limited asylum to Snowden after he fled to Sheremetyevo International Airport. The revelations of a widespread American surveillance program vitiated Obama's criticism of Chinese economic espionage. As the state-owned Xinhua news agency put it, the leaks "demonstrate that the United States, which has long been trying to play innocent as a victim of cyber-attacks, has turned out to be the biggest villain in our age." Relations with Germany and Brazil, important partners, soured. President Dilma Rousseff canceled her planned summit with Obama and used her speech to the United Nations General Assembly in September 2013 to rebuke the United States, calling the activities a "grave violation of human rights and of civil liberties."[15]

China, Russia, and a host of developing countries have used the US surveillance programs to buttress their argument that the Internet should be brought under the supervision of the United Nations.

Typically, the United States has promoted itself as the champion and protector of a borderless, global Internet, one that guarantees the right of all people to express themselves freely wherever they are. Not only do the surveillance programs undercut Washington's criticism of authoritarian states, but for Pratap Bhanu Mehta, one of India's most respected commentators, they imply that Washington feels free to "violate the privacy rights of citizens of other countries without just cause."[16]

In the long run, Snowden's revelations may also make the Internet notably less American. There is no escaping demographics. More than 650 million Chinese and 350 million Indians use the Internet, and hundreds of millions will come online in both countries over the next two decades. But the spying revelations have accelerated the desire of others, including US allies, to reduce their dependence on American technology and Internet companies.

THE WORLD ORDER TODAY

Henry Kissinger, the clarion voice for great power politics, argues in *World Order* that "cyberspace challenges all historical experience." He later continues, "When individuals of ambiguous affiliation are capable of undertaking actions of increasing ambitions and intrusiveness, the definition of state authority may turn ambiguous." In addition, Kissinger is markedly pessimistic about the impact of the Internet on strategy and decisionmaking; information, in his view, has eclipsed knowledge and wisdom. Previously, leaders had time to reflect and the ability to distinguish between what they could and could not control. Kissinger fears that now all problems are something to research on the web rather than to deliberate over carefully and place within a historical context.[17]

The twenty-first-century hacked world order is markedly more complex than that of the burgeoning Cold War in 1947. Then, mountains, rivers, and walls divided friends from enemies. Physical space matters much less in the cyber age, when attackers can act from anywhere with access to a modem or a smartphone. Hackers in Russia can use the Internet to attack neighboring Estonia or the United States nearly 5,000 miles away. For policymakers and the public shortly after the end of World War II, conventional power was relatively easy to chart as a share of world gross domestic product (GDP) and military spending. Now there is an uncertainty about how to measure cyber power. Does economic power stem from producing software, hardware, and content, or can a country specialize in one high-value area? Unlike long-range bombers and missiles, cyber weapons cannot be counted and it is unclear whether it is better to have a large corps of cyber troops or, given the importance of creativity and skill, a smaller number of elite hackers.

During the Cold War, only a few countries had the economic and technological capacity to build nuclear bombs. Even today, only nine countries possess them, and terrorists groups are likely to acquire them only through theft. The general contours and capabilities of each nuclear power's arsenal are well known. Should these weapons ever be used, the attacker's identity would be known before the missiles landed. And the development of so-called secure second-strike capabilities—that is, the ability to respond to a nuclear attack in kind—greatly diminished the incentive to attack first in a crisis. With nuclear parity, neither Washington nor Moscow could launch a nuclear strike without being destroyed in return, or, as the rule went, "whoever shoots first, dies second."

But almost any country as well as skilled hacking groups can launch a digital assault. Admiral Michael Rogers, General Alexander's successor as director of the NSA and head of US Cyber Command, told a House Armed Services subcommittee in March 2015, "We foresee increased tensions in cyberspace. The cyber strife that we see now in several regions will continue and deepen in sophistication and intensity." Approximately twenty-nine countries have formal military or intelligence units dedicated to offensive operations, and forty-nine have purchased off-the-shelf malware; those numbers are increasing every year, though it is difficult to understand the balance of forces and the risk of conflict. As Andre McGregor, a former cyber special agent at the Federal Bureau of Investigation (FBI), says, "With some countries, we're comfortable with knowing what their capabilities are, but with other countries we're still lost."[18]

There may be strong incentives to attack first in a crisis: cyber weapons are "one and done," used once and then they are gone. Once your adversaries see what you can do, they will patch their defenses, or could attack you, making your cyber weapon obsolete before you ever use it. This pressure not to sit on a weapon heightens strategic instability.

The global and interconnected nature of the Internet also means that cyberattacks have the potential to produce unpredicted and inadvertent problems far beyond damage to the intended target. Once set loose, malware can be examined, repurposed, and used by the target or someone else; for instance, hacker websites now make Stuxnet available for download. And unlike nuclear technology, which remained the province of a very small group of scientists and engineers, information and communication technologies are ubiquitous and rapidly changing. Territorial boundaries, once clear and constant, are now relatively less useful markers. The United States and its North Atlantic Treaty Organization (NATO) allies prepared to meet a Soviet tank invasion at the Fulda Gap, a corridor at the border between East and West Germany, but today attackers can route computer attacks through several networks from bases on the other side of the world, inside friendly countries, or even inside the target country.

The most difficult problem is that you may not actually know who is attacking you or what the assailant is planning. Without attribution—without knowing who is behind an attack—it is difficult, if not impossible, to determine whom to punish, which in turn makes it harder to deter an attack in the first place. Cold War stability, however imperfect, expensive, and fragile, rested in part on nuclear deterrence between the superpowers. That stability is eroding. The already high and growing attack levels provide perhaps the clearest evidence that attackers feel like they can operate without consequences.

During the course of an intrusion, attackers can use various tools to hide their identity; they can jump from different computers and route attacks through networks in different countries. They can use widely known and available techniques and malware. Hackers can conduct "false flag" operations, attacks designed to look like they are coming from another group or nation-state. In April 2015, for example, attackers claiming to be from the Islamic State's Cyber Caliphate shut down transmissions from France's TV5Monde television channel and posted jihadist propaganda on websites. Two months later, French investigators and cybersecurity experts reported that Internet addresses linked to the Cyber Caliphate website and techniques used in the attack pointed to a Russian group as responsible for the attack, though the motive remained elusive.

Moreover, when in a system an attacker's intentions can be opaque. Hackers may be there to steal data, prepare for a destructive assault, or both. Someone defending an oil company may not be able to tell if a hacker is looking for industrial secrets or mapping networks to "prepare the battlefield"—that is, to look for weaknesses that an attacker can later exploit in the event that a conflict breaks out.

Hackers can also turn espionage malware into an attack tool. The malware known as BlackEnergy, for example, has a long history. First designed and used for DDoS attacks by criminals and sold on Russian black markets, it then began downloading plug-ins that would steal passwords and IDs for bank websites. A group of Russian hackers used the malware for espionage directed at NATO, the European Union, Poland, Ukraine, private energy organizations, and European telecommunications companies. Yet they could also reprogram it as an attack tool capable of crippling energy supplies, water-distribution and water-filtration systems, or financial transactions.[19]

Even when an attack can be traced back to a country, there is usually uncertainty about its ultimate origin: Was it launched by individuals at the instigation and support of their home government, entirely on their own, or for other criminal third parties? A senior intelligence officer told me, "There is lots of overlap between state and criminal hackers, and what hackers do at home when the work day is done is often the same as what they did for their day job." The fog of digital conflict is thick, and political leaders, in the heat of the moment, could finger the wrong perpetrators, respond disproportionately, and exacerbate a crisis.

Mistaken attribution can inflame already tense geopolitical standoffs. During the summer of 2014, sophisticated hackers broke into the networks of JPMorgan Chase and a dozen other financial institutions. They stole name, address, and e-mail data—but not credit card numbers—for about 83 million US households and small businesses. The scale of the breach was shocking enough, but the attacks further heightened the sense of vulnerability since the financial sector was widely assumed to be the most prepared for cyberattacks. Financial institutions already spend hundreds of millions of dollars on defense and have the most developed mechanism for cooperation and sharing threat information, the Financial Services—Information Sharing and Analysis Center.[20]

The difficulty of attribution was of heightened political importance given the timing of the attacks. The United States and its partners had recently tightened sanctions aimed at crippling Russian companies following Moscow's seizure of Crimea and support for rebels in the eastern part of Ukraine. When asked by President Obama about the attacks, senior government officials reportedly could not answer the question "Is this plain old theft, or is Putin retaliating?"[21]

Although he claimed to have no knowledge of the attack, former NSA head Keith Alexander publicly speculated that the Kremlin had ordered the attacks: "How would you shake the United States back? Attack a bank in cyberspace. If it was them, they just sent a real message: 'You're vulnerable.'" In contrast, Joseph M. Demarest, assistant director of the FBI Cyber Division, while still uncertain about whether the hackers were agents of a government, criminals, or some combination of the two, said, "There's no indication that [the attacks came] as a result of the sanctions." In the end, despite all the speculation, the hacks do not seem to be government sponsored. Law enforcement announced in March 2015 that it would soon indict the people behind the JPMorgan Chase hack and that they were "gettable," meaning that they were in a country with which the United States has an extradition treaty. Russia is not one of those countries, and in July 2015 authorities arrested four people in Israel and Florida for a complex securities-fraud scheme.[22]

While the hacked world order is a break from the past, nation-states have not shaken off all the constraints of historical experience. Elements of the old statecraft remain. Technological sophistication, wealth, and size still matter. New technologies and techniques are, for example, making attack attribution more possible. The White House was adamant that North Korea was behind the December 2014 computer attack on Sony because of the forensic work of US cybersecurity companies and data collected by the intelligence agencies through "technical means." Documents released by Snowden show that the NSA has successfully placed code and monitoring devices in chips, routers, servers, and computers across the globe, giving the agency sweeping views of traffic on the Internet, including on Chinese and Korean computers. Attribution remains a relatively slow, deliberate process, but hackers can no longer assume that they will escape eventual detection and that attacks will not ultimately be ascribed to them.

Nation-states have regrouped to address the diffusion of power that has accompanied the proliferation of communication technologies and the expansion of cyberspace. New trade pacts with Europe (the Transatlantic Trade and Investment Partnership) and Asia (the Trans-Pacific Partnership) include provisions to remove barriers to the cross-border flow of data, prevent the forced localization of data, and reduce taxes on digital services. The United States has made cybersecurity an increasingly important part of its defense treaties with Japan and NATO, and Beijing and Moscow have signed a nonaggression pact with each other in cyberspace. The tools of trade agreements and alliances have been remade for the hacked world order.

THE PERVASIVE INFLUENCE OF CYBER CONFLICT

While often cloaked in secrecy, the maneuvering of states in cyberspace has a direct impact on all of our lives. The long-term effects of how states react to Year Zero will be pervasive. The impact of the Cold War on individuals went beyond the threat of nuclear war, although this alone was certainly consequential enough. The struggle resulted in new relationships between individuals and the state as the two sides created extensive, powerful bureaucracies to compete with each other. The National Security Act of 1947, for example, created the Department of the Air Force, the National Security Council, and the Central Intelligence Agency, as well as the Joint Chiefs of Staff and the position of secretary of defense. The National Aeronautics and Space Administration, the National Science Foundation, and the US Atomic Energy Commission were established to promote scientific competition and economic growth. President Harry S. Truman formally established the National Security Agency in 1952, although it was unknown to the public and referred to within the intelligence community as "No Such Agency." The responsibilities and authorities of the Department of Justice, the Department of Defense, and the intelligence community developed over a time when there was a clearer distinction between internal threats and those that came from "over there" and between criminal and military activity. The demands of digital conflicts are remaking these institutional assumptions. New bureaucracies are created; new authorities are defined, taken, and abused. In the process, the balance between public and private authority, production and power, and transparency and privacy are transformed.

Policymakers and the public have hundreds of years' experience with the deployment, use, and destruction created by conventional weapons. Traditional war is, in military jargon, primarily kinetic. The point is to kill people and blow things up. While cyberattacks are often framed as part of "cyber wars" by the media, you cannot hold territory in cyberspace, no one has ever died directly from an attack, and the danger of widespread physical destruction remains hypothetical. Russia and China might be able to launch an assault on the power grid, but they are also highly unlikely to do so unless they first perceive their vital interests to be under threat. Beijing and Moscow certainly know that Washington would respond with its own cyber weapons or with more conventional military force. Moreover, given the interdependence of the two economies, Chinese leaders would have to be fairly desperate to create economic chaos without high assurance that it would not blow back on China.

As cyberattacks typically pose risks to the integrity of complex systems, they represent a less dramatic but more pervasive threat than the destruction caused by a tank, destroyer, or fighter jet; they tend to wreak less physical destruction and more psychological and social havoc. By changing data, sometimes subtly, sometimes in the open, cyber weapons deceive, confuse, and surprise. They heighten uncertainty about what type of damage they may cause; the uncertainty itself may be the most potent weapon. And cyberattacks often exist in and amplify the space between war and peace. They are used by states, and non-state actors, to coerce, influence, and damage despite there being no formally or legally declared conflict.

In April 2013, the Syrian Electronic Army (SEA), a group of hackers that supports the regime of Bashar al-Assad, took over the Associated Press's Twitter account and sent a fake message about a bomb attack on President Obama, causing the Dow Jones Industrial Average to plunge 146 points in a few seconds and erasing $136 billion in market value. The market quickly bounced back, but the hack demonstrated the power exerted by destabilizing extremely complex systems—high-frequency trading programs that make trades based on keywords within milliseconds. The Associated Press was not the first or the last media organization to get hacked; the SEA attacked CBS, NPR, the BBC, the *Washington Post*, the *Onion*, and the *New York Times* in retaliation for what it calls one-sided coverage of the Syrian civil war. Taking over a social media account is not a complex hack, but it was effective in undermining trust in information systems at the local, national, and international levels.[23]

With the shift away from purely military targets, the battle over cyberspace is remaking the division between the public and the private, between what we expect the government to do and what remains the responsibility of companies, public organizations, and individuals. A defining characteristic of a modern state is a near monopoly on security and foreign policy. Yet for the last three decades, the assumption has been made by both the technological community and the US government that the private sector should take the lead in cyberspace. Even bureaucratic language drawn from an Obama administration document on cybersecurity admitted that the private sector "designs, builds, owns, and operates most of the digital infrastructure."[24]

The stark division between public and private was temporary, if not illusionary, as was the idea that the two were separable when it comes to cyberspace. The year spanning June 2012 to June 2013 destroyed the illusion. Almost everything the United States does in cyberspace requires a blurring of the line between public and private. Private firms own the networks necessary for attacking and defending the telecommunications, energy, and financial sectors. More than 90 percent of American military and intelligence communications travel over privately owned backbone telecommunications networks. Many of the most talented programmers are in the private sector or academia, and private companies develop both attack malware and defenses against such programs. In the face of relentless and seemingly unstoppable theft of intellectual property, some have suggested that companies be allowed to "hack back"—that is, to hack the hackers. In fact, in one survey, more than one-third of respondents admitted that they had already done so, even though it is illegal.[25]

Diplomacy is undergoing a similar transformation to warfare. As is now well known, a number of technologically enabled individuals can disrupt the carefully choreographed diplomacy of states. WikiLeaks, a website that hosts classified and other secret materials, posted thousands of State Department cables leaked by Chelsea Manning in 2010. The Edward Snowden disclosures undermined US strategy in cyberspace and forced Washington to justify and explain its intelligence collection practices to Berlin, Tokyo, Brasilia, and other close partners.[26]

Indeed, privately owned platforms and technologically savvy civil society groups are often central to achieving or blocking diplomatic initiatives. Under Hillary Clinton, the State Department adopted an Internet agenda built on four freedoms: the freedom of expression and religion online, as well as the freedom to access the Internet and thereby to connect to websites and other people. While US government officials pursue these rights at the United Nations and other international institutions, the State Department also relies on private groups to develop software that allows users in Beijing, Tehran, and other locales around the world to avoid censorship. At the same time, sales by technology companies like BlueCoat of surveillance and filtering equipment to Bahrain and Syria can undermine the State Department's Internet freedom agenda, as might corporate decisions like Apple's discontinuation of OpenDoor, an app that allowed Internet users to circumvent China's so-called Great Firewall.

In part, the changing economic base of power and influence drives this blending of the public and private. For the last 250 years, the material source of power was manufacturing. In his "Report on Manufactures," Alexander Hamilton urged Congress to help build a strong manufacturing base so that the United States could become "independent of foreign nations for military and other essential supplies" and trade with Europe on equal terms. By the middle of the last century, there was little doubt the United States had fulfilled Hamilton's dream. In the first year of World War II, the United States produced 18,466 aircraft; by 1944, 96,270 had rolled off the lines. Educational policy, tax incentives, and investments in transportation and other infrastructure all served to support factories at home. US diplomats roamed the world promoting the General Agreement on Tariffs and Trade, as well as its successor, the World Trade Organization, and countless bilateral agreements to encourage the (relatively) free flow of goods, services, and people.

Cyber power has a different source and requires different subsidies, incentives, and support. In the first decade of this century, Israel, a small economy of a little more than 7 million people, sparked a disproportionately large number of successful technology companies. It has more companies listed on the NASDAQ than any country outside the United States, more than China, Europe, India, Japan, and Korea combined. Amazon, Dell, Intel, Microsoft, Google, Cisco, and other technology giants have important research and development centers in Haifa, Herzliya, and Tel Aviv. Israel has benefited from a handful of world-class universities and the immigration of a large number of Jewish Russian scientists and engineers into the country. However, much of the energy and knowledge that drove Israel to become a "start-up nation" came from the military. Almost every non-Arab citizen serves in the Israel Defense Forces (IDF), and veterans of Unit 8200, the IDF equivalent of the NSA, have founded a high number of technology firms. Shvat Shaked and Saar Wilf, for example, took their experience tracking terrorists and turned it into Fraud Sciences—a company, eventually sold to PayPal, that identified online criminals and prevented fraud.

Israeli prime minister Benjamin Netanyahu is applying this model of innovation and entrepreneurship to cybersecurity. "Although the field is not precise . . . we must enter it . . . and become a world cyberpower," Netanyahu told participants in a 2011 conference in Tel Aviv. "This is possible. We're no longer crawling, we're walking, and soon we will be running forward." Netanyahu's efforts have included the establishment of a new National Cyber Defense Authority with a budget of over $500 million and the creation of a cyber threat research cluster in the desert city of Beersheba. The cluster encompasses branches of Unit 8200, Israel's computer emergency response team, private companies, multinational firms, and Ben-Gurion University, the first university in the country with a graduate program in cybersecurity. While still in the early stages, the programs look promising. By the end of 2014, eight Israeli cybersecurity companies had been sold for almost $700 million, and Israel accounted for 13 percent of new global research and development in cybersecurity.[27]

The same model of private-sector, government, and university interaction was responsible for the emergence of Hewlett-Packard, Google, and other US tech giants and, as a result, for a huge amount of US power and international influence. US companies not only developed and sold the computers, servers, software, and routers on which the Internet runs but also became part of what the Harvard political scientist Joseph Nye calls America's soft power, its ability to influence and attract through ideas, institutions, and culture rather than to coerce through force. The rest of the world loved the products, story, and energy of Silicon Valley.

The exposure of NSA surveillance and espionage programs is reconfiguring the interdependence between Silicon Valley and Washington. The double helix that bound them together is being unzipped and its components cut and shuffled. The enzyme activating this process is the global market. US technology companies have billions of customers outside the United States. Greater China, for example, accounted for about $16 billion in revenue for Apple, out of total revenues of $74.6 billion during the first quarter of 2015. "It's an incredible market," said Apple's CEO Tim Cook. "People love Apple products. And we are going to do our best to serve the market." In 2014, Google earned 58 percent of its revenues outside the United States; Facebook, 55 percent; Intel, in 2015, earned over 80 percent abroad. American companies are now more willing to stand up to Washington and to align with the interests of global customers.[28]

Multinational companies and globalization are, of course, not new. GM, Procter & Gamble (P&G), and Coca-Cola are global companies, but their relationships with their customers are relatively limited and transactional. They market and sell a product. P&G wants to know how often people in Caracas wash their hair with Pantene but is unlikely to have information about where Caraqueños go after getting out of the shower, how long they are stuck in traffic, and what they think of a new Italian restaurant.

The technology companies' missions have been much more expansive—Facebook wants to connect the world; Google, to bring order to the world's information—and so these companies have a more complicated, intense personal relationship to their customers that, if they have their way, will extend over years and into almost every aspect of users' lives. Integrating the data from searches, the Android smartphone operating system, and the traffic app Waze, Google knows all of the above information as well as whether a given Caraqueño compared Pantene to Unilever's Suave, if he or she looked up other restaurants before deciding on the Italian one, and quite possibly who the evening's date is—if the Caraqueño did a Google search on that individual.

This means that governments in a number of regions around the world are looking at Google, Facebook, Twitter, and other large US technology companies less as beacons of innovation and invention and more as the handmaidens of the NSA, monopolists, or both. The global technology companies undermine nation-states' conceptions of territoriality. Any change Facebook makes to its privacy settings affects over a billion people around the globe. These decisions get made in Menlo Park, without the input of policymakers in Brasilia or Jakarta, even though they affect tens of millions of Brazilian and Indonesian citizens.

In the abstract, almost everyone agrees that the free flow of data, like more open trade, is good for the economy. According to a 2011 McKinsey study of thirteen countries (the Group of Eight plus Brazil, China, India, South Korea, and Sweden), the Internet has accounted for 3.4 percent of GDP and 7 percent of growth in these countries over the past fifteen years. McKinsey also predicts that by 2025 the potential global economic impact of the Internet of Things will be $2.7 trillion to $6.2 trillion annually and of cloud computing—massive amounts of data stored not on your own device but on remote servers—$1.7 trillion to $6.2 trillion.[29]

But no one lives in the abstract, and the push to impose digital sovereignty is spreading. "Digital sovereignty" is an evocative if vague term that harkens back to twentieth-century conceptions of regulation and state control. It represents the old world imposing itself on the hacked world. Nearly every node of the Internet is located within the territory of a sovereign nation and therefore falls under its laws and jurisdictions. Countries can arrest, intimidate, and beat individual users, try to route all e-mail within their territory, pressure companies to maintain data servers locally, arrest technology company employees, or force companies to submit to security inspections and provide access to source code if they want to sell in domestic markets. For some, digital sovereignty is synonymous with the de-Americanization of the Internet. One French Foreign Ministry official described the US technology companies to me as "the gatekeepers of the digital economy, absorbing the value and ensuring European companies act as subcontractors."[30]

With the combination of massive amounts of data and the growing ability to monitor individuals—on the web, via mobile phones, through closed circuit cameras—we appear to be sliding into a "surveillance society." The question we have to face is, by whom do we want to be surveilled: a government, a corporation, a hacker? There are no limits to our technology. John Villasenor, an electrical engineer at the University of California, Los Angeles, argues that because costs for computer data storage keep plunging, it will be feasible "to record and store everything that can be recorded about what everyone in a country says or does."[31]

The capabilities to collect information have expanded as the potential targets have proliferated. During the Cold War, there was a limited number of secrets, a finite number of Chinese and Soviet diplomats or naval bases. Today, terrorist networks, lone wolves, and anonymous groups of political hackers are unseen and diffuse. The fear is that they can be anywhere, and so national security agencies have an almost boundless ambition and desire to gather all data available. As Deputy Attorney General James Cole has said, "If you're looking for the needle in a haystack, you have to have the haystack."[32]

In addition, defending complex systems from computer attacks requires ever-growing volumes of data. The interconnection of communications, financial, energy, health, transportation, and other vital networks creates more possibilities for failure and more points vulnerable to attack. The defender cannot be everywhere but wants to see more data to predict where the attacker might be. As computer security expert Dan Geer put it in a speech at the 2014 RSA cybersecurity conference, "As society becomes more interdependent within itself, the more it must rely on prediction based on data collected in broad ways, not in targeted ways. That is surveillance."[33]

The United States has incomparable resources, but it may never be as strong in cyberspace as it is today. Cyber power may be a particularly ephemeral form of power. New technology competitors are arising, friends and allies hold different visions of how to manage the Internet, and the gap between the interests of global Internet and technology companies and Washington is growing. Individual users may come to depend more on their own technological prowess to defend themselves from malware than on law enforcement agencies. The global, open Internet, a wellspring of US economic, political, and military power, is fragmenting.

Some of this loss of power is unavoidable, the result of demographics as the center of gravity for Internet users shifts rapidly from the developed to the developing world. As with many transnational challenges, there will be much that the United States cannot control, and new challenges will emerge from the spaces beyond the range of US regulations, norms, and influence. Some of the diminishment of power stems from the logic of international politics, from competitors that seek to balance US power. And some of it is self-inflicted; the United States pursued data and information in service of defending itself from terrorist attacks but at the expense of other diplomatic, economic, and national security interests.

Policymakers have been slow to understand the fallout from and significance of Year Zero. This myopia is partly the result of American Internet exceptionalism, a sense that the United States has a unique, beneficent role in cyberspace. This was not an outlandish view, given the United States' history in creating the Internet and overseeing its global expansion. But this exceptionalism not only led to an exaggerated sense of US power and influence but also blinded decisionmakers as to how other countries defined their own interests and interpreted US actions.

It also left policymakers ill prepared for the technology community's reaction to the Snowden disclosures. As story after story emerged alleging that the NSA undermined encryption, hacked into cables carrying the data of US companies, placed implants and beacons in servers and routers, and generally weakened internet security, Washington struggled to find its feet. Most of the national security justifications offered for the intelligence agency's actions, such as breaking up terrorist plots, seemed unsubstantiated or rang hollow. Policymakers failed to comprehend the depth of Silicon Valley's anger. As one cybersecurity entrepreneur based in Santa Clara told me, "I cannot overstate the loss of trust. You have today large, publicly traded companies that do not even want to take a meeting with people in the administration. They think there is nothing to be gained."[34]

There has always been a cultural clash between the technology and foreign policy crowds, between readers of *Wired* and *Foreign Affairs*. Many of the readers of *Wired* embraced the ideas that "information wants to be free" and that computer technologies would radically empower individuals and make the world a better place. "The Internet," the lawyer and activist Jennifer Granick told the audience at a 2015 hacker conference, "would place our reading, our associations, and our thoughts outside of government control." Granick continued, "The Internet would not just enable communication, but would do so in a decentralized, radically democratic way. Power to the people, not to the governments or companies that run the pipes."[35]

While foreign policy elites were also awed by the ability of the Internet to change the world, they saw it, like so many other spaces, as an arena for regulation, contention, and conflict. They were more likely to think about national advantage and relative gain. They preferred "cyber" as a descriptor over "digital," "connected," or "wired," a prefix off-putting to the *Wired* crowd. As Granick put it, "When I hear 'cyber' I hear shorthand for military domination of the Internet, as General Michael Hayden, former NSA and CIA head, has said—ensuring U.S. access and denying access to our enemies. Security for me, but not for thee."[36]

There was, however, a small space where the ideas and interests of the technology and foreign policy communities overlapped. *Wired* readers agreed with the *Foreign Affairs* crowd that Silicon Valley and Washington should work together to advocate for free speech and open access, reduce international trade barriers, and promote the promises of the information technology revolution globally. This narrow alliance is now on shaky grounds, and those who want to preserve it, or even reinvigorate it, face growing skepticism from inside their own ranks.

While it should continue to promote and espouse the virtues of an open, global, and secure Internet, the United States must prepare for a more likely future—a highly contested, nationally divided cyberspace. Brazil, China, Russia, and others have different visions of the preferred structure and legitimate uses of cyberspace, and chapter two describes both the sources of power in the digital age and the emerging patterns of statecraft—how nation-states get power and what they think they should do with it once they have it. States are confronted with a number of decisions in cyberspace: Should cyberattacks be limited and precise, or disruptive and widely used? Is influence best exerted through counter-narratives or mass disinformation? Is the model for innovation the one developed in Silicon Valley, or does it require more government intervention and direction? The answers to these questions are rooted in history, ideology, and strategic challenges, and they will shape the hacked world order.

The next six chapters are a short history of how these ideas have been put into action; they recount two decades of disruption, destruction, theft, trade, and influence in cyberspace. Chapter three covers disruption and the political uses of cyberattacks, primarily by Russia but also by North Korea. Chapter four looks at a more destructive future, attacks designed to cause physical damage or death, and what can be done to prevent the outbreak of cyber conflict and limit the fallout from it. Chapter five delves into the most prevalent forms of cyberattacks—cyber espionage and the theft of secrets for political and military gain as well as economic benefit. Chapter six looks at how cyber espionage, and NSA surveillance in particular, spilled over into and became intertwined with the desire in Europe to protect user privacy and create competitors to US technology giants. Chapter seven begins with the Twitter war between Israel and Hamas, and then moves on to Chinese and Russian trolls and the online battle against the Islamic State. Brazil's Internet culture and efforts to reform the global governance of the Internet is the centerpiece of chapter eight.

The challenges of the hacked world order are both familiar—other states will pursue policies that limit US power and influence—and unconventional—new actors may exploit unexpected and unknown vulnerabilities in networks to wreak damage and destruction. Policymakers will lose their sense of strategic stability, predictability, and control while gaining new tools of coercion and a wider legitimacy for digital policy.

In order to address the challenges, the United States must at least accomplish three things: enhance defense at home, create a working truce between the government and the private sector, and build a coalition of like-minded countries in the international sphere. Washington will have to funnel new money to research, development, and innovation in cybersecurity; forge agreements with the private sector on the sharing of data; and, with its friends in Europe and Asia, clearly define what behaviors are acceptable in cyberspace and how it plans to respond if lines are crossed. The United States will have to be more limited in its ambitions but more assertive in their pursuit.

The hacked world order will come with social, security, and economic costs. But if it succeeds, the United States can help shape a future in cyberspace that is, if not entirely pacific, marked by continued innovation and the relatively free flow of information in many parts of the world.

Chapter 2

THE ANATOMY OF
CYBER POWER

· ·

D uring a brief period before Year Zero, many assumed that super-hackers and shadowy groups of cyber criminals would dominate the Internet of the future. The technologically enabled network would be more responsive, agile, and flexible than the slow-moving, hierarchical, and bureaucratic nation-state. At the very least, small states, it was supposed, would close the power gap with their larger, more powerful competitors.

Yet, despite the diffusion of capabilities, states have not given way as the most powerful players in world affairs. Individuals and groups have gained absolute power, but in response nation-states have developed new techniques and technologies and remain the predominant actors in terms of relative power. Nation-states still regulate the companies that create the hardware and software of cyberspace; threaten, imprison, fine, and monitor individual users; develop competing technology standards; and require that the physical infrastructure of the Internet be configured to give them more control. The larger and more powerful the state, the more resources it brings to bear.

The fears and desires of several states—the United States, Russia, China, Germany, Brazil, and Israel among them—are shaping the future of cyberspace. While all states want to spur growth, exploit the data of adversaries, and protect their own information, they do not pursue these goals in the same ways. Some see cyberattacks as a limited tool to use carefully; others view them as a much broader political weapon to wield against a range of adversaries. Some states try to construct attractive political narratives on the Internet, and others dissemble and drown out their opponents. During the Cold War, the major powers all had distinct understandings of the world's workings, the role of war, the nature of the enemy, and how to distinguish between friend and foe. In the hacked world order, new strategic cultures of cyber power are emerging.

CHINA'S CYBERSPACE SPIRIT

In 2014, the Pew Research Center asked thousands of technology analysts, business executives, entrepreneurs, and activists what cyberspace might look like in a decade. One of the four biggest concerns these experts expressed was "meddling by countries," and we can assume that high on their list of meddlers was China. During the 2015 Lunar New Year Celebration, at festivities hosted by the Beijing Internet Association, the Cyberspace Administration of China (CAC) debuted a new song to an audience that included media figures and Internet executives. Decked out in tuxedos and fancy red dresses, a choir made up of CAC employees sang a slightly martial tune in praise of the glories of China's Internet. "Cyberspace Spirit" described the Chinese Internet as "a beam of incorruptible sunlight, touching our hearts. Uniting the powers of life from all creation." The song finished with a rousing patriotic call to go out to the rest of the world. "An Internet power: Tell the world that the Chinese Dream is uplifting China," the chorus sang. "An Internet power: I represent my nation to the world." Videos of the performance appeared online, but then some versions quickly vanished.[1]

The man behind both the triumphal spirit of the song and the impulse to delete it was CAC head Lu Wei. Lu's ascent up the ranks of the Chinese bureaucracy has been rapid, as he moved from provincial branches of Xinhua, the national news agency, to become its secretary general and vice bureau chief. Promoted in 2011 to vice mayor of Beijing and chief of the capital's propaganda department, Lu moved up again in April 2013, becoming head of the State Internet Information Office, which regulates China's Internet.

Lu's work and thinking are essential to understanding China's approach to the Internet at home and abroad. From the moment

Chinese users first went online a little more than two decades ago, poli-cymakers and analysts have conceived of the Internet as a double-edged sword, essential to economic growth and good governance but also a major threat to domestic stability and regime legitimacy. Economic development has been a priority; China's first Internet white paper, pub-lished in 2010, described the network's "irreplaceable role in accelerat-ing the development of the national economy." Chinese officials have also stressed the importance of the web in "supervision," the online exposure by Chinese users of official corruption and malfeasance. Posts on Weibo, a Chinese social media platform that combines aspects of Twitter and Facebook, give the central government insights into prob-lems at the local level. Social media also play a role in "public opinion guidance," allowing Chinese officials to methodically disseminate the right kinds of information. With these two uses in mind, Lu encouraged government officials to join social media platforms: "Watch Weibo, open a Weibo account, send Weibo messages, study Weibo," he exhorted.[2]

While declaring that Chinese citizens enjoy full freedom of speech on the Internet, the white paper also stated that the exercise of those rights must not "jeopardize state security, the public interest, or the legitimate rights and interests of other people." The Chinese leader-ship sees itself in ideological struggle with the West and cyberspace as the "primary battlefield." As the *PLA Daily* put it in May 2015, "Foreign forces use this convenient tool of the Internet to build 'value traps,' implement a 'cultural cold war,' and foster 'a fifth column,' befouling leaders, vilifying heroes, mocking the system. . . . [A]ttacks against the army may be said to have reached a state of unbridled brazenness, making the Internet into 'concession' to peddle Western ideology."[3]

To mitigate these threats, the Chinese Communist Party has built an Internet-management system that has two faces. On the exter-nal side, a number of technologies colloquially known as the Great Firewall filter and block offending material from outside China. In a notable instance of the Chinese government exerting censorship out-side China, Beijing appeared responsible for launching a distributed denial-of-service (DDoS) attack on GitHub, a website that hosts code for software programmers and that was also hosting a page from a non-profit organization that helps Chinese users avoid the Great Firewall. Beijing deployed what researchers from Citizen Lab and the University of California, Berkeley, called the Great Cannon, a tool that hijacked the computers of visitors to Chinese websites and directed streams of data at GitHub, knocking it offline for five days.

Within China, blacklists block certain phrases or words; in extreme cases, the government can remove whole regions from the Internet, as happened for ten months after riots in Xinjiang province in 2009. A real-name registration policy requires Chinese citizens to sign up for social media websites using their national identification numbers, making anonymity for most users difficult. Chinese web and social media companies are legally responsible for the illicit or harmful activities of their users—a policy known as intermediary liability—and so they employ huge departments of employees to monitor and censor their customers.

Lu has reinforced this system of control. In May 2013, the State Internet Information Office announced a campaign against "online rumors." Big Vs—influential verified (hence the *V*) users of Weibo—received notice that they faced up to three years of jail time if "defamatory" comments were forwarded more than 500 times or viewed more than 5,000 times. The Big Vs often have millions of followers, so the prospect of one of their posts getting forwarded more than five hundred times and landing them in jail were high. Lu invited prominent Big Vs to appear with him on television, where he harangued them to be more positive in their posts. One prominent user, American businessman Charles Xue, was detained for eight months on what looked like politically motivated prostitution charges.[4]

In February 2014, China announced the creation of a leading small group for cybersecurity to be chaired by President Xi Jinping. Leading small groups are ad hoc bodies that advise the Politburo and implement decisions. They represent efforts to cut through the Chinese bureaucracy, create consensus, and signal the high importance of a policy issue. In the official announcement of the group's formation, President Xi clearly stated cyberspace's strategic value: "Without cybersecurity there is no real national security." Lu was named director of the office of the leading small group and head of the newly formed Cyberspace Administration of China.[5]

Lu's mission expanded to not only maintaining and improving the Great Firewall but also selling China's vision of the Internet to the rest of the world. For much of Barack Obama's administration, China had taken an essentially reactive stance, criticizing US efforts to promote an open, free, and global Internet. When then secretary of state Hillary Clinton delivered three speeches on Internet freedom between 2010 and 2011, asserting that users must be assured freedom of expression and religion online, as well as the right to access the Internet and thereby connect to websites and other people, Beijing responded to the call for these four freedoms negatively and defensively. "Behind what America calls free speech is naked political scheming," read the headline of one article in *People's Daily*. "The United States," the article continued, "applies double standards in implementing freedom of information: for those who have different political views or values, it waves a 'freedom fighter's' club and leads a crusade against them." Another article claimed, "One person's Internet freedom is another's Internet imperialism."[6]

Lu's message to the rest of the world has been more positive, and Beijing is now offering a viable alternative vision of Internet governance based on control. At a meeting of the World Economic Forum in Tianjin, China, Lu told an audience of foreign and Chinese business executives that the Internet, like a car, must have brakes. "Freedom and order are twin sisters," Lu said, "and they must live together." Questioned at another meeting by foreign reporters about why China blocked access to websites such as Facebook, Lu initially denied that it did. But then he said that while China was "hospitable," it could also "choose who can come to our home and be our guest." "I can't change who you are but I have the power to choose my friends," he said. "I wish that all who come to China will be our real friends."[7]

Lu and others have dressed up this right to block Internet content and control access to the domestic market, now a central principle of China's Internet diplomacy, as Internet (or cyber) sovereignty. Sometimes the diplomacy surrounding the principle has been ungainly. For the first time, in November 2014, China organized an international conference on cyberspace, the World Internet Conference in Wuzhen, a historic town near Hangzhou and home to the headquarters of the Alibaba Group, the massive Chinese e-commerce company that set the record for the largest initial public offering ever, raising $25 billion. Lu opened the meeting by telling participants, "We will strengthen communications and seek common ground while resolving differences to establish a multilateral, democratic, and transparent international Internet governance system." "Join us," he continued, "in building up a peaceful, safe, and open and co-operative cyberspace."[8]

Despite highlighting the contradictions of the Chinese Internet—attendees could access Facebook and Twitter freely, while those sites remained blocked in the rest of China—the conference went smoothly, with speeches from Internet executives and representatives of foreign governments. The night before the closing ceremony, at around 11:00 p.m., however, the organizers slipped a draft document under participants' doors. A note accompanying the two-page memo explained, "In light of the views of various sides, we have made this draft declaration. If you want to make revisions to it, please contact the organizing committee before 8 a.m." The document contained nine points, which included encouraging joint efforts on cybersecurity and fighting cyber terrorism, developing the Internet economy, and enhancing connectivity. It also called for respect for the Internet sovereignty of all countries. Not surprisingly, many of the participants balked at signing on to a controversial document passed to them for input only after they had gone to sleep. The conference ended with no final declaration.[9]

A few weeks later, Lu visited Washington, DC, and Silicon Valley. The trip, at least in the eyes of the Chinese press, was a roaring success. Pictures in Chinese newspapers show a buoyant Lu laughing with Jeff Bezos of Amazon and riding in a self-driving car at Google. During a stop at Facebook's headquarters, Mark Zuckerberg showed Lu a copy of Xi Jinping's *The Governance of China* prominently displayed on his desk. During his trip, Lu published a piece in the *Huffington Post* characterizing the relationship between the United States and China as one of "deep fusion and high stakes." Lu wrote, "We should respect each other's cyber sovereignty, Internet governance, major concerns and cultural differences."[10]

China is an outlier only in its size and ambition. Cyberspace does not exist independent of politics, and nation-states have competing visions of how the Internet should be managed at home and governed globally. Some states, however, have more technological, economic, military, and social resources at their disposal and thus are more likely to achieve their vision than others.

THE SOURCES OF CYBER POWER

Lu Wei and his colleagues are not shy in describing their mission as transforming China from a big cyber country into a strong cyber power. The almost daily stories about Chinese hackers breaking into US networks give the impression that China rules cyberspace. Beijing, however, sees itself as vulnerable. While China has the world's largest number of Internet users—more than 650 million—and a vibrant domestic market, policymakers have significant concerns about Beijing's technological prowess, the coherence of its international strategy, and its ability to respond to the growing sophistication of cyberattacks.

But what is cyber power for China or any other country? Here we have to look at both words in the couplet. Norbert Weiner, a math professor at the Massachusetts Institute of Technology, started and named a field known as cybernetics, the study of the structure and processes of regulatory systems. In the late 1940s, he introduced the term "cyber," from the Greek for "governing" or "steering." Science fiction writer William Gibson originally coined the term "cyberspace" in 1982 to capture a new virtual reality—"a consensual hallucination experienced daily by billions of legitimate operators" who jack in through computers and handheld devices. As used by governments and policymakers, the term has multiple meanings; one academic study found at least twenty-eight definitions. Many—like the Internet lawyer Jennifer Granick—hate the word "cyber," thinking it militaristic or outdated. Gibson himself said he chose it because it "seemed evocative and essentially meaningless."[11]

With Internet-enabled cars, thermostats, and other devices by the thousands, there is in fact no separate cyberspace; the online world is increasingly physically present. "The Internet will disappear," Google chairman Eric Schmidt said in January 2015, meaning that the online and offline worlds will merge to such a degree that we will no longer always be able to differentiate them.[12]

Technology writer Timothy B. Lee once tweeted this editing rule: "Never use the prefix cyber—unless you are William Gibson." But governments now widely use the concept of cyberspace to signal the new global political challenges created by the interconnected world. The United States has an International Strategy for Cyberspace, the UK Foreign Ministry hosted an international conference on cyberspace, and China and Israel established a Cyberspace Administration and National Cyber Bureau, respectively.[13]

The word is here to stay in policy circles, and I will use "cyberspace" to mean the global network of interconnected information technologies and the information on it. While this suggests a distinction simply between two layers, the technology and the information, in fact states compete to exert authority and influence over three levels: the hardware, the software, and the information. Nation-states lay new fiber-optic cables and build massive data warehouses; develop malware and subsidize national operating systems and search engines as substitutes for Microsoft and Google; and use fake Facebook and Twitter accounts to spread propaganda and disinformation.

As with other types of power, there are the great cyber powers, the middling and lagging, and those that punch above their weight. The strongest have four components: large or technologically advanced economies; public institutions that channel the energy and innovation of the private sector; adventurous and somewhat rapacious military and intelligence agencies; and an attractive story to tell about cyberspace.

SIZE MATTERS

Economic and technological power is essential. States have an almost unassailable advantage over competitors if their companies develop the routers and servers that carry the Internet's data, the phones and personal computers that people use to communicate, and the apps and web services that serve as gateways to the Internet.

US technology companies dominate the Internet economy. The United States captures 35 percent of telecommunications revenues globally and over 40 percent of net income generated online. In India, the top twenty-five websites are US-based sites such as Google, Facebook, Twitter, and LinkedIn; over 50 percent of the top twenty-five sites in Brazil and South Africa are run by US companies. Google is the leader in search, and its Android operating system is on three-quarters of the smartphones being made in the world.

The shape and structure of the Internet give the United States a great deal of gravity. A small number of Internet providers carry the bulk of data over the "backbone," and a majority of Internet data gets drawn into and routed through the United States, even if this makes little geographic sense. An e-mail sent from Brazil to Peru, for example, might travel to Brasilia, leave Fortaleza on the coast via submarine cable, enter the United States through Miami, pass by California, and then head back down the Pacific to Lima. Former National Security Agency (NSA) director Michael Hayden put it bluntly when justifying some of the NSA's activities by telling the *National Journal*, "This is a home game for us. Are we not going to take advantage that so much of it [data] goes through Redmond, Washington? Why would we not turn the most powerful telecommunications and computing management structure on the planet to our use?"[14]

There is a central paradox for the United States: economic and technological sophistication are also sources of vulnerability. New engines of economic growth and opportunity—the Internet of Things, self-driving cars, smart cities—are open to destructive cyberattacks. Progress brings greater exposure (or, if you prefer the jargon of cybersecurity, attack vectors). As the Chinese economy becomes more technologically advanced, Beijing will face the same challenge of encouraging innovation while protecting technological systems, but for now the United States is uniquely empowered and susceptible.

Even if a country is not recognized as a technology leader, market size matters. The United States invented the Internet, but the future of cyberspace is not American, at least in terms of its users. The global distribution of power will shift. At present, Asia comprises 42 percent of the world's Internet population (the most by region), but it ranks only sixth in terms of penetration rates at 21.4 percent, meaning that an enormous, mostly young population has yet to be connected. China is home to the world's largest number of Internet users—649 million in 2014—but little more than half of the population is online; 60 percent of Internet users in China are under thirty. While Brazil has been on the cutting edge of open-source (or free) software, the influence it exerts over foreign companies and the governance of cyberspace rests in part on the larger and growing number of Brazilian Internet users. Indonesia and South Africa will have a similar sort of influence, though they have, so far, been much less active than Brazil on the global stage.

A Shared Mission

Critical to cyber power is a government's ability to work with the private sector. This interdependence is the source of nation-state capabilities and vulnerabilities and is most prominent in defense; private firms own the vast majority of telecom, energy, and transportation networks. National cybersecurity "has to be a shared mission," said President Obama at a February 2015 cybersecurity summit in Palo Alto. "So much of our computer networks and critical infrastructure are in the private sector, which means government cannot do this alone." A form of this cooperative defense is on view in action every year, on April 7, when Anonymous conducts #OpIsrael, a series of widespread attacks on Israeli websites. Launched the day before Holocaust Remembrance Day, the attacks try to "erase Israel from the Internet" in protest against Israeli policies directed against the Palestinians. In response, S-74, a clandestine hacking group in Shin Bet, the Israeli intelligence agency, reportedly disrupts the attackers, and volunteers from a network of companies and information technology associations also help defend websites.[15]

Spying is also deeply intertwined with the private sector, and signals intelligence programs have been built on the back of private infrastructure. Security expert Bruce Schneier writes, "Surveillance is the business model of the Internet." Google, Facebook, Twitter, and other social media companies collect user data to personalize and develop new products and, most importantly, to generate revenue through marketing and advertising. The more information technology companies collected, the more attractive they became to the NSA and other agencies as both targets and reluctant partners.[16]

The private sector has itself become a potent force in intelligence operations. CrowdStrike, Cylance, FireEye, Kaspersky, and Micro Trend are just a few of the cybersecurity companies that have exposed state-backed hacking programs from in the United States, China, Iran, Israel, United Kingdom, and Russia. "It is no longer spy versus spy," one senior intelligence analyst told me. "The private companies provide all-source intelligence. And they raise the bar for operations. Nations have to be better if they do not want to get caught by the companies."[17]

While security provides the most obvious illustration, the intertwining of business and government is also present in foreign and trade policy. States secure the assistance of technology companies through law, money, or ideology; that is, they can force companies to respond, buy them off, appeal to their better nature, or wield some combination of these tactics. The United States, cooperating with its European trade partners, has, for example, tried to use export-control laws to prevent US companies from selling surveillance technology to authoritarian regimes. It has also tried to shame them.

The challenge for governments wanting to harness the energy and innovation of the private sector is that technology companies increasingly do more business abroad than they do at home. Companies are critical to any solutions, but their economic incentives often lead them to try and find the middle ground between governments. This is especially true with the China market, where the private sector will demand US action on Chinese cyberattacks behind closed doors, but is unwilling to take a public stand in support of sanctions or other actions against Chinese hackers.

Small, technologically advanced states have one advantage. It is easier to create a shared mission, and the institutions needed to support that mission, when everyone knows each other. Personal ties and familiarity help. While one Israeli expert complained to me that too many security agencies were trying to have a say over cybersecurity policymaking, he also said that the "relationship paths between people are much, much shorter than anywhere else."

RAPACIOUSNESS WANTED
The third component of cyber power is adventurous and inventive military and intelligence agencies. Forty-one nation-states have cyber warfare doctrines; seventeen reportedly have offensive capabilities. It is cheap and easy to break into machines, but much more difficult to design an attack that creates real impact. That takes significant intelligence, analysis, and research and development. While poorer states can invest a relatively small amount in developing disruptive capacities, those with the greatest resources will be at the cutting edge. By some estimates, the United States spends three to four times more on cyber offense than it does on defense.[18]

In addition, the more intense the military competition, the more rapid the innovation and development will be. Israel's Unit 8200, dedicated to cyber operations, is the largest unit in the Israel Defense Forces.

As one Israeli official told me, "Security has been part of our DNA from the founding of the state, and cyber is just the newest challenge." In 2013, an Iran expert and a cybersecurity specialist could publish a report calling Iran a third-tier cyber power. Since then, sophisticated cyberattacks designed to derail Iran's nuclear program have appeared, and Iran's own attacks on neighbors and the United States have accelerated the development of Tehran's own capabilities. Andretta Towner, a senior intelligence analyst at the cybersecurity firm CrowdStrike, says, "Iran is not a tier three cyber actor anymore, it's emerging."[19]

It is not enough, however, to recognize the military potential of cyberattacks. A state also has to have the political will and creativity to use them. It has to recognize the art of the possible and have a touch of rapaciousness. I was once in a meeting where a former employee of a three-letter agency—he did not get more specific—said that one principle is essential to understanding cyberattacks: "If you can imagine it, you can do it. It just takes time, money, and some effort." This statement may be slightly hyperbolic, but the steady stream of leaks from Edward Snowden about the weakening of encryption, interdiction of servers and routers, and reprogramming of firmware on hard drives bolsters the argument that the US intelligence agencies indeed have expansive resources and imagination. There appears to be no communication platform that the NSA and CIA have not made the strategic choice to try to exploit, and there must be many possible, but as yet unseen, types of cyberattacks that disable or destroy adversary networks. Referencing the famous quote from science fiction author Arthur C. Clarke that "any sufficiently advanced technology is indistinguishable from magic," the information security researcher known as The Grugq put it this way: "An unlimited black budget, thousands of dedicated people, and decades of effort, is indistinguishable from magic."[20]

THE CYBER STORIES WE TELL

The final component of cyber power is an attractive narrative of cyberspace. Over the last two decades, the United States has advocated, often in tandem with technology and Internet companies, for norms of open access and free speech with minimal government interference and surveillance. While the Internet originated in a defense-sponsored network, the ARPANET, its rapid expansion is owed to private actors and a decentralized model of governance. Strong cybersecurity, especially by companies and individuals, was deemed a value in itself and promoted as an enabler of the free flow of information. The 2011 White House International Strategy for Cyberspace condensed all of this into one phrase, stating that the United States will work toward an "open, interoperable, secure, and reliable information and communications infrastructure."[21]

From the vantage point of much of the rest of the world, the Snowden revelations exposed a high degree of inconsistency, if not hypocrisy, in Washington's stance. The United States promoted itself as the defender of the open Internet at the same time that it engaged in extensive surveillance. Global Internet freedom and national security are not mutually exclusive, but they are not easy to reconcile. While the State Department supported the development of and taught dissidents in Syria to use Tor, a service that allows people to surf the web anonymously, the NSA was trying to break it. Still, even if "open, interoperable, secure, and reliant" does not fit well on a bumper sticker, the ideas remain potent.

While China has embraced the economic potential of the Internet and the need for global cooperation in fighting cyber crime, its narrative is not of an open, global platform but rather of one fragmented by national jurisdictions and regulations. "We live in a common online space," Lu Wei told his guests at the Lunar New Year's festivities. "This online space is made up of the internets of various countries, and each country has its own independent and autonomous interest in Internet sovereignty, Internet security, and Internet development." Many African and Asian countries line up with China behind the idea of multilateral governance of cyberspace and reassertion of sovereign power over digital communications. They are also using technology from the Chinese telecoms Huawei and ZTE to perform deep packet inspection of Internet content. When you send or receive data, your computer packages it in a packet with a header that tells Internet routers what it is, who it is from, and where it is going. With deep packet inspection, the Internet provider monitors the headings of the packets as well as examines the content of the messages, scanning for sensitive key words and blocking access to sites.[22]

Between these two positions, regions and countries can carve out alternate stories. The European Union's treatment of privacy as a fundamental right has translated into widely copied trade policies and regulatory models. "We have a chance to be influential around the world," Giovanni Buttarelli, the European data protection supervisor, told the *Wall Street Journal*. A "growing number of countries" are "looking at us and are likely to follow the European approach." In addition, European diplomats have been instrumental in generating UN resolutions and other international declarations that question the legitimacy of mass surveillance and promote the protection of online rights. Brazil has leveraged domestic experience into international influence. President Dilma Rousseff and others within Brazil have pointed to the Marco Civil da Internet, a civil rights framework for domestic policy-making, as a suitable model for the global governance of cyberspace.[23]

THE TRUE CYBER SUPERPOWERS

Few countries manage to put all four of the building blocks together. China and the United States are the only true cyber superpowers, with Russia standing just in the wings. China and the United States both have large numbers of web users and competitive technology companies. Beijing and Washington have created new political institutions and identified cyber as a strategic priority. Their cyber operations, for the purposes of espionage and sabotage, have pushed the envelope of what is acceptable in cyberspace. And both countries have tried to convince others that their mode of governing the Internet should drive the international conversation.

Russia meets all the criteria of a great cyber power but one. Cybersecurity experts often list Russian hackers as the best in the world. Unlike the Chinese, they are stealthy, leaving no clues that they are in a network. "I worry a lot more about the Russians" than the Chinese, Director of National Intelligence James Clapper told a conference at the University of Texas in 2014. Just over a year later, Clapper told Congress, "The Russian cyber threat is more severe than we have previously assessed."[24]

But Russia does not have a long game. It is losing the competition to produce the technologies and services that are shaping cyberspace. Kaspersky, the Russian cybersecurity firm, is the exception with 400 million users, $667 million in sales, and a record of exposing some of the highest-profile security incidents, including Stuxnet and the Carbanak cyber crime ring. China's Xiaomi is now the world's third-largest maker of cell phones and sold 60 million handsets in 2014. YotaPhone, a dual-screen Russian phone, hoped to sell 1 million in the same year. Telegram, a Russian mobile messaging app, has about 35 million users compared to Tencent's WeChat with 440 million. Chinese technologies are used throughout Southeast Asia, Africa, and Latin America. Russia's dream of a Silicon Valley remains elusive. Anticorruption officers raided the offices of a tech incubator in April 2013, official and unofficial statistics suggest an exodus of technology talent, and investment has evaporated.[25]

Other states and political entities may be able to check two or three of the four boxes. The United Kingdom, Germany, and France have the potential to develop significant offensive cyber power but have so far showed restraint. Israel has technological innovation and military flexibility but is happy to follow the United States' lead in Internet governance. Estonia, the birthplace of Skype and dozens of technology start-ups, punches above its weight. Its government is at the vanguard in designing new domestic institutions for cybersecurity and in defining norms of international behavior.

North Korea and Iran also have outsized influence. Pyongyang has no global technology companies, much less assured electricity for the entire country, and only a small number of people are allowed access to Kwangmyong (bright star), the officially sanctioned intranet at universities, government offices, and a small number of cafes in the major cities. Perhaps a thousand political elites have access to the global Internet, but North Korean hackers are not shy about launching disruptive and destructive attacks. Tehran is developing a technological base and has used cyberattacks as an important part of its asymmetric competition with the United States and its regional adversaries, Israel, Saudi Arabia, and the Gulf states.

THE PACHINKO BOARD OF CYBERSPACE

The new international order, the hacked world order, is emerging from the interactions of these powers. Since there is not a great deal of historical precedent to draw on, analogies in the field are many and, like all analogies, imperfect. Cyberspace is the Wild West or a feudal domain; cyber weapons are like improvised explosive devices, paintball guns, or antiradiation missiles. I have sat through conferences where, over the course of a day, speakers have compared cyber war to the first-ever use of airpower in 1911 by the Italian army's air corps against a Turkish camp at Ain Zara, Libya; the dropping of the atomic bombs on Hiroshima and Nagasaki; the 1960s arms race between the Soviet Union and the United States; the Vietnam War; and the low-intensity conflict against the Taliban in Afghanistan.

Discrepant analogies aside, the list of things states want from cyberspace is fairly consistent. They want to increase access to information and communication technologies to spark economic growth. They want to protect their own information assets and citizens at the same time that they exploit and sometimes damage those of other countries. And they want access to the data of their own citizens for intelligence and law enforcement. We can be certain, however, that the policy tools they design to achieve these desires will not be the same. Technological change and the empowerment of nonstate actors will affect and be interpreted by states differently. And yet, patterns of behavior are emerging.

Five fundamental questions about the uses and characteristics of cyberspace determine the strategic culture of a country's use of cyber power: how a nation-state interprets threats, uses force, exerts influence, spurs innovation, and delineates the national good. These questions are the little pegs on a pachinko board that direct the falling ball in one direction or another. Their answers define the American, Chinese, and Russian ways of cyber statecraft.[26]

INTERNAL AND EXTERNAL HAZARDS

The first question is: What is the balance between internal and external threats? All states see the underside of the Internet, the threat to security and the rule of law. Yet some primarily defend against threats to national security, whereas others conflate national security and regime stability. Or, put another way, liberal democracies and authoritarian states both collect data to prevent terrorist attacks, but authoritarian regimes also classify certain types of content and information as imperiling domestic stability and regime legitimacy.

Both of these security concerns result in governments of all types vacuuming up as much available data as possible. At the same time, they result in different visions of borders in cyberspace. For the United States the goal is to maintain the Internet as a global platform. The promotion of this norm is both ideological and self-interested. The belief is, as President Obama said in a town hall during a 2009 visit to China, that the "more freely information flows, the stronger societies become." Individuals become more creative, governments more accountable, and economies more competitive with an open Internet.

The focus on ideas, however, is only half of the equation. Or as the scholar of Russia Stephen Sestanovich put it in another context, "For the United States, the victory of its ideas has always been hard to separate from the spread of its influence and power." The United States reaps large economic, military, and intelligence advantages from keeping the Internet as a global platform.[27]

To be sure, even in the ideological realm, vision and reality often clash. There are, in Silicon Valley's favored phrase, degrees of friction. Many liberal democracies prevent the flows of certain types of content, and all advanced economies crack down on copyright violation and piracy. France demanded information from Twitter about users who violated French law by publishing anti-Semitic comments under the hashtags #UnBonJuif (a good Jew) and #UnJuifMort (a dead Jew), and Germany blocks neo-Nazi websites. India has asked Twitter, Google, and YouTube to remove posts considered blasphemous or that might incite communal violence.

Authoritarian states and those facing immense domestic pressure revert to the position of gatekeepers. There is no gap between their rhetoric and action because, for these states, the ability to control information is a primary security concern. A July 2010 report from the Chinese Academy of Social Sciences, *Development of China's New Media*, accuses the United States of using Twitter, Facebook, and other social media sites to foment instability. Until 2012, Russia's Internet developed relatively freely. As sentiment against President Vladimir Putin gathered steam in the streets and online, the Kremlin saw the protests as part of an information-warfare campaign and began trying to remove Western influence from the web. Sergei Smirnov, deputy director of Russia's Federal Security Service, told a regional security conference that the CIA and other secret services were using "new technologies" to "create and maintain constant tension in societies." Russia's 2013 National Security Concept warns of the serious danger arising "from the desire of a number of countries to dominate the global information domain space and to expel Russia from the external and internal information market."[28]

DISRUPTION AND DESTRUCTION

The second question is: How do you use force and military power in cyberspace? Much of what happens in cyberspace occurs in the shadows, out of public sight. Government officials have spoken off the record or on background about operations, but no government has taken credit for a cyberattack, and we know as much about the logic behind attacks that did not happen as about the thinking behind those that did. The United States, for example, reportedly planned to freeze Saddam Hussein's bank accounts during the 2003 Iraq War and take out air defenses in Libya in March 2011. In the case of Hussein, policymakers feared that the potential for collateral damage—in a spillover either to connected systems or to trust in the integrity of the financial system—was too high. The restraint proved prudent in Iraq, as cyberattacks against the telephone system did disrupt cell phones in neighboring countries. There was also, more generally, an aversion to providing justification for counterattacks on the United States.[29]

Policymakers are also reticent about what offensive cyber capabilities they possess and how they might use them. When Defense Secretary Philip Hammond announced that the United Kingdom was "developing a full spectrum military cyber capability, including a strike capability," the reaction was shock, not because anyone doubted that the United Kingdom would want digital weapons but because no country had admitted it so publicly.[30]

Even without policy documents and statements, we can see that states, large and small, are acting as if they live in a zero-sum world, where offense overcomes defense and potential adversaries will almost inevitably exploit vulnerabilities. Intelligence collection and force, espionage and sabotage have become blurred. Offense in cyberspace is considered the best defense. It is also a self-help world. While a number of states, including the United States, Russia, and China, talk about the need for international cooperation to develop acceptable norms of behavior, their actions betray a strong skepticism that shared interests or new treaties and agreements will dampen, much less eliminate, the most dangerous competition.

States have used cyberattacks in two different ways. The first is like Stuxnet. These digital strikes are surgical, precise, and, so far, rare. They require exquisite intelligence and are more like special operations than carpet bombing. The vast majority of cyber conflicts will be much more diffuse, a constant hum of low-level skirmishes that violate sovereignty but fall short of armed attacks. They may entail an attack on data at one company, as in the case of the hack of Sony, or DDoS attacks on multiple banks in a country. States find these types of attacks attractive because they are unlikely to provoke military retaliation but still have the potential to create useful political outcomes. They prick, harass, overwhelm, and undermine.

Assistant Secretary of Defense Eric Rosenbach, the Pentagon's principal cyber adviser, calls where all of this happens "the space between": "You have diplomacy, economic sanctions . . . and then you have military action. In between there's this space, right? In cyber, there are a lot of things that you can do in that space between that can help us accomplish the national interest." This gives states a whole lot of room to maneuver, to push the other side up to the point of violent conflict.[31]

It is one thing for a US government official to recognize this space in a speech. But the United States has an entire legal and bureaucratic structure that recognizes a sharp distinction between war and peace, between the powers granted to the military and intelligence agencies during national security conflicts and legitimate activity during peacetime. These dividing lines are blurred in other countries, particularly in Russia, and Moscow is likely to straddle categories, building asymmetric strategies that inhabit and exploit the "in-between" space. Putin has relied heavily on what some have termed hybrid or "nonlinear" war. He has used espionage, sabotage, economic coercion, and propaganda, as well as special forces or militias. In Crimea, special forces operated in concert with cyberattacks on politicians' cell phones. NATO and Ukrainian websites were knocked offline as the Russian media portrayed the government in Kiev as fascist.

DIPLOMATS AND TROLLS

The third question is: How do you exert influence in the digital age? While behind-closed-door negotiations and secret consultations remain important, states now actively engage publics and their diplomatic counterparts through social media. The era of one-way broadcasting is over, and the pace and volatility of public messaging have sped up greatly. Foreign ministries must converse in real time with a wide range of audiences, from private individuals to nongovernmental organizations to journalists.

Twitter, Facebook, and YouTube are now as much diplomatic tools as the public statement and démarche. According to public relations firm Burson-Marsteller, as of June 2014 83 percent of the 193 UN member countries have a presence on Twitter, as do more than half of the world's foreign ministers and their ministries and two-thirds of heads of state and government.[32]

Behind the social media engagements are competing theories of influence and counterinfluence. For the United States and its partners, the twin ideas of networks and narratives animate how diplomats should communicate with foreign publics. Embassies and diplomats have received greater autonomy to engage through social media and to develop relations with civil society organizations. The strategy is to increase global exposure to information that would help dispel animosity and anger toward the United States regarding its policies and actions. It is also an attempt to forge narratives that undermine the arguments and attractiveness of adversaries, especially radical Islamists. Alberto Fernandez, former coordinator of the US State Department's Center for Strategic Counterterrorism Communications, describes his office as engaging in the "war of narratives."[33]

Narrative coherence and network flexibility may not, however, be able to withstand a torrent of misinformation. In the battle for hearts and minds, states may simply flood the zone under contention with rumors, conspiracy theories, and falsehoods. The demand for speed over accuracy on social media often results in bad information driving out good in the marketplace of ideas. Narrative coherence has difficulty standing up to dissembling. Hundreds of Russian trolls have certainly adduced this, posting flattering comments about Putin on news websites, tweeting abuse at critics, and maintaining fake Facebook accounts.

Silicon Valley, Beijing, and Brussels

The fourth question is: What model of technological competition is best adapted for the future? Here there are three competing types: Silicon Valley, Beijing, or Brussels. The Silicon Valley model stresses innovation and entrepreneurship. The state funds basic research and development, but companies and the private sector provide the main engine of growth. Universities not only train the next generation of scientists but act as significant sources of discovery and enterprise. The state acts to keep borders open and competition level, and there is a high degree of trust in the private market's ability to self-regulate. The ultimate goal, absolute gain, rests on the assumption that US companies will be the most competitive.

The Beijing model is mercantilist. The government defines crucial long-term development goals and funds research in these areas. The state intervenes to protect industries and build national champions. While welcome, foreign investment is channeled and molded so as to raise the competitiveness of domestic industries. There is a heavy focus on relative gains and on technological autonomy. The 2006 Guidelines on National Medium- and Long-Term Program for Science and Technology Development, for example, aspire to reduce the "degree of dependence on technology from other countries to 30 percent or less" by 2020. Noting the vulnerability that comes from relying on other countries, especially the United States and Japan, the guidelines declare that China should not purchase any "core technologies in key fields that affect the lifeblood of the national economy and national security."[34]

The Brussels model is more managerial than the Silicon Valley approach and less interventionist than the Beijing one. The state directs its efforts at social goals, managing inequality, promoting social welfare, and, especially important in digital competition, protecting privacy. An overarching ambition of regulation is to create a common market, to lower or eliminate trade barriers within the European Union, and to use the gravity of the European market and shared standards to shape technological trajectories. "We are pursuing a digital vision for Europe," said EU Commissioner for Digital Economy and Society Günther Oettinger. "Only in this way will we be able to set standards in a globalized world, achieve market dominance, and at the same time secure our digital sovereignty."[35]

These are, of course, ideal types. China has tried to recreate Silicon Valley locally; Europeans firms such as Nokia, Opera, F-Secure, SoundCloud, Rovio, Raspberry-PI, Spotify, and Skype are innovative, entrepreneurial technology leaders; and Washington has used security concerns to block Chinese telecoms from domestic markets. But they are the default models that policymakers fall back on.

THE SOCIAL CONTRACT

The final question is essentially domestic but radiates back into the international arena if only because data flows across national borders: What is the balance between individual rights and state interests in the digital age? Every society is confronting the question of what to do with the massive amounts of data generated by cell phones, Internet usage, and networks of cameras and sensors recording the physical world. Within liberal democratic societies, there is an assumption that the ubiquity and permanence of data will force a rewriting of the social contract. States have legitimate security and law enforcement rationales for accessing data, but individual citizens also question whether the benefits of giving ever-increasing amounts of data to the government and companies outweigh the costs. While liberal democracies will have different understandings about rights and responsibilities, there will still be similar understandings about the individual's relationship to the state and shared references to the need for some limits on state power. These visions of the social contract, drawn from British philosopher John Locke and French Enlightenment thinker Jean-Jacques Rousseau, emphasize the recognition of human rights online, government transparency, and checks and balances.

By contrast, the narrative in one-party and authoritarian states is primarily about how to optimize data collection to serve national goals, including economic development and national security. Discussions in the Chinese press about big data, for example, revolve around two questions: How can the government and companies exploit what many call the "new oil" for economic advantage, and what should the Chinese government do to protect consumers from misuse of data and criminal breaches? This concept of the role of the state echoes Thomas Hobbes, whereby the state acts to defend and protect the national interest and, at times, violates individual rights, if necessary, for state preservation.

The history of cyberspace and cyber conflict is short, but the pace of history is rapidly accelerating. Whereas years or months once separated notable cyberattacks, now they come almost weekly, if not sometimes daily. In the onslaught, it is difficult to see any underlying pattern. If history is one damn thing after another, the history of the digital age seems little more than one damn cyberattack after another.

The hacked world order is, however, not completely chaotic. The five fundamental questions identify the contours of the new world and nation-states' motivations. States alternate between political disruption and destruction, platforms and gates, narrative construction and dissembling, mercantilist and innovative intervention, and Hobbesian and Lockean approaches to data and the public good. These approaches are visible as states disrupt, destroy, steal, trade, and influence.

Chapter 3

GUARDIANS OF PEACE, LITTLE GREEN MEN, AND THE ELECTRONIC ARMIES OF THE FUTURE

....

D uring Thanksgiving week in 2014, the employees of Sony Pictures lost access to the company's computer networks and their e-mail accounts due to a massive hack. Management was forced to communicate with employees through phone trees, personal Gmail accounts, and old BlackBerry phones found in a storeroom and speedily rushed into service. Writers worked on legal pads; the payroll department cut checks on old machines. The hackers, operating under the name Guardians of Peace (GOP), uploaded five unreleased Sony films—including *Fury*, a World War II film starring Brad Pitt, and a remake of *Annie*—to file-sharing Internet sites. The group not only stole one hundred terabytes of internal data but also damaged two-thirds of the company's servers and computers. Sony Entertainment CEO Michael Lynton told the *Wall Street Journal*, "It took me 24 or 36 hours to fully understand this was not something we were going to be able to recover from in the next week or two."[1]

On December 1, the FBI announced that it was investigating the breach and, eighteen days later, that the Guardians of Peace were really North Korean hackers. Pyongyang had previously expressed outrage over the Sony film *The Interview*, starring Seth Rogen and James Franco. Six months before, a Foreign Ministry spokesman had called the movie, which depicts the assassination of supreme leader Kim Jong-un, "the most blatant act of terrorism and an act of war that we will never tolerate." "If the United States administration tacitly approves or supports the release of this film," the spokesman continued, "we will take a decisive and merciless countermeasure."[2]

The Kim regime's ability to deliver these merciless countermeasures through cyberattacks is a bit of a paradox. Known as the Hermit Kingdom due to its isolation from the outside world, North Korea is popularly perceived as a technological backwater. The per capita gross domestic product in South Korea is over $33,000; it is less than $2,000 in North Korea. A stark photo of the Korean Peninsula taken from the International Space Station captures the country's poverty: bright lights illuminate South Korea and China; in between, darkness cloaks North Korea. Internet access, allowed only to a small cadre of political elites with special permission, is among the lowest in the world. As of 2014, the entire country had only 1,024 Internet protocol (IP) addresses—fewer than in a couple of New York City blocks.

The feebleness of the North Korean economy has not stopped the regime from seeing cyberattacks as an important tool; they are cost-effective, allow North Korea to attack targets away from the peninsula, and operate (so far, at least) at a level that will not provoke military responses. As Director of National Intelligence James Clapper put it, "Cyber is a powerful new realm for them, where they believe they can exert maximum influence at minimum cost, and this recent episode with Sony has shown that they can get recognition for their cyber capabilities." Moreover, the lack of communication technologies within the country means North Korea is relatively immune from digital strikes itself. There just are not many targets for such attacks.[3]

Given the strategic and tactical efficacy of cyber offense, North Korea is dedicating scarce resources to Bureau 121, an elite force run by the Reconnaissance General Bureau, the military's spy agency. Defectors claim hackers are recruited at a young age, trained, and given special privileges, housing, and higher status. "There is a pyramid-like prodigy recruiting system," says one defector, "where smart kids from all over the country—students who are good at math, coding and possess top analytical skills—are picked up to be grouped at Keumseong High School." After graduation, they go on to technical universities such as Kim Il-sung University and Kim Chaek University of Technology. Some members of Bureau 121 are supposedly based at Chilbosan Hotel in Shenyang, the capital of Liaoning province, China. The website for the hotel boasts of a sauna, fitness room, karaoke, and broadband Internet; one TripAdvisor reviewer raved that the "crowning jewel is the in-house North Korean restaurant that can bring you delicious Korean food right to your room."[4]

Four days after the FBI announcement, the Guardians of Peace sent an e-mail to Sony employees and their families, threatening, "What we have done so far is only a small part of our further plan." James Franco and Seth Rogen went on *Saturday Night Live* to make fun of the hack. Rogen interrupted Franco during the monologue to tell him, "It is much, much worse than we thought." He announced that the North Koreans had leaked embarrassing photos, while the screen showed images of Rogen in pantyhose and of Rogen and Franco recreating the *Rolling Stone* cover of John Lennon and Yoko Ono, with Rogen in his underwear. The GOP continued to release batches of stolen data, including salaries, Social Security numbers, passwords, and sales plans, as well as two years' worth of the e-mail correspondence of a number of Sony Pictures executives. E-mails making racially insensitive comments about President Barack Obama, disparaging Angelina Jolie and other actors, and highlighting the gender gap in pay for male and female actors came to light. The costs of expunging the hackers and repairing the damage from the hacks had reached $35 million by March 31, 2015.[5]

As the December 25 release date for the movie approached, the hackers threatened theaters with physical violence. In a note accompanying another cache of released data, the Guardians of Peace wrote, "Remember the 11th of September. We will clearly show it to you at the very time and places 'The Interview' be shown [sic]." Despite the Department of Homeland Security's assurance that the threats had no credibility, on December 17, after theater owners said they would not show the film, Sony canceled the movie's theatrical release. Two days later, the FBI issued a press release concluding that the "North Korean government is responsible" for the intrusion into Sony's networks. This was the first time the US government had explicitly and directly named another government as responsible for hacking.[6]

President Obama, in his end-of-year news conference, criticized Sony for pulling the film. "I'm sympathetic," said the president, "that Sony as a private company was worried about liabilities, and this and that and the other. I wish they had spoken to me first. I would have told them, do not get into a pattern in which you're intimidated by these kinds of criminal attacks." The president asserted that the United States will "respond proportionally, and we'll respond in a place and time and manner that we choose. It's not something that I will announce here today at a press conference."[7]

With bad publicity mounting, Sony reversed its decision and released *The Interview* in select theaters and online with support from Google and Microsoft. A few days after the president announced that the United States would retaliate, North Korea disappeared from the Internet. With no traffic coming from the country, Internet experts said the event looked like a distributed denial-of-service (DDoS) attack, and people began speculating that the United States was behind it. The State Department refused to comment on the disappearance, but State Department spokeswoman Marie Harf told reporters, "Some [responses] will be seen. Some may not be seen." Speaking a few months later, unnamed sources cut through the coyness. The US government, according to these sources, had not crippled North Korea's Internet infrastructure; a group of individual hackers and vigilantes had brought down the country's network. The United States did, however, launch precision computer attacks on targets used by the leadership.[8]

On January 2, 2015, the United States levied economic sanctions on the Reconnaissance General Bureau, the Korea Tangun Trading Corporation, and the Korea Mining Development Trading Corporation (North Korea's primary arms dealer and main exporter of ballistic missiles and conventional weapons). The United States also reportedly asked the Chinese government for help with North Korea, but public statements from Beijing were noncommittal. Officials stated that while China opposed cyberattacks and would engage in "constructive cooperation" with the international community, there was no proof North Korea was behind the Sony hacks. Foreign Ministry spokeswoman Hua Chunying said, "We need sufficient evidence before drawing any conclusion."[9]

A SMOKING GUN?

The Sony hack is almost too perfect as both narrative thriller and parable. Ruthless tyrant with outlandish hair from one of the world's poorest countries hacks major company, causing millions of dollars in damage, destroying computers, and creating a threat to free speech so severe that George Clooney organizes a petition in support of showing the movie (which no one in Hollywood will sign). The attack exposes boorish behavior and crude language from studio executives and provokes a response from the president. All this over a sophomoric movie by Seth Rogen and James Franco. At the same time, the hacks exposed gaping holes in how the United States thinks about and responds to cyberattacks, raising questions about when and how to identify an attacker, what counts as evidence of an attack, what the threshold of an attack is, and what role the government should play in defending the private sector.

The first step in responding to an attack is identifying the culprit, but almost from the moment North Korea was named as the primary suspect behind the Sony hacks, doubters emerged within the cybersecurity community. As the information security researcher known as The Grugq wrote, "The problem with attribution in the cyber realm is that the evidence is entirely under the control of the attacker." As a result, "the attacker can mimic, spoof, falsify or remove any evidentiary data available to the defense." Even if the attacks could be traced back to North Korea, it was difficult to know if the attackers were working on their own or with support from government officials. Many hackers freelance. In the earliest communication with the company, the hackers did not seem very interested in Sony's release of *The Interview*. Instead, the first e-mail, signed by a different group than the GOP, attempted to extort money from the company. The e-mails only began mentioning the movie in later statements after the press had speculated that North Korea was behind the attacks.[10]

In fingering North Korea for the crime, the FBI released several pieces of evidence. The malware employed in the attack used similar lines of code, algorithms, and data-deletion methods as DarkSeoul, a June 2013 attack on South Korean banks and television broadcasters. In addition, North Korean hackers had previously used the Internet infrastructure employed in the attack. In particular the code that deleted files communicated with IP addresses that North Korean hackers had used before.[11]

But to some doubters, these facts hardly amounted to a smoking gun. Marc Rogers, a longtime hacker and director of security for DEF-CON, the world's largest hacker conference, remained skeptical: "We don't have any solid evidence that implicates North Korea, while at the same time we don't have enough evidence to rule North Korea out." Rogers argued that most malware is publicly available, and a huge amount of code sharing goes on in the hacker underground. It is not uncommon to see the same malware across different attacks, so Rogers did not view as conclusive evidence that the Sony hackers had used the same malware as was used in DarkSeoul. Moreover, as Rogers and others noted, common criminals widely used the IP addresses allegedly used by the North Korean hackers. The addresses were in Thailand, Poland, Italy, Bolivia, Singapore, Cyprus, and the United States, and anyone could exploit them and cover their tracks.[12]

Further revelations eventually quieted the doubters. Responding to critics, FBI director James Comey, in a speech at Fordham University, said that the North Korean hackers "got sloppy" and failed to use proxy servers that would hide their identity. "Several times," Comey continued, "either because they forgot or because they had a technical problem, they connected directly and we could see them." Yet the most convincing evidence the FBI had was not available to the general public. The skeptics, in Comey's words, "don't have the facts that I have, don't see what I see." As Comey explained, "We have a range of other sources and methods that I'm going to continue to protect because we think they're critical to our ability—the entire intelligence community's ability—to see future attacks and to understand this attack better."[13]

Even if Comey intended to protect these other sources and methods, Edward Snowden's revelations and other leaks to the press soon revealed some of them. An Internet tapping system, known as XKEY-SCORE, allows the National Security Agency (NSA) to trace a hacker's location or at least the location they used to launch an attack. According to a *New York Times* report published in early January 2015, the NSA had also gained access to North Korean computers even before the Sony hack. In some cases agents sat on Chinese and Malaysian networks that North Korean hackers liked to use and watched them attack. This information in the *New York Times* built on a 2013 *Washington Post* story that the United States had placed "covert implants" in tens of thousands of computers, routers, and firewalls around the world. Three-quarters of these operations targeted potential adversaries such as China, Iran, Russia, and North Korea, and the plan was to extend the surveillance to millions of machines. This would have given the United States some overview of North Korean actions.[14]

The NSA also exploited South Korean intelligence in a process called fourth-party collection, or, even better, "drinking from someone else's milkshake," which entails using the data other spies gather from a third party—say, the NSA taking data Chinese spies have stolen from the United Nations. The NSA noticed the South Koreans were spying on the United States (allies spying on allies) and, in the course of breaking into South Korean computers, found that they had also been targeting the North Korean cyber espionage programs. While the United States may have seen the initial spear-phishing e-mail to Sony that got the hackers in, officials who spoke to the *New York Times* said they did not realize how thoroughly the North Korean hackers had mapped the company's networks or the severity of the attack planned.[15]

The leaks and the Snowden revelations eventually settled the question of whether the North Koreans were behind the Sony hacks, but they damaged US ability to spy on potential adversaries. Pyongyang (and Moscow and Beijing) certainly took countermeasures against the NSA; information and insight were lost. The leaks did, however, create one possible positive outcome: the suggestion of a degree of NSA omniscience might deter attacks on the United States. In testimony about six months before the Sony hack, Admiral Michael S. Rogers obliquely acknowledged this possibility. His logic went like this: if Snowden has convinced potential attackers that the NSA sees all, then they will think the agency can attribute attacks to them and eventually retaliate. The Chinese and Russians at least would pause before launching destructive attacks. Fears of omniscience, unfortunately, had much less impact on the North Koreans (or the Iranians).[16]

VANDALISM OR WAR?

Leaks and the "just trust us" approach to attribution are, however, likely to have unintended consequences. If you are going to name a nation-state and levy economic and legal sanctions, should you meet some minimum level of attribution? Put another way, what happens when Beijing says it has evidence that a contractor in Arlington, Virginia, broke into Chinese networks and that it is thus sanctioning Boeing, but cannot reveal the most damning evidence? More generally, is it possible to create a standard of attribution? Should the level of attribution differ, for example, depending on the severity of the event?

Not only did US officials have problems in agreeing how to identify those behind the Sony attack, but they had difficulty describing the attack itself. In an interview with CNN a few days after his end-of-year press conference, President Obama said he considered the hack not "an act of war" but rather "an act of cybervandalism." Senator John McCain rejected the characterization: "It's more than vandalism. It's a new form of warfare." These sharply contrasting stances reflected more than the domestic divide between the president and one of his most vocal critics on national security matters. They revealed how the Sony hack confounded previous categories because it existed in an in-between space, one that US cyber policy had not really prepared for.

The Pentagon's cybersecurity strategy, released in July 2011, described two major types of threat. Along with network attacks that disrupt the military's ability to operate, the document warned that "computer-induced failures of power grids, transportation networks, or financial systems could cause massive physical damage and economic disruption." For at least twenty years, government officials and cybersecurity experts had been warning of a coming cyber Armageddon that would arrive like a destructive bolt from the blue, causing physical damage and death. Cybersecurity expert Winn Schwartau used the phrase "electronic Pearl Harbor" in congressional testimony in 1991, and numerous government officials have repeated it in different forms ever since. Former secretary of defense Leon Panetta was particularly fond of "cyber Pearl Harbor," using the term multiple times in 2011 and 2012. The White House's 2011 International Strategy for Cyberspace warns that the "United States will respond to hostile acts in cyberspace as we would to any other threat to our country." An off-the-record comment may, however, best sum up the US position. One unnamed military official told the *Wall Street Journal*, "If you shut down our power grid, maybe we will put a missile down one of your smokestacks."[17]

The other threat, while less visible, could, in the Pentagon's phrasing, be the "most pervasive." "Every year," the 2011 cybersecurity document claimed, "an amount of intellectual property larger than that contained in the Library of Congress is stolen from networks maintained by U.S. businesses, universities, and government departments and agencies." In his fifth State of the Union, President Obama touched on both types of threats, mentioning "foreign countries and companies [swiping] our corporate secrets" and enemies "seeking the ability to sabotage our power grid, our financial institutions, our air traffic control systems."[18]

The Sony hack existed outside these two types of threat. It did not cause death or physical destruction. The hackers stole data, but not to advance the economic interest of a foreign company or government. They meant to embarrass and hurt Sony. While it clearly damaged Sony's economic interests and reputation, the hack, unlike the widespread theft of intellectual property for technology companies, did not undermine economic security. Rather the goal was the coercion of one company.

The Obama administration struggled in the early days of the crisis to define the attack, leading to uncertain and confusing signals to domestic agencies and foreign partners. What President Obama described as cybervandalism was soon redefined as a threat to core US values and national security. North Korea had launched a cyberattack that violated US sovereignty and was "an attempt to interfere with freedom of expression," in the words of Christopher Painter, State Department coordinator for cyber issues. The joke version of this point, circulated on the Internet, was a modification of the Motion Picture Association of America rating screen you see before a movie: "The following MOVIE has been approved for AMERICAN AUDIENCES by the Democratic People's Republic of Korea." If Sony had not canceled the release of *The Interview*, there likely would have been no official US response. Sony might have represented an extreme case of a company falling prey to hackers, but it would not have been unique.[19]

Once Sony did withdraw the movie, the United States chose to act not only to defend freedom of expression but also to prevent other countries from thinking that they could launch cyberattacks to create political outcomes. "Many nation-states, groups, and individuals seem to have come to the conclusion that there is little price to pay for engaging in these behaviors," said Admiral Rogers. "Nation-states, groups and individuals are going to watch how the U.S. responds to this as a nation."[20]

The North Korean hackers were innovative in targeting a private company for national political interests. But they were not the first to see disruptive cyberattacks as a useful tool of political coercion. Their neighbors to the north had pioneered that tactic over the previous decade.

THE FIRST CYBER CONFLICT

The first major cyber conflict began on April 27, 2007, at around 10 p.m., as the operators of Estonian government websites discovered they were under attack.

Relations with Moscow had been tense since January, when the Estonian government announced its intentions to move a statue commemorating World War II from the center of the capital, Tallinn, to the outskirts of the city. The acrimony between the two countries had historical roots. In 1918, Estonia gained its independence from Russia, but its freedom only lasted twenty-two years, as the Soviet Union invaded in 1940. The Soviets deported tens of thousands from Estonia and other Baltic states in June 1941. When the Nazis launched Operation Barbossa and invaded the Soviet Union, some Estonians initially welcomed the Germans as a liberating force.

This bitter history swirled around the monument. Many Estonians viewed the statue, a Red Army soldier, helmet in hand, mourning his fallen comrades, as a symbol of the Soviet occupation. Russian politicians, as well as the sizable population of ethnic Russians in Estonia, saw the move as an insult to the memory of the 27 million who died in the Great Patriotic War. Estonian policymakers cast the decision to move the statue as a solution to a public-order problem: it would reduce the clashes between war veterans, Estonia-born Russians, and more conservative, nationalistic Estonians who gathered in the shadow of the "Monument to the Fallen in the Second World War" to argue about the meaning of the war and share memories of the Soviet occupation of Estonia. The move was also a clear effort to free Estonia from the Soviet legacy and to align the country with Europe.[21]

Throughout early 2007, Moscow made its displeasure about the statue's impending move known and exerted diplomatic pressure. High-ranking Russian officials threatened a boycott of Estonian goods. In the weeks before the scheduled move, Russian Foreign Ministry officials warned of serious consequences to the bilateral relationship.

The day before the move, 1,500 people gathered in downtown Tallinn to protest. After a small group tried to break through a police line protecting the memorial, the protest turned violent. Demonstrators threw rocks and bottles. The police responded with stun grenades. Around three hundred people were arrested amid widespread vandalism and looting. Estonian officials called the protests the worst riots since the country declared its independence from the Soviet Union in 1991. One defense official told me, "For the French those types of riots might be a common weekend, but they were new to us." In Moscow, members of Nashi, a pro-Kremlin youth movement, blocked off the surrounding streets and attacked Estonia's embassy. Russian Foreign Ministry officials responded with surprisingly vitriolic rhetoric, calling the statue's move disgusting, blasphemous, inhuman, and sacrilegious.[22]

That night the attacks on websites began. Hackers defaced the sites of the Estonian president, Ministry of Foreign Affairs, Ministry of Justice, and parliament. The website of the Reform Party, the lead political partner in the coalition government, displayed a fake letter of apology for moving the statue. Estonian prime minister Andrus Ansip and other leading politicians were spammed (sent large amounts of junk mail), and the e-mail services of the Estonian parliament had to be temporarily shut down.

Around April 30, hackers stepped up the intensity and sophistication of their attacks. During the first wave, hackers in online chat forums raged against the Estonians and provided information to others on how to launch a ping attack, a simple request for a response from a web server, repeated hundreds of times per second, eventually leading to a crash. The second wave was more like carpet bombing, using networks of hijacked computers called botnets to launch attacks. Some of these botnets included up to 85,000 commandeered computers and were located in Belgium, Canada, Egypt, Germany, Russia, Turkey, the United States, Vietnam, and elsewhere. Websites that typically received 1,000 visits in a day became overwhelmed on receiving more than 2,000 visits a second. The attacks broadened out, targeting media and banking sites. The Estonian news outlet *Postimees Online* went down. Once blocked, the hackers quickly adopted new tools or shifted the attacks to come from a new geographical location, maneuvering around walls as quickly as the Estonians built them.[23]

The attacks reached their apex around May 9, as Russia was officially commemorating the end of World War II and President Vladimir Putin was declaiming that those who "defile the monuments to the heroes of this war are insulting their own people and spreading enmity and new distrust between countries and peoples." At one time, fifty-eight Estonian websites were down. The online services of Estonia's largest bank, Hansabank, were unavailable for ninety minutes on May 9 and for two hours the next day. In order to deal with the massive amounts of data flowing in from abroad, Estonia had to temporarily disconnect itself from the outside Internet. The Internet within Estonia was accessible, but Estonians living abroad were cut off from their bank accounts and news services. Over the next week, the attacks would stop and start; they concluded entirely on May 18 at 11 p.m. (12 p.m. Moscow time).[24]

While Estonian officials did not know that the removal of the statue would be the trigger, they expected the use of cyberattacks against them one day. As Lauri Almann, undersecretary in the Defense Ministry during the 2007 attacks, said, "We were expecting attack because we were so dependent on IT [information technology]." After its independence from the Soviet Union in 1991, the country embraced IT and the Internet not only as key to economic development but also as an emblem of what Estonia wanted to become—open, inclusive, and Western, not Russian.

By most measures, few would have guessed that Estonia would become a major technology player, a highly wired society, and the home of Skype. At the time of independence, only half the population had a phone line. Still, there was some base to build on. The Institute of Cybernetics, founded in 1960, provided an important educational foundation, and Estonian programmers had played a significant role in the Soviet space program and in developing software for the Telegraph Agency of the Soviet Union, the organization that collected and distributed news to Soviet newspapers and radio and television stations. More importantly, newly independent Estonia recognized communication technologies as a means to overcome its lack of physical infrastructure and leapfrog over a generation of legacy technologies. In 1996, the government declared its intention to make Estonia a global test site for the information society.[25]

By 1998 all schools were online, and in 2000 the government declared Internet access a human right. The country adopted a system of e-governance that included cabinet meetings going paperless and using a web-based document system. Since 2001, Estonians have been issued national identification cards that provide digital signatures. At the time of the attack, over 95 percent of bank transactions were conducted via the Internet, health forms were stored in the digital cloud, and Estonians could vote and file income taxes online. Yet the dependence on the Internet was more than just practical or economic. As Linnar Viik, a lecturer at the Estonian IT College, government adviser, and founder of several software and mobile communication companies, put it, "For other countries, the Internet is just another service, like tap water, or clean streets. But for young Estonians, the Internet is a manifestation of something more than a service—it's a symbol of democracy and freedom."[26]

Estonia's vulnerability, on the economic, political, and psychological levels, made it an easy target for cyberattacks. In the days before and after the statue's move, online Russian-language forums hummed with calls for retaliation against Estonia. Estonian intelligence and police officers closely monitored these discussions, which provided information about targets, dates, and exact times for coordinated attacks. Defenses, moreover, had been in preparation in the preceding years. In 2006, for example, the government had signed a memorandum of understanding with the banks and Internet service providers (ISPs) to coordinate responses to computer attacks. The Estonian Computer Emergency Response Team (CERT), established in 2006, had run emergency exercises in March 2007 right after national elections. These exercises tightened already strong links among people working in IT across the government as well as between the government and the private sector.

Estonia shared with Israel and Finland a great advantage in building cyber power: size. In a country with only 1.3 million people, most government officials and IT specialists were already acquainted or could be quickly introduced. The US embassy in Tallinn, in a cable titled "Estonia's Cyber Attacks: Lessons Learned," argued that "Estonia's CERT, the [Government of Estonia's] Cyber Defense Unit, and private IT Security Managers all knew each other for years before the crisis and were, thus, able to work closely together."[27]

Estonia's size also meant that it never believed it could deal with the attacks alone. It had to seek help from the outside world. As Viik told me, the "answer of how to solve the security problem was never more, better technology. It was collaboration." In a lucky coincidence, two technical conferences were scheduled in Tallinn during the week of May 3, bringing Estonian operators into close contact with European and American experts. Hillar Aarelaid, head of CERT, had dinner with Kurtis Lindqvist, head of Netnod, a Stockholm-based nonprofit that runs Internet exchange points and one of the domain name root servers. Lindqvist would be instrumental in helping convince foreign ISPs to block the botnets attacking Estonia. CERT contacted over one hundred countries to ask them to block attacks, and American, Finnish, German, Israeli, and Slovenian security experts also helped process information, filter and block attacks, and provide bandwidth to divert or remediate the attacks that continued to get through. As the attacks dragged on for almost three weeks, observers from the US Department of Defense, NSA, US Navy, and Secret Service arrived in Tallinn.[28]

The big question was how Estonia's political and military allies would respond to the attacks. Estonia's president, foreign minister, and defense minister all raised the emergency with European Union and NATO officials. Estonia joined NATO in 2004 and thus came under the Washington Treaty's Article 5 mutual-security guarantee—the alliance would treat an armed attack on any one member as an attack on all and respond to defend the victim. While the cyberattacks were not "armed" in the traditional sense, since they did not involve physical force or cause destruction or death, they were clearly designed to exploit vulnerabilities to achieve political aims, especially as they occurred in concert with diplomatic pressure from Moscow. Or as Estonia's minister of defense Jaak Aaviksoo put it, "The attacks cannot be treated as hooliganism, but have to be treated as an attack against the state."[29]

None of the members of NATO believed that the attacks justified military action, though NATO sent technical experts to Tallinn during the crisis. Senior officials told the press that they were taking the attacks "very seriously," since they went "to the heart of the alliance's modus operandi." But throughout the crisis, NATO and EU officials were very careful never to directly accuse Moscow of responsibility for the attacks. Estonian officials were less circumspect. The minister of justice asserted that some of the data packets in the flood had been traced to IP addresses belonging to Moscow offices of the Kremlin, and Prime Minister Andrus Ansip directly blamed the Russian government.[30]

Besides the immediate political context of the attacks and Moscow's clear motive to support them, additional evidence suggested that Russian authorities were behind some parts of the attack. There were the above-mentioned IP addresses and the fact that Russian hackers had used the same botnets in previous attacks. The size and sophistication of some of the attacks also suggested the need for some coordination. On May 4, two routers belonging to the Estonian government and the telecom company Elion were attacked and crashed almost immediately. The addresses of these routers were not publicly available, and so a successful attack on them required intelligence support. Two years after the attacks, Sergei Markov, a deputy of the Russian State Duma, identified the perpetrators of the attacks as members of the pro-Kremlin youth group Nashi, a conclusion that a secret 2009 NSA study also reached.[31]

Despite breathless reporting about Europe's first "cyber war," the lasting impact of the attacks was minimal. Estonia did not reverse its decision to move the statue, and the attacks did not result in long-term damage to critical infrastructure or the economy. Estonia was briefly cut off from the rest of the world, but the Internet remained accessible within the country. The damage of the attack was instead highly psychological, putting Estonia's digital vulnerability in stark relief.

The attacks also accelerated the development of domestic institutions, and Estonia used its experiences "on the front line" to develop a diplomatic platform and promote itself as an international leader in cybersecurity and Internet governance. Conflict served as a base for cyber power. With regard to the workings and interworking of agencies and ministries, Estonia found that ad hoc, informal processes worked well, while the official responses to the attacks were often muddled and confused. There was no consistent policy across the different ministries. Decisions were made and policy justifications found afterward. One Estonian bank official told me, "The technical means we found to fight the attacks were not directly illegal, but stretched the definition." As a result, Estonia adopted a comprehensive cyber strategy in 2008. The country also built on the spirit of voluntarism and collaboration demonstrated during the crisis, developing the Cyber Defense League, a unit of programmers, computer scientists, and software engineers whose mission is to "protect Estonia's high-tech way of life." The unit is part of Estonia's Defense League, a volunteer reserve force that outnumbers the full-time military. By 2014, Estonia was spending €40 million a year on cybersecurity, about .5 percent of the country's spending.[32]

ESTONIA + MILITARY INVASION = GEORGIA

A year after the attacks on Estonia, cyberattacks accompanied conventional warfare in the conflict between Russia and Georgia. Russia harnessed disruptive attacks launched by third-party hackers to military force.

After the fall of the Soviet Union, a region in the Caucasus a little bigger than Rhode Island known as South Ossetia, which had been a special autonomous area within Georgia, declared its independence. A separatist government ruled parts of South Ossetia, while other sections of the region remained under Georgian control. A brief war erupted in 1991–1992; the Russians brokered a cease-fire that included stationing peacekeeping forces from Georgia, Russia, and Ossetia in the region.

It was a tenuous arrangement, and when elected president in 2004, Mikheil Saakashvili set returning South Ossetia to Georgian control as an early priority. He also pushed for Georgia's entry into NATO, triggering harsh warnings from Moscow. In 2006 residents of South Ossetia overwhelmingly voted for independence from Georgia. In the summer of 2008, Georgian and South Ossetian forces exchanged fire, and more than 8,000 Russian troops conducted exercises on the border. On the evening of August 7, the Georgian military entered the South Ossetian capital, Tskhinvali, claiming to be responding to bombardments by South Ossetian soldiers. The Russian response was swift. The next day Russian tanks, artillery, and reconnaissance forces entered Tskhinvali, and aircraft conducted airstrikes on Georgian positions and the port city Poti. Russian ground forces moved into Georgia, drawing close to the capital, Tbilisi.

Two and a half weeks after the conflict ended, Russia recognized an independent South Ossetia. The Five-Day War killed hundreds and left thousands in temporary refugee shelters. Though not a very large military conflict, it was significant in the Kremlin's larger strategic thinking. Charles King of Georgetown University writes that historians will look back at the conflict and "mark a time when Russia came to disregard existing international institutions and began, however haltingly, to fashion its own." It was also an important test case for the use of cyberattacks in a limited military conflict. As Eka Tkeshelashvili of the Georgian National Security Council put it, "Russia invaded Georgia on four fronts. Three of them were conventional—on the ground, through the air, and by sea. The fourth was new—their attacks via cyberspace."[33]

Even before Russian troops crossed over into South Ossetia, Georgian government websites came under attack. At the end of July, hackers took down the website of President Saakashvili for twenty-four hours. Cybersecurity experts found Russian language and the message "win+love+in+Rusia" embedded in the code. On the evening of July 7, before Russian troops engaged in direct conflict, a large number of governmental websites went down. Hackers knocked the country's largest commercial bank and media outlets offline and defaced the websites of the Georgian president and Ministry of Foreign Affairs with a collage of photos of Mikheil Saakashvili and Adolf Hitler. Forums used by Georgian hackers were attacked in an effort to prevent retaliation.[34]

From the beginning, someone or some group appeared to be coordinating the attacks. Yet, as with the Estonian case, no conclusive proof linked the Russian government to the hackers. The Kremlin had obvious political and military motives to take down Georgian websites, but the attacks were coordinated on public forums, available to anyone with a computer and an Internet connection. Russian-language websites such as StopGeorgia.ru distributed instructions on how to flood websites and provided a list of targets. Users could download a utility called DoSHTTP, enter a web address, and click the "Start Flood" button. When Georgia blocked access from Russian Internet addresses to mitigate the attacks, forum administrators told users how to get around the barriers by routing through Eastern European countries.[35]

Moscow denied responsibility. To show how "open the field is to anyone with a grudge against Georgia," technology writer and author Evgeny Morozov described in a piece for *Slate* how he became a soldier in the Georgia-Russia cyber war. Morozov visited a few sites, including StopGeorgia.ru, and within an hour was participating in the attacks. Moscow used the proliferation of these tools to shift attention to patriotic citizens who could have launched the attacks, ignoring the role its propaganda played in tarring Saakashvili as Hitler and the Georgian government as fascist and in stoking the nationalist anger that motivated individuals to go online and find programs to attack. Yevgeniy Khorishko, a spokesman for the Russian embassy in Washington, said, "There are people who don't agree with something and they try to express themselves. You have people like this in your country." Suddenly, the freedom to launch a cyberattack had become equated with freedom of expression.[36]

Again, there was enough circumstantial evidence to point the finger at Moscow. Georgian National Security Council chief Eka Tkeshelashvili told *Wired*, "There's plenty of evidence that the attacks were directly organized by the government in Russia." Perhaps the most persuasive argument of official involvement was that StopGeorgia.ru went up with a full target list only a few hours after Russian troops crossed the border. This would have taken some preparation and suggests that the site's organizers had been tipped off on the timing of the military operations.[37]

A number of countries and companies worked to keep Georgia online. The Polish and Estonian computer emergency response teams offered support. Lauri Almann, Estonian deputy minister of defense, helped Georgia come up with a response to the attacks. Tulip Systems, located in Atlanta, Georgia, and run by Nino Doijashvili, a Georgian expatriate, hosted the websites of the Ministry of Defense and the president. The website of the Ministry of Foreign Affairs was relocated to an Estonian server. Blogspot, the Google blogging platform, hosted additional Georgian government websites as well as the news site Civil.ge.[38]

Georgia had successfully executed what two defense analysts called a cyber "left hook": "When Estonia experienced cyberattack, it essentially defended in place; Georgia, on the other hand, maneuvered." The hackers wanted to limit the government's ability to communicate. Georgia partially mitigated the strategic impact of the attacks by streaming its communications through the United States. While deft, this move took place without US government approval and partially drew the United States into the conflict. The DDoS attacks followed the sites to the United States; Tulip's chief financial officer told the press, "We're absolutely being bombarded." Google, with much larger infrastructure and bandwidth at its disposal, was barely affected.[39]

Compared to Estonia, Georgia was more dependent on Russia for Internet connectivity. More of Georgia's connections to the Internet passed through Russia; Estonia could disburse traffic through high-capacity data links to Finland, Sweden, and Latvia. Moreover, Estonia had its own Internet exchange point (IXP), a key point of Internet geography in which different network carriers interconnect. This allowed Estonia to disconnect from the outside world but keep communications running domestically. Without an IXP, Georgia had to isolate itself from international attacks and cut off domestic traffic. As Jason Healey, a cybersecurity researcher at Columbia University, describes it, "Estonia made a deliberate sacrifice to jump offline; Georgia was pushed."[40]

Despite their intensity, the attacks on Georgia were not extremely disruptive. Georgia was a much later adopter of communication technologies than Estonia. Estonia had fifty-seven users per one hundred people in 2007; Georgia had only seven. Very few critical services like finance and energy were connected to the Internet. The main impact of the attacks was interruption of official and internal communications, hindering the Georgian government's ability to coordinate its response and handicapping Tbilisi's efforts to inform the world of its side in the conflict.

UKRAINE

One of the more important outcomes of the Georgian conflict was that it taught Moscow that an international response was unlikely for digital assaults that remained below a certain threshold. The Military Doctrine of the Russian Federation, adopted in 2010, two years after the Five-Day War, describes one characteristic of contemporary conflict as the "intensification of the role of information warfare." The modern military, according to the doctrine, must wage information warfare "in order to achieve political objectives without the utilization of military force." If military force is used, the information and cyber operations become tools to shape "a favorable response from the world community."[41]

This description captures what happened during the Ukraine crisis, which started after protests broke out in Kiev in response to President Viktor Yanukovych's suspension of an association agreement with the European Union in November 2013. The protests went on for months, forcing Yanukovych to make concessions in a deal brokered by Germany, Poland, and France but which Russia refused to sign off on. Despite the deal, protesters continued to call for Yanukovych's resignation, and he fled the capital on February 21. The United States and European Union quickly recognized a new government; Russia denounced the interim president, Oleksandr Turchynov, as illegitimate and condemned his appointment as a coup.

Nationalists in Crimea urged Moscow to defend them from the "fascists" in the west of the country, and on February 26 pro-Russian forces began seizing parts of the peninsula. Many of the forces carried Russian-made guns, spoke Russian, and wore Russian-made uniforms without military insignia. Moscow denied that these fighters were from the Russian military; the Russian press referred to them as volunteers, self-defense militias, or "polite men." Ukrainians called them "little green men" after the color of their uniforms. On March 16, Crimea voted to secede from Ukraine, and the next day Putin recognized the region as a "sovereign and independent state." On March 18, Putin acknowledged the little green men assisted Russian forces, and the Russian Defense Ministry eventually issued a victory medal to soldiers involved in the "return of Crimea." The city of Belogorsk in Russia's far east erected an iron statue of a masked soldier holding a kitten to celebrate the annexation of Crimea.

The little green men were part of a strategy of hybrid war that included irregular forces, Russian military exercises on the Ukrainian border, diplomatic pressure, misinformation, and cyber operations. Months before the involvement of Russian irregulars, as pro-Russian and pro-Western protestors battled in Kiev's Maidan Square, a complex program known as Snake or Ouroboros, after the serpent in Greek mythology that eats its own tail, targeted and siphoned data off Ukrainian government networks. The program had bits of Russian embedded in the code, and timestamps within the malicious software show it was compiled during office hours in the GMT+4 time zone, which includes Moscow. Of the fifty-six computer networks infected by Snake globally, thirty-two were in Ukraine.[42]

Once the move to secession began, the little green men quickly cut communications inside and from Crimea. Armed men seized a facility run by Ukrtelecom JSC, Ukraine's telecom provider, and severed landline, mobile, and Internet services. The cell phones of Ukrainian parliament members were interfered with, and the Ukraine government website was knocked offline for seventy-two hours. On March 8, DDoS attacks hit the National Security and Defense Council of Ukraine and the Ukrainian state-run news agency Ukrinform. On March 16, a group calling itself CyberBerkut, named after the security squads used by former president Yanukovych, attacked NATO websites. Former Ukrainian and Russian security personnel headed CyberBerkut.[43]

Ukrainian hackers struck back, temporarily disabling websites for the Kremlin, the Russian central bank, and Russia's Foreign Ministry. OpRussia, a group that identifies itself with Anonymous, attacked Russian business and government sites, including the websites for the Russian air force, the Kamchatka region, and the Federal Drug Control Service of Russia. The pro-Kremlin, English-language website Russia Today was briefly hacked; the word "Nazi" was prominently inserted into headlines describing Russian actions. Someone took over the Twitter account of Russian prime minister Dmitry Medvedev and sent messages saying that he was resigning out of shame over the government's actions. Another message said, "Crimea isn't ours. Please retweet." The Ukrainian Cyber Troops, led by the Kiev-based hacker Yevhen Dokukin, broke into two Russian Interior Ministry servers and accessed closed-circuit television cameras in rebel-held areas of eastern Ukraine to monitor the movement of Russian troops and military hardware.[44]

There was also a flare-up of cyberattacks from both sides around the secession vote. A wave of forty-two DDoS attacks hit Ukrainian government websites during the vote. CyberBerkut broke into the computers of the election commission, posting network maps, system logs, and the contents of election commission members' mailboxes. A day after the vote, 132 separate DDoS blasts slammed Russian sites. As the fighting continued in eastern Ukraine, and Russia and the West traded diplomatic barbs, the two sides probed and tested each other. NATO scrambled interceptor aircraft more than one hundred times. Four Russian Tu-95 strategic bombers flew through the Baltic and Black Seas to Portugal. Hackers, reportedly from Russia, breached unclassified networks at the White House.[45]

In the beginning phase of the conflict in Ukraine, Russia could have inflicted a great deal more pain on Ukraine through attacks on financial, transportation, or telecommunications networks. Ukraine was wired when still part of the Soviet Union, so Moscow has great access to and influence over much of Ukraine's telecommunications infrastructure (though the country does have good connections to international networks). The low level of cyber activity may have been the result of a crude deterrence. Moscow may have worried that Ukrainian hackers could strike back, and so limited the scope of its own attacks. Ukraine was a key part of the USSR's technology and military complex and has a sizable community of hackers, many with links to criminal enterprises, as well as a large expatriate community of IT professionals. "Ukrainian hackers are well-known in the world," Valentyn Petrov, an information security official at the Security Service of Ukraine, told the *Washington Post*. "Our country is a potential source of cyber threats to other countries."

More destructive attacks, however, would potentially have a political cost. A full-scale cyberattack against Ukraine would be indiscriminate; it could spread beyond Moscow's control, affecting all inhabitants, and so possibly alienate Russian speakers in Ukraine, a critical constituency for the Kremlin. Moscow could get what it wanted with irregular troops, military exercises, and diplomatic pressure.[46]

The limited use of computer attacks also makes sense if we place cyberattacks within a larger strategy of information warfare conducted through a mixture of rumor, innuendo, misinformation, and fact. Cyber is not a superweapon; it is one tool among many. TV producer and author Peter Pomerantsev describes a weakened Kremlin, unwilling and unable to take on the West directly, that has "weaponized" information, culture, and money. It uses information as a weapon to confuse, divide, and subvert liberal democracies. Russia targeted journalists in Crimea and blocked media that it saw as unfriendly to Moscow's narrative of the crisis. It spread rumors through official and unofficial outlets. The effort to spread misinformation was so broad that the State Department felt the need to issue a counter fact sheet, "President Putin's Fiction: 10 False Claims About Ukraine."[47]

Russian politicians and military leaders see themselves as victims of information attacks from the Western media, nongovernmental organizations, and the Internet itself. In their view, they are simply fighting back. Dmitry Kiselev, host of *Vesti Nedeli* (News of the Week), which airs on Russia-1, a state-owned channel, told an interviewer that information wars have become "the main type of warfare." In April 2014, President Putin was widely quoted as claiming the Internet to be a "CIA project" and saying that a popular search engine in Russia, Yandex, had come under Western influence. Cyberattacks were just one means to manipulate information in a war that had many fronts.[48]

As the conflict drags out, Russia's calculus may change. Destruction may follow disruption. Since the West was not going to use military force to defend Ukraine's territorial sovereignty, it had to find diplomatic and financial instruments to pressure the Kremlin. The United States and its allies imposed travel restrictions on individuals and financial sanctions on Russia's largest banks, blocked the assets of defense industries, and prohibited financing for and transactions with energy companies. At a NATO conference in September 2014, the alliance agreed to create a new response force and to deploy prepositioned equipment and supplies along the eastern border with Russia. NATO also increased fighter jet patrols over the Baltics and the number of ships in the Baltic, Black, and Mediterranean Seas.

These moves were meant to reassure Poland, Estonia, Lithuania, and Latvia, but the reality for the small countries on Russia's border was bleak. Putin allegedly told European Commission president José Manuel Barroso, "If I want to, I can take Kiev in two weeks." The time-line for Estonia—a country of a little over 17,000 square miles right on the border—would be even quicker. No matter how much it boosted its conventional defenses, it could not stop a Russian military invasion.[49]

Estonia could not increase its physical geography to slow Russian tanks down, but in the traditional language of military strategy, it could create defense in depth on the Internet. Estonia increased in size (and connections) in cyberspace. In May 2014, the government announced a "digital country" initiative. Anyone who could pass a quick background check and come up with $64 (€50) could become a digital citizen of Estonia and receive an e-card allowing him or her to open a bank account or an online business. Many of those who apply are likely to be US or European citizens, and so an attack on Estonia's digital infrastructure would quickly become the concern of Washing-ton, London, and Berlin.[50]

Estonia also opened "digital data embassies," databases and ser-vices deemed vital to the state's operation replicated in countries friendly to Estonia. These embassies would be able to operate any-where in the world no matter if Estonian territory were seized or invaded and, again, create a web of responsibility with more powerful friends. Jaan Priisalu, director-general of Estonia's Information Sys-tem Authority, argued that host countries "take responsibility for the [physical] security of an embassy, so likewise they might also assume responsibility for the security of the virtual embassy in the network."[51]

NATO: NO WEAPONS OF ITS OWN, NO STRATEGY TO USE THEM

While NATO responded to Russian incursions into the Baltic coun-tries' airspace and coastal waters with increased air and sea patrols, the alliance also had to craft a response to the DDoS attacks and cyber espionage. In November 2014, NATO conducted the largest cyber war exercise in its history. More than 670 people from twenty-eight countries participated in scenarios that included hackers taking over airborne warning and control system surveillance aircraft as well as an attack designed to influence public opinion. One scenario involved a made-up conflict taking place in the Horn of Africa; the participants of the digital war game were in Estonia, and the target of the exercise was unmistakably Russia.[52]

The Crimea crisis forced to the forefront a question that had been simmering since the 2007 attacks on Estonia: How should the alliance respond to cyberattacks on one of its members, especially those that threaten vital interests but do not cross the threshold of an armed attack? As noted before, under Article 5 of the Washington Treaty, members would consider an armed attack against one to be an armed attack against all. In 2007, Estonia asked for NATO assistance but did not invoke the clause as attacks unfolded over April and May. Estonian officials knew the alliance would not treat the DDoS attacks as an armed attack. But when NATO met in June, a month after the attacks on Estonia ended, a new cyber defense framework was high on the agenda, and many were looking for greater clarity on the threshold for cyberattacks.

The summit did bring some forward motion in cyber policy. NATO created a Cyber Defence Management Authority to coordinate defense and, in a tsarist-era military barracks in Tallinn, established the NATO Cooperative Cyber Defense Centre of Excellence, a cybersecurity research and training center. The question of what would constitute an armed attack on allies in cyberspace, however, was put off.

In 2010, a group of experts led by former secretary of state Madeleine Albright completed a document to help guide the development of a new "strategic concept" for NATO. The group warned that the "next significant attack on the alliance may well come down a fibre optic cable." To defend against this threat, the group wrote, "NATO must update its approach to the defense of Alliance territory." The NATO Council, the political decisionmaking body within the alliance, however, rejected the idea that a computer attack on critical infrastructure might be considered the equivalent of an armed attack. The declaration from the 2012 NATO summit in Chicago only reaffirmed the alliance's commitment to "improv[ing] its capabilities to detect, assess, prevent, defend, and recover in case of a cyberattack against systems of critical importance to the Alliance."[53]

When NATO leaders met again in the summer of 2014, the reluctance to recognize that offensive cyber operations could have catastrophic effects had evaporated. The Ukraine crisis and the widening recognition of the sophistication of cyberattacks had a bracing effect. The summit document declared, "Cyberattacks can reach a threshold that threatens national and Euro-Atlantic prosperity, security, and stability. Their impact could be as harmful to modern societies as a conventional attack. We affirm therefore that cyber defense is part of NATO's core task of collective defense."[54]

The declaration did not say, however, under what circumstances an attack would trigger collective defense. As Jamie Shea, deputy assistant secretary general for emerging security challenges at NATO Headquarters, explained, the policy does not set any detailed criteria for the activation of Article 5. Instead the alliance will decide on a case-by-case basis, with judgment based on the impact of an attack.[55]

The declaration did nothing to change NATO's ability to respond to those threats. While the alliance has been improving its defenses, NATO's offensive capabilities are limited, though it could respond through conventional strikes. "Our mandate is pure cyber defense," said former NATO secretary general Anders Fogh Rasmussen. "Our declaration is a start but I cannot tell you it is a complete strategy." NATO has no weapons of its own. Some member states have weapons but no strategy to use them in concert with NATO activities. According to the *New York Times*, the United States and United Kingdom had not even briefed NATO on the capabilities of the NSA, US Cyber Command, or UK Government Communications Headquarters.

In October 2014, criminal hackers, reportedly working at the behest of the Kremlin, broke into unclassified networks at the State Department and the White House. Another set of hackers exploited zero-day vulnerabilities in Adobe and Windows, searching for information on sanctions policy. US government officials reported a dramatic jump in the number of attacks from Russia directed at government agencies as well as attempts to steal intellectual property and business plans from the financial and energy industries. One cybersecurity company reported a rise from just dozens of attacks per month on American companies to 10,000 intrusions in the first three months of

2015 alone. These criminal hackers were apparently targeting US and European companies in the wake of and as a response to sanctions.

While long known for being far stealthier than their Chinese counterparts, Russian hackers no longer seemed to care if they were uncovered. The Kremlin's intention? To remind the White House of two things: (1) if NATO is involved in conflict in Ukraine, Russia has a way of reaching out to touch the United States at home; and (2) Moscow has a method to retaliate for economic sanctions. If the sanctions continue to hurt the Russian economy, the Kremlin seemed to be saying, we have a way of hurting the US economy. The US government engaged in its own signal sending, leaking to the press about the hacks and the attackers. Washington's message? We know who is behind this, and do not think we will not respond if the attacks grow more threatening.

In the hacked world order, disruptive cyberattacks (and espionage, which I discuss in chapter five) will be prevalent. They already accompany almost every outbreak of regional tension—Israel and Hamas, Turkey and Armenia, Japan and China, China and Vietnam, China and Philippines, and Korea and Japan. In many instances, these attacks are the equivalent of a protest outside of an embassy, nationalistic expressions of anger that are little more than an annoyance for the victim and often act as a safety valve for restless populations of the attacker state.

In other instances, the cyberattacks will be more directed efforts at political coercion, although so far they have had limited effect. Sony eventually released the film, and Estonia moved the statue. Still, they will remain attractive to Russia and others that have expansive views of cyber conflict, especially if they can use proxies to launch the attacks and retain plausible deniability. They are much less appealing to the liberal democracies, which tend to both keep a tighter rein on offensive cyber capabilities, keeping them within traditional military structures, and make a sharper distinction between war and peace, military conflict and other forms of statecraft.

States will learn to live with these attacks, just as they have learned to cope with and adapt to many other forms of low-intensity conflict. The primary concern will be that these cyber conflicts will escalate and become ones that cause physical devastation or undermine the integrity of sensitive financial data. The opportunities for and destructiveness of these types of attacks is only going to increase. More things are being connected to the Internet—more sensors, medical devices, consumer goods, and cars. If the hacked world order is going to have any semblance of stability, the United States, Russia, and China will need to do better than signaling through noisy cyberattacks and leaks to the newspapers.

Chapter 4

BREAKING THINGS AND THE SEARCH FOR ORDER

T he vast majority of cyberattacks so far have been disruptive. They knock computers offline or interfere with communications. Increasingly, nation-state attackers destroy data. And very rarely—only once as far as the public knows—do states try to destroy things through digital assaults. But that is changing. Militaries, not wanting to be caught flat-footed, are rushing to develop powerful cyber weapons without any agreement on how and when they might be used or even a deep understanding of the consequences they might unleash. Cyberspace is "uncharted waters," as President Barack Obama observed after his June 2013 summit with China's President Xi Jinping: "You don't have the kinds of protocols that have governed military issues, for example, and arms issues, where nations have a lot of experience in trying to negotiate what's acceptable and what's not."

ENTERING AND BREAKING

Charlie Miller really seems to enjoy what he does, and he is very, very good at it. What he does is break into things. *Forbes* described him as "probably the world's most prominent Mac hacker." In one month in 2010, he publicized twenty security vulnerabilities in Apple's software, and from 2008 to 2011, he won an annual hacking competition in Vancouver called Pwn2Own ("pwn" is hacker speak for "to gain control" or "to own") by finding vulnerabilities in Apple's Safari browser and the iPhone operating system.[1]

Miller was the first in his family to attend college, and after receiving a doctorate in math from the University of Notre Dame, he spent five years at the National Security Agency. He first worked on making and breaking codes but was eventually trained to hack. Asked in an interview for his hometown St. Louis newspaper what he did while still at the secretive intelligence agency, his answer reflected the language of his former employer: "Executed numerous computer network exploitations against foreign targets." That is, he broke into other countries' computers. Like many skilled government hackers, he left for the private sector, working at a computer security firm and becoming a "white hat" hacker—someone who looks for vulnerabilities before the bad guys find them.[2]

Miller later moved on to Twitter, but one of his hobbies, supported by a grant from the Defense Advanced Research Projects Agency, is demonstrating how to hack a car. Modern automobiles contain dozens of computer systems that control everything from airbag deployment to oil-pressure monitoring and can run up to 100 million lines of code. Herb Lin, who ran the cybersecurity program for the National Research Council of the National Academies and is now at Stanford University, once described his new car, with its three-hundred-page owner's manual, as "software on wheels." Not only do cars run more software (or vice versa), but their systems are increasingly interconnected. The speedometer, brakes, and seatbelts all talk to each other and to systems outside the car.

Working with Chris Valasek, the director of security intelligence at a Seattle consultancy, Miller hacked the software running on a Ford Escape and a Toyota Prius. (They didn't bother showing that you could hack into a car through Bluetooth, keyless entry, or diagnostic systems, because other researchers had already done that. Researchers from the University of California, Santa Barbara, and the University of Washington, for example, hacked into a vehicle using the emergency-assistance system.) The two created false GPS and speedometer readings, cut the power steering, and accelerated the Ford Escape. A video on YouTube shows them gleefully jerking its steering wheel back and forth from a laptop in the backseat. In July 2015, they raised the stakes, hacking a Jeep from ten miles away, blasting the radio, turning the air-conditioning and wipers on, and slowing the vehicle to a standstill as it drove along Interstate 64 outside St. Louis. A week later, Chrysler recalled 1.4 million vehicles susceptible to attacks on the Uconnect dashboard computer. (In August 2015, Miller and Valasek were hired by Uber to work in Pittsburgh, where the company has based its self-driving car and robotics research.)[3]

We might be tempted to see the hacking as a bit of a stunt. Cars are still relatively hard to hack—it took Miller and Valasek a year to find the Jeep's vulnerabilities—and, unlike phones or PCs, which operate on a few main operating systems, autos run custom software that differ by make and model. Their connections to the Internet are limited and infrequent. Moreover, as a former NSA hacker, Miller possesses skills that few can match.

But this was more than a prank. The next generations of Tesla and Audi, for example, are connected to AT&T networks, and the National Highway Traffic Safety Administration is working on a vehicle-to-vehicle communication program to allow cars to automatically relay information wirelessly to one another to increase safety. In March 2015, Eric Evenchick, a twenty-five-year-old former intern at Tesla, introduced the CANtact at the Black Hat Asia security conference. The $60 device connects to a port under a car's dashboard. Used with free, open-source software, the CANtact makes hacking cars faster and easier for amateurs. Evenchick did not build the tool for malicious purposes, but to help hobbyists. "I wanted to build a tool I can get out there, along with software," Evenchick told *Wired*, "to show that this stuff isn't terribly complicated."[4]

Automobiles are not a unique case. They are a leading indicator of the new vulnerabilities emerging as the Internet of Things—factory equipment, robots, drones, kitchen ovens, office copiers, electrical grids, hospital beds, medical implants, agricultural irrigation systems, and thousands of other things fitted with sensors that collect data and communicate with each other and with computers over the Internet—spreads to every sector of the economy. Cisco Systems predicts that 75 billion devices will be connected to the web in 2020.[5]

These devices will be everywhere. As the Internet becomes more enmeshed with the physical world, complexity multiplies, and the potential destructive consequences of an attack spike. Very few of the new web-enabled devices have security baked in from the beginning, and hackers will hijack them to do things they were not designed for, creating numerous unintended outcomes. The network itself will become a destructive weapon. Dan Geer, a computer security expert and chief information security officer for In-Q-Tel, the CIA's venture capital firm, argues, "By now it is obvious that we humans can design systems more complex than we can then operate." "The more techno-logic the society becomes," Geer continues, "the greater the dynamic range of possible failures."[6]

This vulnerability will be an almost irresistible target for nation-states and for terrorists and criminals. Though Stuxnet is the only known cyberattack to cause physical destruction, the idea that these attacks could become more widespread is not science fiction. In 2007, Idaho National Laboratory conducted a test in which hackers opened and closed a diesel generator's circuit breakers. The video of the test shows the huge machine bucking three times and then black smoke pouring out. After hackers entered the networks of a German steel mill in 2014, the resulting unscheduled shutdown of the factory dam-aged the blast furnace. In May 2015, an Airbus A400M military plane crashed outside Seville, Spain, killing four of the six crew members. Critical data had been accidentally wiped before the flight when the software that controls the engines was being installed, and the soft-ware failure caused three of the four engines to freeze.

Nation-states have huge budgets. They have large intelligence ser-vices and can mobilize hundreds if not thousands of hackers to map systems, break into computers and servers, and design destructive mal-ware. What Miller and Valasek can accomplish in their spare time is scary. That danger, however, is dwarfed by the destructive potential of the United States, China, Russia, Israel, and a few others.

CYBER DETERRENCE AND THE GREAT POWERS

Facing the threat of a deadly attack and a growing sense of vulnera-bility, the United States has followed a three-pronged strategy as much as from a lack of better alternatives as from a deeply held conviction that it will work. It has tried to deter attacks before they happen, in part through the buildup of offensive cyber weapons; talked with friends and adversaries about international norms or rules of acceptable state behavior in cyberspace; and shored up defenses at home through a combination of legislative and executive actions. The success of these efforts depends on the cooperation of allies; the ambitions, assumptions, and maneuvering of adversaries; and the reactions of the private sector.

Over the last decade, the United States has struggled to create a credible deterrent against cyberattacks. It has developed offensive capabilities and increasingly spoken publicly about them. While the Defense Department's 2015 cyber strategy emphasizes the defensive nature of Cyber Command, it also recognizes offensive missions. "If directed by the President or the Secretary of Defense," states the strategy, "DoD must be able to provide integrated cyber capabilities to support military operations and contingency plans." Washington has also deployed diplomatic tools, economic sanctions, and law enforcement in an effort to convince would-be attackers that there are costs to penetrating US networks. Moreover, it has stressed denial—making it so hard for the attacker to get in that the attack no longer seems worth it—and resilience—the ability to recover quickly when an attack succeeds. As Deputy Secretary of Defense William Lynn III wrote in 2010, "Deterrence will necessarily be based more on denying any benefit to attackers than on imposing costs through retaliation."[7]

The results, so far, have been mixed at best. The great powers appear deterred from committing destructive attacks on each other. Former NSA director General Keith Alexander told the Senate Armed Services Committee in 2013 that states like China and Russia would think twice before launching a major digital assault on vital infrastructure because "a devastating attack on the critical infrastructure and population of the United States by cyber means would be correctly traced back to its source and elicit a prompt and proportionate response." Former defense secretary Robert M. Gates made the same point in a speech at the Council on Foreign Relations: "Although attribution can be difficult, eventually, we figure it out, where the attack came from. And there's a home address, if the Chinese, or the Russians, or somebody else does it to us."[8]

While the absence of destructive attacks is notable, no one can be certain if Moscow, Beijing, and Washington will continue to exercise restraint if vital interests are threatened. In addition, this is a very narrow deterrent leaving a great deal of room for maneuver. It does not stop China and Russia from cyber espionage. Moreover, the limited deterrence does not prevent the big powers from scoping the battlefield. As Admiral Michael S. Rogers told a congressional hearing, "We believe potential adversaries might be leaving cyber fingerprints on our critical infrastructure partly to convey a message that our homeland is at risk if tensions ever escalate toward military conflict."[9]

The tolerance for these fingers in networks depends highly on the political context. For the defender, it is extremely difficult to distinguish espionage from attack preparations. As Mike Jacobs, a former NSA director for information assurance, writes, "If you are engaged in reconnaissance on an adversary's systems, you are laying the electronic battlefield and preparing to use it." Forbearance is much less likely in a time of crisis. The defender may assume that an attack will immediately follow preparation and feel pressure to respond quickly.[10]

This compression of decisionmaking time is exactly the opposite of what you want in a crisis and could easily lead to mistakes and escalation. During the "reset," the effort to lessen tensions between Moscow and Washington during President Obama's first term and the presidency of Dmitry Medvedev, the two sides took some first steps to reduce the chance of miscalculations. They shared views on military uses of cyber, regularized information sharing between their respective computer emergency response teams, and established a crisis hotline. With the return to office of Vladimir Putin, the conversations became testier and then stalled out over Ukraine, just when they were needed most. Now the two sides have resorted to an indirect and dangerous type of messaging. Leaks to the press in April 2015 about the hacking of the White House and State Department mail systems, allegedly by Moscow-backed criminal hackers, represented an attempt to signal Russia about the need for restraint.[11]

Things may be even worse in the Sino-US relationship. Several years ago, I attended what's called a track 1.5 meeting between Chinese and US officials; officials meet with academics and think tankers outside formal channels. The US side asked the Chinese what they would do if they saw a massive cyberattack coming out of the United States. After some caucusing among themselves, the Chinese responded that they would call the Department of Defense (DoD) on the hotline. The US side was nonplussed. There was no hotline between the Chinese Ministry of Defense and the Pentagon, at least not one that operates like they do in the movies. You couldn't pick up the receiver, see a light flash, and then hear a voice in China. Rather, calls had to be scheduled, often seventy-two hours in advance, and there was no guarantee that anyone in Beijing would actually pick up the phone. In fact, that's exactly what officials did not do in April 2001 when a US spy plane crash-landed on Hainan Island after a collision with a Chinese fighter jet. Admiral Joseph Prueher, ambassador to China at the time, later complained that no one in either the Foreign or the Defense Ministry answered or returned his phone calls as the two sides tried to find a way out of the diplomatic impasse.

Even when the two sides do manage to talk, they often speak past each other. There are dueling exceptionalisms in cyberspace. In the American version, the United States has a singular role in promoting and preserving an open Internet, both because it created the network and because it is uniquely committed to a foreign policy that expands individual freedom and human rights. China regards itself as uniquely peaceful since it believes it has never invaded another country. China also contends that it is the biggest victim in cyberspace. In this view, the Chinese see any criticism of Beijing's actions as motivated by what they call the "China threat school," an attempt to stir up distrust, increase the Pentagon's budget, and contain China's rise.

In April 2014, Pentagon officials briefed their Chinese counterparts on how the United States would use cyber technology to defend itself and how it might conduct offensive operations against potential adversaries, including China. The greater transparency was meant to assure Beijing of Washington's good intentions. Just weeks before the briefing of the Chinese, Secretary of Defense Chuck Hagel had delivered a similar message. Speaking at General Alexander's retirement ceremony, Hagel claimed that the United States would not militarize cyberspace and would "maintain an approach of restraint" to cyber operations.[12]

But with these briefings, the United States clearly intended both to assure and to deter. Chinese defense planners, like their counterparts everywhere, make decisions based more on a potential adversary's capabilities than on its stated intentions. Moreover, there is often a disconnect between what policymakers and war fighters say. At the same retirement event for General Alexander, Admiral Cecil D. Haney, head of US Strategic Command, spoke of the US "capability to protect the asymmetric advantages we have by operating in cyberspace and giving us that assured access and the ability to deny others its use." The plan to deny others use of and access to cyberspace does not sound reassuring to China.

Because China's Internet infrastructure is relatively self-contained, Chinese policymakers may have felt themselves comparatively less vulnerable to attacks. That confidence must have evaporated in the light of Edward Snowden's revelations about the NSA's skills. Articles in the Chinese press worrying about the exposure of industrial control systems to damaging attacks are now common. A shared sense of vulnerability is good motivation for the two sides to speak to each other. Unfortunately, bilateral negotiations were suspended because of the Department of Justice's (DoJ) indictment of five Chinese hackers for cyber espionage (discussed in more detail in the next chapter).

During the Cold War, Washington and Moscow held numerous exchanges so each side would understand the "red lines" for employing nuclear weapons. The great powers need to develop a similar framework for cyberspace. Washington, Moscow, and Beijing have an interest in identifying legitimate targets and thresholds. At this point, all would likely agree that a cyberattack with "kinetic effects" equivalent to those of a conventional armed attack would be treated in the same manner, allowing for individual and collective self-defense. One Cyber Command officer once told me that Pearl Harbor and the September 11, 2001, terrorist attacks, both of which caused about 3,000 fatalities, give an indication of what would push the United States to war, but there will be no hard-and-fast rule here. Decisions to retaliate or not will always be political, just like they are in conventional conflicts.

It will be necessary, but much harder, for the three to develop an understanding about attacks below this threshold. China may consider an attack that disrupts the stock market for a day or destroys the data of several midsized banks in the Midwest a relatively restrained act of signaling; the United States could see it as an escalation demanding a response. Designating financial markets as off-limits for preplanted logic bombs—malicious software that goes off once predefined conditions are met—or direct targeting during a conflict would be a small step toward boosting confidence among all three parties, though an agreement like this is unverifiable and may quickly fall by the wayside if the parties come to blows.

The three powers also have a shared interest in preventing the proliferation of sophisticated attack weapons among terrorists and criminals. Currently, terrorist groups have the interest but lack the capacity to launch destructive assaults. In October 2015, an assistant secretary from the Department of Homeland Security announced that hackers from the Islamic State were trying to break into the power grid. They were using unsophisticated tools, and one FBI agent summed up the efforts as "Strong intent. Thankfully, low capacity." But this will change over time as terrorist groups either attract more talented hackers or buy more advanced malware on black markets.

The United States can only accomplish so much. Talking to Moscow and Beijing may help reduce the chances of destructive cyberattacks on critical infrastructure; it will not end espionage. Other types of cyber conflict among China, Russia, and the United States will not cease, just as nuclear deterrence did not prevent numerous proxy wars in Africa, Latin America, the Middle East, and Southeast Asia. As attribution improves, states will become stealthier. The smart state will contract the attack out, using a proxy or criminal gang. In fact, a fairly stable standoff in cyberspace may encourage greater adventurism in the areas of cyber espionage and in politically motivated attacks.

OFFENSE AND THE LITTLE POWERS

If the United States and the other great powers are settling into an unsteady arrangement, Washington has clearly failed to deter smaller states like Iran and North Korea from launching destructive attacks on data and business operations. Even after the United States delivered a warning in October 2012 that it could locate and hold them accountable, Iranian hackers continued and eventually expanded their attacks to include the probing of critical US infrastructure.

Moreover, less than two years after the warning, in February 2014, hackers supported by Tehran and angered by owner Sheldon Adelson's comments about exploding a nuclear weapon in Iran, shut down the servers of the Las Vegas Sands Casino, wiped hundreds of computers clean of data, and disabled the systems that monitor payouts at the slot machines and gambling tables. Calling themselves the "Anti WMD [weapons of mass destruction] Team," the hackers posted on the casino's website pictures of Adelson with Israeli prime minister Benjamin Netanyahu, employees' personal information, and a warning stating, "Encouraging the use of Weapons of Mass Destruction, UNDER ANY CONDITION, is a Crime" (which means that Iran, not North Korea, launched the first destructive attack on the United States).[13]

Looking at this history of failed deterrence, many experts have argued that as a response the United States should take the offensive. "We focus[ed] primarily on the defensive piece initially. I thought that was a sound investment," Admiral Rogers told the Senate Armed Services Committee in March 2015. "But I think now, we're at a tipping point." Defense "will be both late to need and incredibly resource-intense," he continued, concluding, "We also need to think about how can we increase our capacity on the offensive side here, to get to that point of deterrence." Shawn Henry, former executive assistant director of the FBI's cyber-crime branch once put it more colorfully: "You can only be punched in the face so many times before you fall to your knees. There needs to be more offense and less defense."[14]

Increasing offensive capacity alone will not increase deterrence. You have to talk about your cyber weapons and your plans to use them. As retired Marine Corps general and former vice chairman of the Joint Chiefs of Staff James Cartright argued, "You can't have something that's a secret be a deterrent. Because if you don't know it's there, it doesn't scare you. We've got to get that done, because otherwise everything is a free shot at us and there's no penalty for it." Senator Angus King of Maine made the same point in March 2015. Alluding to *Dr. Strangelove or: How I Learned to Stop Worrying and Love the Bomb*, the classic movie on the absurdities of the Cold War, King argued, "If you build the doomsday machine, you've got to tell people you have it. Otherwise the purpose is thwarted."[15]

Yet talking is not enough. The visible use and testing of nuclear and conventional weapons have made their physical effects well known to all. The United States and the Soviet Union conducted a combined

1,745 known underground and atmospheric nuclear tests between 1945 and 1991, along with countless launch exercises from submarines, bombers, and missile silos. Offensive cyber capabilities, however, are essentially invisible. You cannot march a cyber weapon in a parade or detonate one over a Pacific atoll. The results of an attack are unpredictable. It may be a dud, failing to have the expected impact. You might be able to conduct a cyberattack in a test bed or under other controlled circumstances, but potential adversaries may discount such displays, convincing themselves that their systems are configured differently and do not have the same vulnerabilities.

States will have to use digital weapons and then claim responsibility or at least demonstrate that they can and will use them. Even then, cyberattacks are unlikely to succeed as a deterrent on their own. Look at Iran. Based on the numerous leaks to reporters, public reporting on malware by cybersecurity companies, and the Snowden revelations, it seems likely no other country knows US cyber capabilities better. Iran has endured a barrage of cyberattacks but continues to develop and use its own cyber weapons.

With regard to states willing to come as close to the red line as possible, the United States will have to disrupt attacks before they happen or reach US networks. In cybersecurity circles, this is often known as active defense, an expansive and often vague term. Some use it to refer to a second layer of defense consisting of real-time efforts to detect and mitigate threats in one's own networks after an attacker has managed to get past the firewall and other security measures. Others have in mind more offensive operations, like shutting down servers in Europe being used to launch attacks. General Alexander told a congressional committee in 2009, "My own view is that the only way to counteract both criminal and espionage activity online is to be proactive." Referring to a possible exploitation in which Chinese got inside critical US computer systems, Alexander continued that he would "want to go and take down the source of those attacks." A third group uses the term to mean combined prevention and disruption.[16]

A real-world example, cheered by some advocates of active defense, captures some of the ambiguity. A Russian hacker was placing malware on Georgian websites and stealing sensitive and secret files. Georgian security experts created a decoy file called "Georgian-NATO

Agreement" embedded with its own spyware. Once the hacker opened the decoy file, the camera on his computer began taking pictures and sending them back to Georgia. The spyware also collected the documents on the hacker's hard drive, including one, written in Russian, containing a target list. The Georgians, however, did not damage the computer the hacker was using.[17]

In several instances, Cyber Command officials have publicly stated that they needed greater clarity on whether they had the legal authority to conduct active defense operations. Cyber Command can do anything it wants on its own networks but requires presidential approval for operations on other networks. Snowden documents suggest, however, that some authorities exist for more aggressive activities. Some of the documents discuss teams from the FBI, CIA, and Cyber Command working next to the NSA with overlapping legal authorities for "any kind of active operation that's not defensive." Unnamed US officials described these actions to the *Washington Post* as "moving toward the use of tools short of traditional weapons that are unattributable— that cannot be easily tied to the attacker—to convince an adversary to change their behavior at a strategic level."[18]

THE NARROW AND BROAD VIEWS OF CYBER ATTACKS

Active defense and deterrence require extraordinary levels of intelligence gathering (which would seem to require ever-greater hacking from the NSA). Deterrence in particular rests on perception and psychological factors—what measures a defender is willing to take, what cost a defender can impose on an attacker, and what the attacker hopes to accomplish. During the Cold War, US nuclear strategists went back and forth over what combination of targeted cities (known as countervalue targets) and missile, bomber, and submarine forces (counterforce targets) would have the greatest likelihood of influencing Soviet leaders. They made these decisions based on history, culture, and decades-long experience negotiating with the other side. In the end, they often still misjudged what the leaders across the table deemed important.

Today, unpacking motivations and ambitions is even more difficult. The decisionmaking chain that connects political and military leaders to the Chinese or Russian hacker sitting in front of a computer is essentially unobservable to outsiders. What we know about the development of US offensive operations is unlikely to help much and may lead to mirror imaging, or the assumption that an adversary will behave in a certain way because that is how the United States has acted under similar circumstances. Already we can see different approaches, with the United States adopting a narrow vision of cyber conflict that stands in sharp contrast with the more expansive view in Moscow and Beijing.

Since their beginning, first in units like the US Air Force's 609th Information Warfare Squadron, then in the Pentagon's Joint Task Force—Computer Network Operations (JTF-CNO), and now in Cyber Command, offensive operations (not NSA cyber intelligence) appear to be tightly controlled and legally prescribed. In an oral history, Major General James D. Bryan, the first commander of the JTF-CNO, estimated that the group, which became operational in the fall of 2000, was at "about a 70/30 split between defense and offense." The 30 percent on offense was, however, taking up close to 70 percent of Bryan's time "because it was so sensitive and classified. . . . [E]very time I turned around, somebody wanted to give me another polygraph to read me onto a program." The group only totaled 150 members.[19]

Offense and defense were split between two groups, the Joint Functional Component Command—Network Warfare and the Joint Task Force—Global Network Operations, before Cyber Command absorbed both in 2010. Cyber Command is currently set to grow by the end of 2016 to 6,200 military, civilian, and contractor personnel, but the total number of Chinese and Russian cyber operators is likely to be much larger.[20]

After years of silence, the Pentagon has gradually become relatively more forthcoming, acknowledging the existence of cyber weapons but providing few details. In July 2011, the Defense Department released a strategy that institutionalized war fighting in cyberspace. It declared the military would treat cyber like air, sea, space, and land as a domain of warfare in which the United States would equip, train, and fight. The 2015 version goes further, stating that there "may be times when the President or the Secretary of Defense may determine that it would be appropriate for the US military to conduct cyber operations to disrupt an adversary's military related networks or infrastructure so that the US military can protect US interests in an area of operations." In other words, the United States might attack other countries. Of the three types of troops that make up Cyber Command—national mission forces, cyber protection forces, and combat mission forces—the first two focus on defense, the last on offense. The combat mission forces will help commanders in regional commands—for example, in the Pacific or Afghanistan—plan and execute attacks. By 2018, there will be 133 teams: 13 national mission forces, 68 cyber protection, and 27 combat mission (plus 25 in support and analysis).[21]

Transparency has also been forced on the Pentagon. Leaked by Snowden and published by the *Guardian*, the October 2012 Presidential Policy Directive (PPD) 20 argues that offensive cyber operations "can offer unique and unconventional capabilities to advance U.S. national objectives around the world with little or no warning to the adversary or target and with potential effects ranging from subtle to severely damaging." PPD 20 instructs the military and intelligence agencies to identify targets of "national importance" where cyberattacks offer a "favorable balance of effectiveness and risk as compared to other instruments of national power." The United States can hold these targets back in case it needs them in a conflict. The risks to balance against the effectiveness of digital assaults include judgments about whether the attacks will provoke retaliatory strikes against the United States, destabilize the Internet, or create undesirable norms of international behavior.[22]

The president tightly controls the authority for offensive operations, according to PPD 20. Any operation with "significant consequences," defined by the memo as causing "loss of life, significant responsive actions against the United States, significant damage to property, serious adverse US foreign policy consequences, or serious economic impact on the United States," requires specific presidential approval. We can also surmise from some of the design decisions in Stuxnet that there is considerable legal oversight of US offensive operations. As noted earlier, the malware was designed to attack only one specific installation so that it would not create collateral damage. It also had a "kill switch" command embedded in the code. On June 24, 2012, Stuxnet stopped functioning.[23]

The Russian and Chinese views of cyber operations are more encompassing and less restrictive. Their hackers are on a much longer leash, if leashed at all. Russian defense planners refer not to cyber operations but rather to information warfare in which cyber plays a part. A 2011 document, the first official public statement of the Russian military's role in cyberspace, describes information warfare as a confrontation involving attacks that damage "information systems, processes, and resources," undermine "the political, economic, and social system," and create "massive brainwashing of the population for destabilizing the society and the state." It also calls on the Russian military to establish a system of effective deterrence, collect information on threats, and develop countermeasures to prevent and resolve military conflict. The document makes no mention of offensive cyber activity, but the assumption that information warfare is a constant during hostilities and peacetime runs through it and other Russian strategies. This means that Russian leaders, in effect, consider a whole range of what looks like malicious activity to the United States to be an expected part of everyday competition.[24]

The Russian definition of cyber competition is more expansive than that of the United States, and pinning down who the operators are in the Russian system is much harder. Unlike the United States, Russia relies on criminals, patriotic hackers, and other proxies, as seen in the conflicts with Estonia, Georgia, and Ukraine. In early 2012, Russian deputy prime minister Dmitry Rogozin announced plans to create a new service in the Russian military. "We are discussing the creation of a cyber command," he said. "Russia is following the U.S. and NATO, which established cyber commands long ago." Initial outlays for Russian cyber forces were reported to be $500 million, but the Kremlin will have political and tactical reasons to continue outsourcing hacking even as it builds capacity in the military.[25]

The use of third-party hackers also provides a useful smokescreen for Beijing. Officially China maintains that it has no cyber troops, but the most recent version of *The Science of Military Strategy*, an authoritative study by a research institute of the People's Liberation Army (PLA), admits the existence of three types of these forces. First, PLA network warfare forces carry out attacks and defense. Second, specialists in the Ministry of State Security (the equivalent of the CIA) and

Ministry of Public Security (their FBI) have the authority to conduct attacks. Finally, "external entities" can be organized for digital assaults. For both Russia and China, the structures of cyberattack will be more complex than for the United States.[26]

This detour into the thicket of Russian and Chinese doctrine and organization serves as a reminder that the punishment for hackers will not be one-size-fits-all. Even if someone in the CIA or NSA understands what Xi Jinping wants for China when he talks about the "China Dream," the relationship between the small leading group on cybersecurity and the hackers, the intelligence agencies, the PLA, state-owned enterprises, and other actors is opaque at best. In some instances, it may make sense for the United States to sanction a state-owned enterprise and threaten economic interests. Directly taking over a computer in Zhongnanhai, the central leadership compound, might focus the mind of a high-level Chinese official. Cyberattacks that threaten regime stability, perhaps by weakening the control over information, may garner the most attention. The drop of the Shanghai stock market by 64.89 points on the twenty-third anniversary of the Tiananmen Square massacre (which occurred on June 4, 1989) may have been a weird coincidence or a very savvy psychological operation, revealing to the Chinese leadership their vulnerability to a disruptive attack.[27]

Disruption and punishment do not have to come through cyberattacks. Criminologists talk of two types of deterrence, specific and general. In the specific model, offenders realize the consequences of their behavior and do not commit another crime. General deterrence targets potential lawbreakers; they see what happens to drug dealers, for example, and decide not to engage in the same behavior. Washington may make attacks more or less visible depending on whom it hopes to deter. A retaliatory strike discussed by neither Washington nor the victim will be a specific deterrent. An attack that creates destruction for all to see and attribute will be both a specific and a general deterrent, as will openly levied diplomatic, economic, and financial measures.

In fact, financial and trade sanctions may become the go-to tool for deterring cyberattacks, as they have for so many other US foreign policy objectives. The general appeal of sanctions—they offer a seemingly proportional response and are more palatable than either military intervention or inaction—explains why the United States used them against North Korea after the Sony attacks. In April 2015, President Obama issued an executive order that laid the groundwork for more active use of economic sanctions against Chinese, Russian, Iranian, and North Korean hackers, as well as nonstate actors. Declaring "significant malicious cyber-enabled activities" a "national emergency," the order enables the Treasury secretary to sanction individuals and entities with punishments that could include freezing their financial assets and barring commercial transactions with them. This was a big step, a concrete effort to raise the cost of hacking, although how often the government will deploy such sanctions remains to be seen.[28]

RIGHT AND WRONG IN CYBERSPACE

Even if ineffective, as they often are, sanctions against another country also send a message about what the rules of the hacked world order should be. At the most obvious level, by sanctioning PLA hackers, the United States would signal to friends and adversaries the importance of the idea that states should not steal intellectual property for the benefit of their own companies. But the tools themselves are also an exercise in rule setting, a sign that Washington believes visa restrictions, economic fines, and criminal indictments, not cruise missiles or destructive cyberattacks, are appropriate, proportional responses to cyber espionage.

The fight over these rules, also called norms, is the second part of the US strategy in cyberspace. Cyberspace rules tend to be fuzzier than treaties, but they have important consequences. They allow states to justify certain types of behavior and draw the lines between what is and is not acceptable with strategic interests in mind. Under the right circumstances, norms can help nation-states regulate the outbreak and intensity of conflict.

The United States and Russia met secretly in 1996 in Moscow to discuss an agreement on disarmament in cyberspace, and for many years Moscow has submitted to the United Nations draft treaties on the issue. These drafts called for the banning of logic bombs and deception in cyberspace. Russian diplomats also wanted potential treaties to cover what they called "information terrorism"—that is, any use of the Internet that might threaten domestic stability.

After the 1996 meetings, US diplomats spent most of the next decade and a half vocally opposing the idea of treaties for cyberspace. The resistance from the United States and many of its friends in Europe and Asia was both ideological and practical. The Russian definition of information security would consider hacktivists who circumvented censorship technology and promoted the free flow of information to be terrorists. US diplomats were also deeply skeptical of the applicability of traditional arms-control approaches to cyberspace. Intercontinental ballistic missiles can be counted, nuclear facilities inspected, short-range missiles positioned away from borders, and biological and chemical weapons prohibited. These measures are clearly not possible for code sitting on a personal computer, smartphone, or thumb drive. The most strenuous method of testing a network's defenses is to attack it, so states will continue to develop and test new offensive code. Moreover, as the country with the most advanced digital assault capabilities, the United States was likely to see itself as the party with the most to lose from any arms-control agreement.[29]

But Washington has supported one international treaty that it thinks should be expanded, though it deals with law enforcement. The Council of Europe's Convention on Cybercrime (also known as the Budapest Convention) criminalizes computer crimes such as fraud and child pornography and prohibits illegal access and interception, data and system interference, and intellectual property theft. States that sign the treaty agree to cooperate in the investigation and prosecution of crimes, though they can opt out if the request infringes on sovereignty, security, or other critical interests—fairly broad categories. As of September 2015, forty-five countries have ratified the treaty, but China and Russia are among the scores that have not. Claiming the treaty violates state sovereignty, Russia opposes a provision that lets foreign investigators work directly with network operators and avoid government officials, while countries like India and Brazil do not like that they were not part of the convention's creation and are skeptical of its European provenance.

In Washington's view, the absence of new international treaties does not mean that there will be a free-for-all in cyberspace. A large body of international law, state practice, and precedent, known as international humanitarian law or the laws of armed conflict, already lays out the conditions under which states can resort to military force (*jus ad bellum*) as well as how they should fight (*jus in bello*)—whom they can attack, what types of attacks are justified, and how to treat noncombatants.

According to Washington, these rules, developed over centuries of warfare, apply to cyberspace. In 2012, Harold Koh, then legal adviser to the State Department, delivered a speech at Cyber Command in the form of ten questions and answers. Koh first asked, "Do established principles of international law apply to cyberspace?" He answered yes: "Cyberspace is not a 'law-free' zone where anyone can conduct hostile activities without rules or restraint." Koh then ticked through many fundamental questions related to the laws of armed conflict: Can a cyberattack constitute a use of force? Can states invoke the right of self-defense in response to a cyberattack? Should the principles of proportionality, neutrality, and distinction apply in cyberspace? Are states legally responsible for action taken by proxies? Koh argued that the US government answered all these questions in the affirmative.[30]

Koh then recognized three difficulties, or what he called "unresolved questions," in applying laws developed for conventional battlefields to cyberspace. First is the question of effects. While it is easy to see how malware that causes a dam to fail and creates a flood that kills several hundred people is similar to destroying the dam with a missile, some cyberattacks do not have a parallel in the physical world. Destroying or manipulating the data of a stock exchange could cause serious economic and political disruptions without physical effects. Some might think that such an event constituted an armed attack, others that, while not an armed attack, it could still be considered a use of force.

Regardless of legal interpretations, policymakers will determine whether to consider an attack as armed or a use of force based on the political or military context. The United States would likely consider an attack that turned traffic lights red a nuisance. But a former Israeli government official told me that, given the country's dependence on mobilizing reserves for defense, analysts had imagined scenarios— say, another war across the Lebanese border—in which a Hezbollah cyberattack made the already horrendous traffic in Tel Aviv worse. The Israelis concluded that they would consider Hezbollah's turning all the traffic lights red as an armed attack.[31]

Koh's second unresolved question had to do with how to separate legitimate military targets from civilian ones, an extremely difficult challenge given how intertwined information and communication networks are. It is easy to imagine an attack that cuts power to a military base doing the same to a neighboring hospital. As in conventional war, weaker parties are likely either to pretend to be civilians or to hide among them, increasing the chances that a strike will cause collateral damage. Third, Koh noted that while legal tools exist to help deal with the attribution problem, particularly the use of proxies, the solutions are likely to be technical and political, not found in international law. Koh concluded his speech by noting that such challenges are not unique to cyberspace. "These questions about effects, dual use, and attribution are difficult legal and policy questions that existed long before the development of cyber tools, and that will continue to be a topic of discussion among our allies and partners as cyber tools develop."

Because so much cyber activity happens below the level of armed attacks, states need additional guidelines besides international law. One of the more important discussions about international principles has been happening since 2005 as a small group of experts gather to discuss cyber threats at the United Nations. The group, which includes representatives from China, Russia, and the United States, signed an expert report in 2013 agreeing that international law applies in cyberspace and that states are responsible for and must act against cyberattacks that come from within their territories. In 2015, the same group agreed that during peacetime states should not attack each other's critical infrastructure or target each other's cyber emergency responders and that they should assist other nations investigating cyberattacks.

Despite this apparent consensus, Moscow and Beijing are deeply skeptical of US efforts. Both take the push for norms as evidence that the United States does not want to constrain itself with binding arms treaties. Speaking of the development of offensive capabilities in the West, Dmitry Rogozin, deputy prime minister for defense and space industry, argued that it came as no surprise that "the U.S. has no strong motivation to sign any global treaties on not using cyber weapons, especially not with Russia, which potentially could be the object of cyberattacks."[32]

Almost immediately after signing the 2013 expert report, Beijing began backtracking. Chinese officials, when referring to international law, stressed the importance of sovereignty without mentioning the laws of armed conflict. During the 2015 meeting of the UN group, China's representative proposed taking out all references to international law in the upcoming report. Chinese officials explained to me that they were sure the United States wanted other countries to accept the applicability of the laws of armed conflict to cyberspace so that it would be free to attack China. Beijing saw the application of international law as a sure sign of the militarization of cyberspace.

Unfortunately for Washington, the Snowden disclosures severely handicapped US efforts at persuasion by exposing a gap between action and rhetoric. While many opposed whatever Washington said for ideological and geopolitical reasons, others more sympathetic are now inclined to ask if the United States disproportionately benefits from an open and global Internet. They also wonder if Washington's commitment is simply utilitarian, to be jettisoned once it no longer furthers US economic, political, and military objectives.[33]

SELF-HELP

Deterrence and rule definition are slow, uncertain processes. In the short term, states have to help themselves—they have to shore up defenses at home. In the United States, at least in short hand, the division of duties has been as follows: the Defense Department protects military networks (the .mil suffix); the Department of Homeland Security (DHS) defends government networks (.gov) and critical infrastructure, with assistance from the NSA and Cyber Command if needed; and the private sector (.com, .org, .edu, .net) is essentially on its own. Demarcating these boundaries has not been easy because most of the infrastructure of cyberspace is in private-sector hands. There is also fear that government intervention will stifle innovation and that the need for control and access to data will trump privacy concerns.

The difficulty of drawing the line between the government's responsibility to protect domestic networks and the private sector's obligation to invest enough to defend itself spans liberal democracies in the hacked world order. With a state-owned economy and close ties to the private sector, Chinese leaders have more tools on hand to mobilize companies, and the legal barriers to intervention are low or nonexistent. In the United Kingdom, however, there has been considerable debate about whether the Government Communications Headquarters or the Cabinet Office should lead cybersecurity strategy and how best to facilitate cooperation with British firms. German chancellor Angela Merkel created the Nationaler Cyber-Sicherheitsrat (National Cyber Security Council) in 2011 to strengthen cooperation within the government and with the private sector. Israel experienced a long-running battle between its internal intelligence service, Shin Bet, and the civilian National Cyber Bureau. "Shin Bet would not tolerate any other organization taking any security role," one Israeli official told me, "but also really doesn't want to be responsible for defending all of the civilian economy."[34]

As policymakers become more alarmed about the possibility of destructive cyberattacks, however, they are redrawing the lines. When news of the Sony attack first began to leak, many in the cybersecurity community had little sympathy for the company, which had long known it was a target for hackers. The hacker collective Anonymous brought down the company's PlayStation network and stole the personal details associated with 77 million accounts in 2011; over the next six months, there were twenty-one major cybersecurity incidents, including a breach at Sony Entertainment that resulted in the theft of passwords and home addresses for over 1 million accounts. Some of the documents the North Korean hackers leaked revealed substandard cybersecurity practices. A file named "Passwords" stored thousands of passwords; many Excel spreadsheets, Word documents, PDFs, and zip files contained unencrypted passwords for Sony Pictures' internal computers. One firewall and 148 routers and servers went unmonitored by the security team.[35]

These failures appear to bolster the argument for why the bulk of responsibility for defending against attacks on the private sector should remain with the private sector. Surely companies cannot expect the government to step in when they have not done the minimum to protect themselves. Saying that the government will eventually save the day encourages companies to continue to underinvest in their own defense, perpetuating the problem. But Matthew Green, a research professor at Johns Hopkins University, cautions against drawing a

direct line from Sony's negligence to firmly placing the responsibility on private actors, given that the attacker was a nation-state: "Even
working and monitored Intrusion Detection Systems are hardly a silver
bullet when it comes to detecting sophisticated attacks like this one."[36]

In other words, nation-states will always win against companies. If
we accept this point and believe there exist threats, backed by nation-
states, to the nation's critical infrastructure and the competitiveness
of the US economy, we cannot legitimately expect the private sector to
defend itself. The goal of policy, then, is to find the sweet spot where
companies invest more in protecting themselves from common threats
and the government has a clear idea of when to step in.

LONG-RUNNING DEBATES AND LITTLE PROGRESS

The United States set the fundamental outline of its cyber defense
strategy in the late 1990s. Since then there has been a frequent rehashing of old debates. Three questions keep circulating: Who should take
the lead in defending the private sector—the NSA, a civilian agency,
or businesses themselves? How do you best encourage public-private
cooperation, particularly sharing between the government and private companies of reports of successful penetrations, Internet protocol
addresses used by attacking computers, hacker techniques, and other
threat information? And what role should regulation play in ensuring
that private companies invest in adequate security?

Released in May 1998, Presidential Decision Directive 63, the first
national cybersecurity strategy, served as a preliminary answer to these
questions. It focused on critical infrastructure protection, public-
private partnerships, and threat sharing. The 2003 National Strategy to
Secure Cyberspace also concentrated on defending critical infrastructure and better public-private coordination of the preceding policies.

In the last days of his administration, President George W. Bush
launched the Comprehensive National Cybersecurity Initiative (CNCI).
The directives establishing it were classified, reflecting the high (and
mostly unnecessary) degree of secrecy surrounding cybersecurity planning. When evaluated after President Obama declassified an outline
of the plan's twelve objectives, the program did truly appear comprehensive. The initiative covered education and cybersecurity awareness,

research into "leap-ahead" technologies, and development of deterrence strategies, though sections on developing offensive cyber weapons remained classified. It also described an effort to deploy an intrusion-detection system across federal networks, known as Einstein. And the CNCI, once again, called for better coordination between the government and private sector regarding critical infrastructure defense.[37]

Indicating the high importance his administration gave to cybersecurity, President Obama ordered a sixty-day review of plans and programs, including the CNCI, just a month after his inauguration. In a May 2009 speech, the first a president had devoted entirely to cybersecurity, he announced the results of the review and called the cyber threat "one of the most serious economic and national security challenges we face as a nation." The president announced a new approach, one starting from the top, "with a commitment from me." The country's digital infrastructure would "be treated as [it] should be: as a strategic national asset. Protecting this infrastructure will be a national security priority." President Obama also raised the issue of privacy. "Let me also be clear about what we will not do," he said. "Our pursuit of cyber security will not include—I repeat, will not include—monitoring private-sector networks or Internet traffic. We will preserve and protect the personal privacy and civil liberties that we cherish as Americans."[38]

CYBERSECURITY TURF WAR

The headline of the new administration's approach was the appointment of a "cyber czar," a cybersecurity coordinator in the White House. Filling the position was unexpectedly difficult, reflecting the limits of the job. The position, eventually placed within the National Security Council and the National Economic Council, lacked budget authority and bureaucratic influence over the DHS and DoD behemoths. The initial frontrunner for the job was Melissa Hathaway, who had launched the CNCI under Bush and shepherded the sixty-day Obama cybersecurity review process. Hathaway had come to the White House with former national intelligence director Mike McConnell, and so her ties to the previous administration may have been a handicap. There was also reporting that Hathaway alienated some of the president's economic advisers by advocating for regulation of private firms and utilities to ensure they secured their networks. Several people turned down the job—the *Washington Post* reported that thirty had interviewed for it—until Howard Schmidt, a former director of information security at Microsoft who also had extensive government experience, finally accepted the position in December 2009.[39]

During the first months of the Obama administration, bureaucratic turf battles over cybersecurity and the protection of the private sector began to emerge in public. While Homeland Security was legally the lead agency, there were doubts about its ability to fulfill its responsibility. The NSA had a much bigger budget and a deeper well of technological expertise. Specific statutes set forth the legal authority for the FBI's and NSA's roles in cybersecurity, but DHS authorities rested on a patchwork of presidential directives and policy memos. Most damaging, confidence in the DHS among the private sector was (and remains) low. "DHS will never own the cyber mission," according to former representative Jane Harman (D-CA). "The bottom line problem is that the private sector doesn't trust DHS." Given these weaknesses, it was not surprising when Director of National Intelligence Dennis Blair testified in February 2009 that the NSA should take over cybersecurity responsibilities. "The National Security Agency has the greatest repository of cyber talent," he said. "There are some wizards out there at Fort Meade who can do stuff."[40]

Many within DHS balked at the pace of change, and turnover was high as a number of officials resigned, including Rod Beckstrom, head of DHS's National Cyber Security Center. In his resignation letter, Beckstrom expressed frustration at the lack of funding and at bureaucratic impediments. Moreover, he cautioned, "the NSA currently dominates most national cyber efforts." He viewed this concentration of network security and monitoring power in one government agency as a threat to the democratic process. In a follow-up interview, Beckstrom also warned that the predominance of the NSA hindered cooperation with the private sector. "In intelligence environments like the NSA, you seek out and gather information, and then you classify it," he said. "It's the opposite of collaboration."[41]

In an effort to reassert the civilian side of the cybersecurity equation, prominent White House and DHS officials tried to reframe the debate. Howard Schmidt announced, "There is no cyberwar," adding, "I think that is a terrible metaphor and I think that is a terrible concept." Senior DHS officials argued that while conflict and exploitation were certainly present, cyberspace was "fundamentally a civilian space—a neighborhood, a library, a marketplace, a school yard, a workshop." Security should be distributed to different agencies and private actors, and DHS had an important role to play.[42]

While the NSA and DHS officially came to an uneasy truce, the intelligence agency keeps pushing for a greater role. A memorandum signed by Homeland Security Secretary Janet Napolitano and Defense Secretary Robert M. Gates spelled out responsibilities, where the NSA would provide technical expertise in case of an attack on critical infrastructure and the DHS would direct operations. Individuals from DHS were stationed at Fort Meade, while experts from the NSA went to the operations center at Homeland Security. General Alexander and then admiral Rogers have been very careful in their public statements to stress that NSA and Cyber Command support DHS in defending government and critical infrastructure. Still, if stopping cyberattacks requires seeing them in real time, then there are reasons to believe the NSA's role will only grow larger.[43]

THE GOVERNMENT AND INFORMATION SHARING: BETTER AT TAKING THAN GIVING

While the DHS and NSA maneuvered over who would play the lead role in defending critical private-sector networks, the larger question about government responsibilities shifted continually. In a 2013 speech, White House cybersecurity coordinator Michael Daniel tried to clarify, describing the government's role in what he called the "new normal"—persistent intrusions, violations of privacy, thefts of business information, and degradation and denial of service to legitimate entities trying to do business or get their message out on the Internet. In almost all cases of the new normal, as Daniel described it, private companies were responsible for their own network defense; the government's job was to help them protect themselves. Some cyberattacks would provoke a government response, just as the federal government reacted to a devastating flood or tornado. But Daniel did not say precisely where the threshold lay. The Defense Department's 2015 strategy tried to further narrow the scope of the US military's response to include those attacks that cause "loss of life, significant damage to property, serious adverse U.S. foreign policy consequences, or serious economic impact on the United States." It estimated that these made up 2 percent of all attacks.[44]

My Council on Foreign Relations colleague Rob Knake, a former National Security Council official, calls the approach laid out in the Daniel speech the Home Depot model: You can do it; we can help. A primary form of help the government can offer is information sharing. The logic is relatively straightforward. DHS, NSA, and Cyber Command collect a huge amount of malware and data on hacking tactics, techniques, and procedures. Private companies have a wealth of information about the attacks they face. Sharing data between the government and the private sector and among private companies would prevent attackers from using the same techniques against hundreds of organizations. It would force hackers to up their game.

Yet the information does not flow like it should. The intelligence agencies have typically been more interested in taking information from than sharing it with the private sector, primarily because they do not want to compromise secret sources and methods. "Government only inhales, it never exhales," says Jason Healey. "It will take all the information, but it will find any excuse to not share." For private companies, the benefits of reporting a breach are abstract and the potential financial losses from a drop in stock price or investor confidence real. Antitrust and privacy regulations make companies hesitant to share information. They want liability protection before they pass user data to the government. In addition, private companies often have competitive reasons not to share. For AT&T, Verizon, and other telecoms, as well as for the specialized cybersecurity companies, threat intelligence is a product to offer to customers.[45]

Despite widespread support by industry and both political parties, information sharing legislation has been remarkably difficult to pass. The Cyber Intelligence Sharing and Protection Act (CISPA), for example, passed in the House in 2012 but never moved on to the Senate (in any case, President Obama threatened a veto). Opposition to the bills, mainly from the privacy and civil liberties communities, revolved primarily around how broadly or narrowly to define cyber threats, the role of the NSA, the sharing of threat data with law enforcement agencies, and the process for redacting or minimizing private user data. Reenergized by the Sony attacks, Congress tried again in 2015. Two bills, the Protecting Cyber Networks Act in the House and the Computer Information Sharing Act in the Senate, reenacted the debate over CISPA, with supporters arguing that private companies need liability protection to share threat information and critics decrying a perceived lack of privacy protection and the introduction of new surveillance powers.

In the face of legislative gridlock, President Obama issued two executive orders. The first, on October 2013, instructed the DHS, DoD, and DoJ to increase the "volume, timeliness, and quality of cyber threat information shared with U.S. private sector," including warnings to companies being targeted. This order merely directed the government to do what it was already authorized to do. The second, announced at Stanford in February 2015, created a special portal at DHS for sharing classified threat intelligence with the private sector. It also promoted new organizations that will link businesses from the same geographic locations or sectors of the economy to resolve security issues and share threat information.[46]

To be sure, information sharing is no panacea. It will help with much of the background noise and with fairly low-level criminal and some state-based attackers. But it will not do much to protect critical infrastructure from sophisticated state-backed hackers since they are likely to exploit unknown vulnerabilities. The DHS cannot share threat intelligence on an attack it has never seen before. As Jeff Moss, founder of the Black Hat and DEFCON hacker conferences, argued, "Information sharing allows better and faster bandaids but doesn't address the core problem." But for low-level attacks, Band-Aids are at least something.[47]

FROM KILL SWITCH TO VOLUNTARY FRAMEWORK

The story of the effort to design cybersecurity regulation plays out in the same desultory fashion as that of information sharing. Cyberattacks generate what economists call negative externalities—costs imposed on unrelated third parties due to individuals' or companies' economic activities. For any one firm, underinvesting in security often makes economic sense. The chances of sustaining a destructive attack seem low, and the investment needed to prevent one almost always exceeds the potential direct and liability costs it would incur. Benjamin Dean, a researcher at Columbia University, found, for example, that the actual expenses stemming from the high-profile breaches of Target, Home Depot, and Sony amounted to less than 1 percent of revenue, and with insurance payments and tax deductions, the total cost was even less. When firms underinvest, however, the costs often get passed on to others. After hackers stole information on 106 million accounts from Home Depot and Target, banks and credit card companies absorbed most of the costs. What is true of theft in the retail sector is even more the case with critical infrastructure. If hackers were to take down the power grid for an extended period, the costs would spread to companies throughout the economy as every business suffered.[48]

In the face of these potential costs to society, the government must find ways to increase private investment in cybersecurity. Requiring adherence to standards—in the same way that business owners and building contractors must conform to the fire code—would seem the most direct way to do this. But what seems straightforward is not. Both the causes of most fires and the best practices for fire prevention are well known. Hackers by contrast are constantly developing new methods, and so industry fears that government regulations are doomed to lag behind the evolving threat and will ultimately generate check-list security—top-down, one-size-fits-all standards that are costly to implement and stifle innovation. As Bruce Josten, a lobbyist for the US Chamber of Commerce, wrote in a letter to senators in reference to a potential cybersecurity bill, such legislation "could actually impede U.S. cyber security by shifting businesses' resources away from implementing robust and effective security measures and toward meeting government mandates." That Chinese hackers had penetrated its network two years before—a thermostat communicated with an Internet address in China, and a printer put out pages with Chinese characters—did not smack of irony to the chamber or soften its opposition to comprehensive cyber legislation.[49]

Over the last five years, cybersecurity proponents have gradually narrowed what they hope to accomplish in the face of opposition from industry and congressional conservatives hostile to the idea that government has any positive role to play in the economy. Two bills—one introduced by Senators Joseph Lieberman (I-CT) and Susan Collins (R-MA), the other by Senators Jay Rockefeller (D-WV) and Olympia Snowe (R-ME)—became exemplars of cybersecurity legislation's ability to generate heat and outrage, yet fail to accomplish much to make the country safer. Both bills, addressing what their authors thought was missing in a potential response to a catastrophic attack, would have authorized the president to declare a national cyber emergency if the energy or communications grids were knocked down; they would then require companies to follow an emergency plan developed by DHS, which might include the government ordering the disconnection of certain networks from the Internet.

These plans to empower the president to shut down Internet traffic generated huge opposition. Critics protested against what they called Internet "kill switches" and described the bills as threats to free speech and Internet access. Proponents warned of attacks that could kill thousands. The White House argued the provisions were unnecessary; Section 706 of the Communications of Act of 1934 gives the president the power to suspend or amend "any facility or station for wire communication" in the event of "war or a threat of war, or a state of public peril or disaster or other national emergency."[50]

Further drafts of the Protecting Cyberspace as a National Asset Act (the Lieberman-Collins bill) and the Cybersecurity Act (the Rockefeller-Snowe legislation) removed or severely limited the kill-switch provisions. The debates, dominated by those at the extreme ends of the spectrum, did little to advance the goal of making critical infrastructure industries safer. By August 2012, the legislative efforts had died. Even a watered-down version of the Cybersecurity Act, which set voluntary standards, failed to make it out of the Senate.

In response, in an October 2013 executive order President Obama called for development of a "cybersecurity framework"—a voluntary set of cybersecurity best practices developed by the National Institute of Standards and Technology with help from the private sector. Work is under way, and once the practices are identified, DHS will work with the Department of Energy and other agencies, as well as industry groups, to ensure their implementation. The government has worked to identify the best set of incentives, such as tax breaks, federal research grant money, and legal protections for participants, to push companies to join the voluntary program. To be truly useful, these programs will require even greater transparency and direction from the government since the objective is to have companies spend more money not just on defense but on the types of defense that actually work.

Executive orders have a note of finality to them, but actually they are more like bookmarks. They indicate that Congress has failed to reach a consensus on what should be done. Some have criticized executive orders, saying that they do not go far enough and, in particular, do not provide liability coverage to companies sharing information (only Congress can do that). And since the next administration might not renew them, they create uncertainty in terms of business investment.

This uncertainty, unfortunately, is the big takeaway from the short history of the federal government and cybersecurity. After two decades, what the private sector can expect from government and what it should be prepared to do on its own remain undetermined. All that is clear is that the threats and the demands on government to do more are growing.

Even as the government was reorganizing and restructuring to foster information sharing and cybersecurity, the private sector was acting on its own. In October 2014, Microsoft, Cisco, Symantec, FireEye, and six other firms cooperated to expose a Chinese hacking group that was targeting Fortune 500 companies, journalists, environmental groups, and government agencies worldwide. During the same week in February 2015 that President Obama announced his threat-sharing initiative, Facebook, with Dropbox, Pinterest, Tumblr, Twitter, and Yahoo as early partners, announced it was setting up, without government involvement, a platform for companies to submit threat information about common attacks. Over six months, ThreatExchange signed up over ninety companies, but no federal agencies. As of September 2015, government agencies were not participating in ThreatExchange, and they will not "until there is legislation that clearly defines how information from sharing platforms can be used by these parties," Mark Hammell, manager of Facebook's Threat Infrastructure team, told the *Christian Science Monitor*.[51]

The current division of responsibility for cybersecurity between the government and the private sector is not firmly set, especially in the liberal democracies. A destructive attack could easily result in a shift toward greater government intervention, with the intelligence agencies in the lead. Or in response to future revelations about NSA surveillance, the technology companies may chart an even more independent path, pursing legal and technical measures that stress their autonomy from Washington.

The needle could be pushed in one direction or another by other events as well. Countries and companies face persistent threats from nation-state attackers looking to steal intellectual property, business strategies, and trade secrets. Everybody is spying on everybody else. There is little cost and much to gain, and states will continue to conduct cyber espionage for a very long time. How states respond to this threat to their own companies could not only draw the public and private sector closer together, but also remake international trade relations.

Chapter 5

EVERYBODY SPIES

··

CHINESE HACKING EXPOSED

On June 26, 2014, the FBI unsealed an indictment against Su Bin, a Chinese national living in Canada for hacking into the networks of US defense contractors. Working with two unnamed conspirators, Su had allegedly targeted and exfiltrated data related to the C-17, a military transport aircraft, as well as the F-22 and F-35 stealth fighter jets. Two days later, the Royal Canadian Mounted Police arrested Su. His two partners remained in China. As of September 2015, Su remained in Canadian custody, and none of the allegations against him have been proven.[1]

According to the affidavit submitted by Special Agent Joel Neeman, Su and the others began targeting Boeing in Orange County, California, in early 2009. In January 2010, the two unnamed conspirators e-mailed Su a list of file names from the company's computers related to the C-17. By August 2012, the two hackers claimed to Su that they had stolen 630,000 files related to the aircraft, which included detailed drawings of the plane, measurements of wings, fuselage, and other parts, outlines of the pipeline and electric wiring systems, and flight-test data.

As with many hacks, the attacks, according to the affidavit, began with spear-phishing e-mails. The hackers had the names, e-mail addresses, and phone numbers of Boeing employees. Using that information they crafted e-mails that appeared to come from colleagues or business acquaintances and contained an infected PDF attachment or bad link, much like the ones I regularly receive from Richard Haass imposters. A recipient's opening the document or clicking the link established a connection with another computer controlled by the hackers. From that command-and-control computer, the hackers installed malware that allowed them to gain access to other computers on Boeing's networks.

These multiphased attacks, often called advanced persistent threats, are in fact less advanced and much more persistent. Once users start checking who e-mails are from and not opening anything they are not expecting, the effectiveness of the attacks goes down. But if the attackers try you enough times, varying their tricks, you might eventually make a mistake. The hackers trying to break into the computers of Kevin Mandia, head of Mandiant, a cybersecurity company that exposes Chinese attacks, tried multiple avenues, including fake e-mails from clients, customers, and journalists, among others. They also sent him fake invoices from the car service he frequently used. In that case, an operative may have followed Mandia to public events and watched what limo he got into afterward.[2]

Su Bin, who headed Beijing aviation company Lode Tech, apparently did the spying for money. Su was allegedly selling the information to Chinese aeronautic companies. In an e-mail to his partners, he asks for their patience regarding payment, promises a big payout soon, and complains that Chinese aircraft companies are "too stingy." But the hackers' greed overlaps with their patriotism and Chinese strategic needs. The hackers explicitly boast in their e-mails of their contribution to China's military modernization. The state-controlled Xi'an Aircraft Industrial Corporation is developing its own military cargo jet, the Y-20, and some of the data from the C-17 may have helped accelerate progress on the plane. Although the hackers complained that it was hard to get data out of Boeing's networks—they had to bundle it differently and change the file formats—the operation only took a year and cost 2.7 million renminbi, or less than $450,000. Considering the C-17 is the third most expensive plane that the Department of Defense has ever developed, with research and development (R&D) costs of $3.4 billion, the hackers were clearly not far off in bragging that their hack showed "cost effectiveness and enormous achievement."[3]

While the Chinese government may have benefited from the hackers' work, there was little indication that it directed their alleged actions. Some hackers may work independently and sell information to state-owned enterprises; the Chinese government or military may instruct or directly employ others.

In May 2014, just a month before Su Bin's indictment, the Department of Justice charged five Chinese hackers with stealing the business plans, internal deliberations, and other intellectual property of Westinghouse Electric, United States Steel Corporation, and other companies. Online three of the hackers went by the names UglyGorilla, WinXYHappy, and KandyGoo; in the real world they are known as Wang Dong, Wen Xinyu, and Gu Chunhui.

The DoJ's explosive claim was that Wang, Wen, and the three others were members of the People's Liberation Army (PLA) General Staff, Third Department, Unit 61398, located in Shanghai. They sought competitive gain, or, as former Attorney General Eric Holder put it, "to advantage state-owned companies and other interests in China, at the expense of businesses here in the United States." This was a watershed event: the first instance of charges against an alleged state cyber actor.[4]

The indictment incensed the Chinese government. Senior Chinese military officials felt particularly burned because the announcement came on the second day of General Fang Fenghui's meeting with Joint Chiefs of Staff chairman General Martin Dempsey. According to the Chinese, General Fang, chief of the PLA's General Staff, had received no advance warning that the indictments were coming. One Chinese officer told me that Fang was preparing a "beautiful report" for President Xi Jinping on the benefits of cooperation and exchange between the two militaries when Dempsey called to tell him of the indictment. Not surprisingly, he never delivered the report.[5]

For elite hackers, UglyGorilla and partners left a lot of online tracks. Security analysts consider the Chinese particularly noisy in networks, especially compared to the Russians. UglyGorilla posted to Chinese online bulletin boards and social media sites using the same e-mail addresses and accounts, making it easier to track him. He also showed off, seeding malicious code with his hacker handle and leaving the initials "UG" in the logs of thousands of compromised computers. Chen Ping, who targeted US telecommunication and satellite companies and is allegedly part of another PLA hacker group, Unit 61486, posted pictures of his girlfriend, birthday parties, and his office in a PLA building to photo-sharing sites. The indictments and arrests were just the beginning of the US government's struggle to find an effective policy response to a pervasive threat to national and economic security.[6]

WHAT AGENCIES HAVE NOT BEEN HACKED?

Units 61398 and 61486 are two of approximately twenty Chinese cyber espionage groups that go after political and military intelligence, as well as information that will bolster China's economic competitiveness (cybersecurity companies looking to garner press attention for their reports and products often give these groups much more expressive names, such as Putter Panda, Comment Crew, and APT 1). According to a *Washington Post* report and numerous other studies, Units 61398 and 61486 and other groups have stolen information from over two dozen Defense Department weapons programs, including the Patriot missile system and the US Navy's new littoral combat ship. In response to a question about attacks on defense contractors, Lieutenant General Vincent Stewart, director of the Defense Intelligence Agency, told a congressional hearing, "I do not believe we are at this point losing our technological edge, but it is at risk based on some of their [Chinese] cyber activities."[7]

While China has been modernizing its military for over two decades, Chinese defense planners worry about a conflict with what they often call a technologically advanced adversary, by which, of course, they mean the United States. The conflict could break out over Taiwan or a collision between the two navies in the South China or East China Seas. Chinese defense spending is now estimated at over $130 billion a year (the United States still spends more than four times that amount), but the PLA is untested, not having fought in a conflict since its 1979 war with Vietnam. In the same time, the US military has taken part in at least eight major conflicts and numerous deployments of more limited forces. China hopes stealing military secrets will offset US technological and operational advantages.

The $400 billion F-35 is already the most expensive weapon program ever, and China's attacks have forced contractors to redesign specialized communications and antenna arrays for the stealth aircraft and to rewrite software to protect systems vulnerable to hacking. Department of Defense officials say that the most sensitive flight control data were not taken because they were stored offline, but the fuselage of China's second stealth fighter jet, the J-31, bears a suspicious resemblance to that of the F-22 and F-35. US Pacific Command's Admiral Samuel Locklear jokingly told a reporter, "Chinese military equipment looks surprisingly similar to American weapons."[8]

After the 2014 revelation that hackers had gained access to the computers of the US Transportation Command, the organization that provides transportation and distribution of goods to war fighters all over the world, Senator Tom Coburn (R-OK) asked Obama administration witnesses at a hearing, "Can you tell me which departments of the federal government haven't been hacked?" He then answered his own question: "The fact is, they've all been hacked."[9]

In July 2014, media reported that Chinese hackers had gained access to the servers of the Office of Personnel Management (OPM), which contained the personal information of tens of thousands of federal employees. A little less than a year later, the OPM hack was revealed to be even worse than first acknowledged. The hackers compromised 22 million records, including security background checks and data on intelligence and military personnel, as well as the fingerprint data of 5.6 million people. Chinese hackers gained access to Standard Form 86, which includes information perfect for blackmail—records of financial trouble, drug use, alcohol abuse, and adulterous affairs. The records would also allow Chinese counterintelligence agencies to identify spies working undercover at US embassies around the world. China's Ministry of State Security reportedly combined medical data stolen from Anthem insurance, travel records from United Airlines, and OPM security files to create a more complete picture of US officials. "This is not the end of American human intelligence," said Joel Brenner, former senior counsel at the National Security Agency, "but it's a significant blow." In September 2015 the *Washington Post* reported that CIA agents had been removed from the US embassy in Beijing as a cautionary measure.[10]

The United States is not the only target of this massive espionage network. In search of military secrets, the hacker units have broken into computers belonging to BAE Systems, Britain's biggest defense company; Japan's Mitsubishi Heavy Industries, which manufactures weapons for the Japanese Self-Defense Force; India's Eastern Naval Command and Defence Research and Development Organization; and, between 2009 and 2011, Elisra Group, Israel Aerospace Industries, and Rafael Advanced Defense Systems, the companies responsible for building the "Iron Dome" missile shield, which protects Israel from rocket attacks from Gaza and Lebanon.[11]

Electronic spies are also on the lookout for political information. Chinese hackers have targeted the offices of the Dalai Lama; Tibetan exile centers in Brussels, Dharamsala, London, and New York; and the embassies, foreign ministries, and other government offices of Germany, India, Indonesia, Romania, South Korea, Taiwan, and others. China-based actors allegedly stole documents from the Japanese Agriculture, Forestry, and Fisheries Ministry related to trade negotiations over the Trans-Pacific Partnership. They hacked the computers of the 2008 Barack Obama and John McCain campaigns and of the UK Foreign Office, House of Commons, and Ministry of Defense. Chinese hackers reportedly accessed the computers of former Australian prime minister Julia Gillard and ten federal ministers, including the foreign minister and defense minister.

In July 2015, Secretary of State John Kerry told CBS News that it was "very likely" the Chinese and Russians were reading his emails, and that he writes all of them with that threat in mind. As even the highest levels of the US government failed to keep hackers out, civil society groups and the private sector seemed doomed to be penetrated and exploited by state-backed attackers.[12]

I KNOW WHAT YOU THINK ABOUT ME

Digital spying is a tool to shape political narratives as well as to gather information on agencies, institutions, and individuals who might influence the debates on topics of importance to Beijing. The government wants to know what will be said and decided before it becomes public. In the days and weeks after the radical Sunni Islamic State in Iraq and Syria (ISIS) seized Iraq's largest oil refinery, for example, Chinese hackers targeted Middle East experts at the Brookings Institution, Center for Strategic and International Studies, Council on Foreign Relations, and other think tanks for an understanding of how the United States

EVERYBODY SPIES • 117

might respond and what effect that may have on Chinese investments in the Iraqi oil industry.

Hackers have penetrated the Gmail accounts of dozens of civil society organizations, human rights activists, and journalists in the United States, China, and Europe. As Citizen Lab, an interdisciplinary lab that researches information technology, security, and human rights at the University of Toronto, notes, the threats to these groups can be as high as they are for the private sector and governments, but activists lack the resources to protect themselves. Tibetan groups find that each mode of communication they use—Skype, Twitter, Gmail, WeChat, KakaoTalk—gets penetrated, increasing their exposure to detention and physical harm. Tibetans report being in the middle of Skype conversations and hearing the click computers make when capturing and recording a picture of the user looking at the screen. Preventing breaches and getting the hackers out of systems once they are discovered also entails financial costs. The Chinese are, in effect, able to reach across borders and intimidate activists. Even though Tibetan monks promoted an education campaign to reduce vulnerability to spear-phishing that played off Buddhist teachings and called for Tibetans to "detach from attachments," the end result is what Citizen Lab calls "malware fatigue," the feeling among targets that a threat has existed forever and cannot be escaped.[13]

When in October 2012 the *New York Times* published a story on the wealth of the family of Wen Jiabao, China's former prime minister, hackers attacked the newspaper. *Bloomberg* followed in June with a series looking at the business empires of the families of other Chinese leaders, including the new Communist Party chief, Xi Jinping, and the computer networks of *Bloomberg*, the *Wall Street Journal*, and the *Washington Post* were all attacked.[14]

MOSCOW TIME AND NEVER ON RUSSIAN HOLIDAYS

Stories of Chinese hackers may dominate the US press, but of course China is not the only country that spies. In March 1998, the Defense Department detected serious attacks on its networks. Dubbed "Moonlight Maze" by US officials, the operation lasted for almost three years and affected computers at the National Aeronautics and Space

Administration, the Departments of Energy and Defense, and several government research agencies. The attacks, which occurred from 8 a.m. to 5 p.m. Moscow time and never on Russian holidays, were eventually traced to Internet servers located twenty miles from Moscow. The Kremlin greeted US complaints with denials of involvement.[15]

In 2008, someone put an infected USB thumb drive into a military laptop at a US base in the Middle East. The drive contained sophisticated malicious computer code, allegedly developed by Russia, that uploaded itself onto a network run by US Central Command, which oversees operations in Afghanistan and Iraq. This classified network was "air-gapped"—that is, not connected to the rest of the Internet and so thought to be protected from remote attacks. It was not immune, however, to curiosity (or stupidity) or the desire for convenience. You find a thumb drive, you wonder what's on it, and you stick it into your computer. Or, if you need to transfer large files between unconnected networks, you use a thumb drive and thereby close the air gap. After infecting one computer, the code downloaded itself to another thumb drive, and the process started again. The breach was considered so serious that Admiral Mike Mullen, chairman of the Joint Chiefs of Staff, briefed both President George W. Bush and Defense Secretary Robert M. Gates on the incident.[16]

The response to the attack, an operation code-named "Buckshot Yankee," was a milestone in US cyber policy, laying the bureaucratic groundwork for military power. The Joint Task Force—Global Network Operations was responsible for defending the DoD networks, but in the course of the operation DoD officials discovered that the NSA had much of the technical capabilities to analyze, reverse engineer, and stop the malware. To address this gap, the NSA merged with the military side of cyber. This blending of offensive and defensive capabilities with intelligence is central to how the United States thinks of cyber power. In addition, the Pentagon elevated the role of cyber in the military and created US Cyber Command.

In October 2014, several cybersecurity companies, along with Google and US intelligence agencies, revealed sophisticated malware that targeted NATO, the Organization for Security and Co-operation in Europe, the governments of Hungary, Poland, and Georgia, the European Commission, and European defense contractors. The tool, alternately called Sofacy, Sednit, or Sourface, encrypted stolen data and sent it out through the e-mail server to avoid monitoring. Operating since 2007, the malware could change itself to avoid detection, insert itself into a USB thumb drive to infect computers not connected to the Internet, and stop itself running when it recognized that it had been reverse engineered, a sign that it had been detected. Security researchers found Russian-language settings within the program.[17]

THE UNITED STATES: COLLECT IT ALL

China spies. Russia spies. The United States, however, may be the farthest-reaching, most invasive, and accomplished spy of the great powers. Documents taken by Edward Snowden reveal the outcome of the convergence of two phenomena: the global terrorist threat and the evolution and pervasiveness of digital technologies.

ADDICTED TO DATA

The president and other policymakers (and their Chinese and Russian counterparts) have become addicted to data and as a result more demanding of their intelligence agencies. Every day the president receives an intelligence briefing, and up to 75 percent of the information contained in the report comes from cyber spies, according to Mike McConnell, director of national intelligence under President George W. Bush. Moreover, the FBI, Department of Homeland Security, and other customers want more access to secret intelligence.[18]

At the same time, there is now a wealth of digital information available to the NSA and its main partner, the Government Communications Headquarters (GCHQ). Collecting information used to be time-consuming and expensive. Intelligence agencies could only follow and search the homes, tap the phones, and intercept the mail of a limited number of high-value targets. Now intelligence agencies can go to Google, Facebook, and cell phone carriers and gather huge amounts of data with little effort. Moreover, falling storage costs and rising computational ability mean that the intelligence agencies can amass, store, sort, and analyze data from large populations. Without much hyperbole, we can say that the NSA now has the ability not only to spy on a suspect in Lahore, but to reap much of the Internet data that flows from Pakistan. The goal becomes, in the words of one PowerPoint slide released by Snowden, "Collect it All," "Process it All," "Exploit it All," "Partner it All," "Sniff it All," and "Know it All."

The United States has three means of accessing digital information: establishment of legal authorities that compel technology companies to create and retain the digital records of their customers and to turn that data over to the state; interception and collection of data made possible by the United States' position at the center of the global Internet; and computer exploitation and other "close access" efforts to place vulnerabilities in servers, computers, and other devices.

Section 215 of the Patriot Act authorizes the NSA to collect the metadata—the time and number but not the content—of millions of phone calls within the United States. The data is stored and, with a judge's permission, can be analyzed for links to foreign terrorists. Executive Order 12333, signed by President Ronald Reagan in 1981 and amended three times since, allows for collection of metadata and content outside the United States for foreign intelligence purposes. The data of US citizens collected "incidentally" can be retained. While metadata does not contain private information, the holder who collects enough of it will have a very good picture of what the user is doing—perhaps better than could be gleaned from the content of a few recorded phone calls.

Under a program known as PRISM, the NSA, with permission from a secretive court established by the 1978 Foreign Intelligence Surveillance Act (FISA), can request data on specific foreign individuals from the major technology companies under a strict gag order. The court comprises eleven judges appointed by the chief justice of the US Supreme Court without any confirmation from the executive or legislative branches. Revisions to the law in 2008 allowed for mass acquisition of data for the purpose of fighting terrorism or espionage. Collection is limited to targets outside the United States, or, put another way, who the NSA is 51 percent sure are not US citizens. In 2012, the FISA court considered 1,856 NSA applications for electronic surveillance and physical searches for "foreign intelligence purposes." It denied none but requested modifications on forty. In 2013, the government filed 1,655 cases; the court again denied none and requested modifications on thirty-four.[19]

The first news stories on PRISM portrayed the NSA as having a direct line to company data and the companies as willing partners, but there is no direct link, and there was considerable pushback. Yahoo, for example, initially resisted participation in PRISM, arguing that the requests required a warrant and were overly broad, violating the US Constitution. The court ruled against the company, and Yahoo had to comply with the demands or face fines of up to $250,000 a day.[20]

The PRISM program collects data "downstream," or at the companies themselves. Another slide released by Snowden suggests that the NSA also actively gathers data "upstream," targeting data traveling on undersea cables and other communication infrastructure. The NSA and GCHQ also reportedly tapped into the fiber-optic lines connecting Yahoo and Google data centers in an operation code-named "MUSCULAR." The companies have data centers in Europe, Asia, and South and North America and can shift data from one center to another on private cables to speed up services for users. Heat-sensitive cameras, round-the-clock guards, and biometric verification of identities protect the centers themselves, but tapping the lines gave NSA access to real-time data.[21]

These programs are the dragnet. The NSA has also allegedly worked to undermine encryption. During the 1990s, encryption—the use of mathematics to scramble and encode data—moved out of the shadows and slowly shifted from the purview of governments and spymasters to commercial markets. Private companies started to develop encryption of their own for use in online sales and other transactions. It is now ubiquitous; we all see it when we visit a website and the padlock appears in our browser's URL bar. It protects credit cards, mobile phone communications, and health records. But as these codes began entering markets, the NSA and FBI started worrying about terrorists and criminals "going dark," using encryption to blind the seeing eye of intelligence and police agencies. There were also national security concerns that US companies might end up selling encryption technologies to countries that the United States wanted to spy on.

In the ensuing debate, the NSA tried to extend its authority over private and public cryptography, but Congress put the official power in the hands of the National Institute of Standards and Technology (NIST), the federal agency that works with the private sector to develop and define standards, technologies, and measurements. NIST, however, was not well positioned to go toe-to-toe with the NSA. NIST's budget, roughly $850 million in 2014, pales in comparison with the NSA's, estimated at $10.8 billion, as does its technical expertise. The NSA threw its weight around and apparently tried to weaken encryption on two fronts, by undermining the standards and mathematical processes that are the basis of encryption and by inserting "backdoors"—hidden vulnerabilities that let outsiders monitor a computer—into software and hardware.

Encryption requires a random-number generator. The random number makes it almost impossible for an attacker to know how a message was encoded and thus makes it difficult to break. The NSA and NIST promoted the use of a generator, Dual_EC_DRBG, which computer science researchers thought insecure almost as soon as it was publicized. In 2006 a number of papers showed the generator was extremely slow, and in 2007 Dan Shumow and Niels Ferguson, computer science researchers who worked for Microsoft, discovered that Dual_EC appeared to come with a secret key that would allow someone to decrypt the code that it had helped create. Despite this and other public warnings about its insecurity, NSA continued to vouch for Dual_EC_DRBG and allegedly paid the cybersecurity company RSA Security $10 million to include the algorithm in its popular BSAFE software library, used to increase security in personal computers and other products.[22]

The NSA also seems to have worked with software companies to build access points into their products. It told companies in the late 1990s that if they wanted to export products, the NSA would have to get a look at them first. According to documents released by Snowden, the NSA forced transparency on technology companies through court orders to hand over their encryption keys. Microsoft, for example, allegedly helped the NSA gain access to web chats on the new Outlook .com portal. In addition, the NSA targeted hardware. NSA technicians introduced backdoors into intercepted routers and other pieces of equipment, which were then repackaged and shipped to the customers. Leaked photos show a team carefully unwrapping the tape around a Cisco router to implant a beacon. The NSA spends around $250 million a year on these efforts to break encryption.[23]

The NSA also relies on zero-day exploits. Before the Snowden disclosures, many security experts assumed the government was sitting on zero days to use for attacks instead of sharing them with the public so that vulnerabilities could be patched and the security of all improved. A report produced about six months after the first Snowden revelations revealed the assumption to be correct. Appointed by the president, the members of the President's Review Group on Intelligence and Communications Technologies acknowledged that the government was exploiting these vulnerabilities and argued in favor of disclosing them, in most cases, to the public. The remaining zero days should only be used for "high priority intelligence collection."[24]

In April 2014, an unnamed government source told the *New York Times* that President Obama had decided that most vulnerabilities should be revealed, though a large loophole remained: sensitive zero days could be stored for possible use for "a clear national security or law enforcement need." In a blog post explaining the White House policy, Special Assistant to the President and Cybersecurity Coordinator Michael Daniel struck a similar balance. While he argued that the review process "is biased toward responsibly disclosing the vulnerability," Daniel described the national security benefits to holding on to some zero days. "Disclosing a vulnerability can mean that we forego an opportunity to collect crucial intelligence that could thwart a terrorist attack, stop the theft of our nation's intellectual property, or even discover more dangerous vulnerabilities that are being used by hackers or other adversaries to exploit our networks."[25]

Daniel insisted in an interview with *Wired* that the NSA was not sitting on a large number of zero days. "The idea that we have these vast stockpiles of vulnerabilities stored up—you know, *Raiders of the Lost Ark* style—is just not accurate." But the NSA is thought to be perhaps the largest purchaser of zero days from defense contractors, information security firms, and individual researchers. Vupen, a French security firm, sold exploits under a subscription plan. The NSA reportedly has 2,000 zero days on hand designed for China alone and in 2013 spent $25 million on software vulnerabilities from private contractors. Vast may mean different things to different people, and it seems certain that the US government retains a significant number of zero days for national security reasons.[26]

THE NSA's ENGINEERING FEAT: HACKING HARDWARE

Undermining encryption, installing backdoors, and buying zero days rends the fabric of trust that is the basis of the Internet, heightens US companies' suspicion, and drives a wedge between Silicon Valley and Washington. The United States also conducts more focused cyber espionage on friends, enemies, and potential adversaries. Given the global nature of US security interests, it appears that almost every country, except the members of the Five Eyes alliance—the intelligence-sharing agreement among Australia, Canada, New Zealand, the United Kingdom, and the United States—is a potential NSA target. Within the National Security Agency, the Tailored Access Operations (TAO) group is the top operational unit, designing custom-fit implants and gaining access to the hardest targets. TAO specialists reportedly broke into and read e-mails sent over BlackBerry's supposedly safely encrypted e-mail servers. By the end of 2013, according to a report in the *Washington Post*, the NSA controlled at least 85,000 implants in machines around the world. The budget for this program, code-named "GENIE," totaled $625 million and resulted, according to one former government official, in the NSA having access to 2 petabytes of data an hour, or nearly 2.1 million gigabytes, the equivalent of hundreds of millions of pages of text.[27]

The United States also apparently has developed its own malware. Flame targeted approximately 1,000 computers in Iran, Sudan, and the Middle East. At twenty megabytes, Flame was much larger than other malware and twice as large as Stuxnet, was designed to work for a limited time in a limited geographical region, and contained some of the same code as Stuxnet. Set loose sometime in 2006, the malware was modular, meaning that its designers could add functionality as time went on. One module called Shredder instructed a breached computer to remove all traces of the infection, one stole documents, another recorded key strokes and screen shots, and still another used Bluetooth to filch data and audio from smartphones or other Bluetooth-enabled devices in the vicinity. An additional module connected to Flame, Wiper, erased data and forced Iran to disconnect networks at the oil ministry and the Kharg Island oil terminal.[28]

In 2015, Kaspersky Labs exposed a spy ring it called the Equation Group for its strong reliance on encryption and other obfuscation techniques. The details and techniques of the operations revealed patience, an impressive level of skill, and a huge budget. The group targeted at least forty-two countries, with Afghanistan, India, Iran, Mali, Pakistan, Russia, and Syria at the top of the list. Most impressively, the group hid spyware deep within hard drives made by Western Digital, Seagate, Toshiba, and other manufacturers. Hiding malware deep in the firmware, in a hard drive's operating system, which launches every time the computer is turned on, was a real engineering feat. The malware created a secret vault that could survive the wiping and reformatting of the drive. In effect, the infection was impossible to remove. Although Kaspersky Labs did not come out and say who it thought was behind the Equation Group, a former NSA employee confirmed that the spyware was one of the agency's most highly prized programs.[29]

The United States has impressive capabilities, many derived from its position at the center of the Internet and the strength of its technology sector. Building, launching, and maintaining spy satellites, planes, and ships to conduct signals intelligence is expensive. During the Cold War, the United States conducted risky operations to tap submarine cables in the Barents Sea and the Sea of Okhotsk. Deep-sea divers, entering the water from nuclear subs, attached listening pods that recorded magnetic waves from the cables. The competition between the United States and the Soviet Union to develop surveillance and spying technologies spurred each to new heights. China and other states fell behind.[30]

ECONOMIC ESPIONAGE: CHINA IN A CATEGORY ALL ITS OWN

The diffusion of communication technologies has radically remade spying. Computer networks allow technologically inferior countries, small states, and even individuals to conduct surveillance operations that were once solely the purview of big states. The development of cyber espionage tools and the movement of information online has somewhat leveled the field. Cell phones and computers are now ubiquitous, and so countries no longer need the capability to build and deploy bugging devices globally. In 2013 and 2014, security firms revealed several Iranian campaigns, one that controlled 16,000 systems located in the United Kingdom, the United States, and other locations around the world and another that breached the networks of airlines, energy companies, defense firms, and the US Navy–Marine Corps intranet. As Alex Karp, CEO of Palantir Technologies, put it, "Software and technology has democratized espionage."[31]

The democratization of spying is more than a national security concern. Since much cyber espionage targets commercial secrets, business plans, research results, and other intellectual property, it is a steady strain on our national economic health. Many countries are perpetrators. The Office of the National Counterintelligence Executive (ONCIX) names France, Israel, and Russia, among others, as states collecting economic information and technology from US companies. During the 1980s and 1990s, Air France's business class seats were rumored to be bugged, and Pierre Marion, former director of France's Directorate-General for External Security, said with regard to spying on the United States, "In economics, we are competitors, not allies."[32]

But the ONCIX places China in a category all its own: "Chinese actors are the world's most active and persistent perpetrators of economic espionage." China is so relentless because it does not want to get caught in a technology trap, where Chinese producers dominate the labor-intensive, low-value end of production and continue paying expensive royalties to European, Japanese, and US patent owners. If Chinese companies continue to rely on technology from outsiders, in the view of the *Global Times* newspaper, part of the Communist Party–run People's Daily Group, they run the risk of "perpetually remaining second-tier manufacturing specialists that lack the innovation needed to become true global technology leaders."[33]

In support of the move from "made in China" to "invented in China," Beijing has committed significant resources to science and technology. The twenty-year plan for science and technology development envisions China becoming an "innovative nation" by 2020 and a "global scientific power" by 2050. Scientific R&D funding has increased by 12 to 20 percent annually for each of the last twenty years, and China passed Japan in 2010 as the world's second-largest spender on R&D. Of all degrees awarded by Chinese universities in 2011, 41 percent were in science, technology, engineering, or math, almost three times the rate in the United States. Chinese scientists now stand behind only their US colleagues in the number of science and technology journal articles published annually and will likely overtake them within a few years.

But Beijing is displeased, or at the least impatient, with the quantity and quality of innovation produced by this staggering investment. In addition, a sense of historical grievance, at least among some Chinese policymakers, derives not only from the history of aggression by European imperial powers and Japan, known as the century of humiliations, but also from Western efforts to deprive China of access to critical technologies during the Cold War and after the Tiananmen Square massacre. As a result, covert efforts—industrial espionage directed at high-technology and advanced manufacturing companies to raise economic competitiveness—accompany the overt science and technology programs.

Much of this is old-fashioned industrial spying, people walking out the door with secrets. In the case of American Superconductor, which developed software that controls the flow of electricity from wind turbines, an employee allegedly stole source code and helped Sinovel Wind develop a copy. The Chinese firm, the largest manufacturer of wind turbines in China, offered the employee a $1.7 million contract, an apartment in Beijing, and "girlfriends." Once Sinovel had access to the source code, it no longer needed to do business with American Superconductor. It stopped making purchases, and American Superconductor soon had to announce it had lost its biggest customer, responsible for close to $210 million in revenue. In other cases, employees have sold to Chinese firms the secrets of the white pigment chloride-route titanium dioxide developed by DuPont, files from Motorola Solutions, and the chlorinated polyethylene process from Dow. In May 2015, the Department of Justice indicted six Chinese professors and engineers for stealing microelectronic designs on behalf of Beijing.[34]

The relationship between cyber and traditional commercial spying mirrors that between cyber and traditional political espionage: it is easier, happens at a much greater pace, and produces a greater haul. In 1791 Treasury Secretary Alexander Hamilton proposed to Congress a scheme to offer money and other inducements to British engineers, German mechanists, and the like to move to America in order to increase the "extent of valuable acquisitions to the population, arts, and industry." Japanese engineer Iwama Kazuo helped Sony build its first transistor in 1954 by sending letters filled with technical details he had observed on the factory floor or gathered in conversation with his counterparts from Western Electric. Industrial age espionage happened over years and decades; cyber espionage takes place over hours and days.

Two Kinds of Companies

Cybersecurity experts often quip that there are two kinds of companies: those that have been hacked and those that do not know it yet. A third party, often law enforcement, discovers somewhere between 70 and 80 percent of data breaches. In 2013, federal agents, often the FBI, notified more than 3,000 US companies that their computer systems had been hacked. Many victims do not have a sense of the threat, why they are attractive targets, or what valuable data they have stored. They fail to monitor their own networks and so do not see what comes in and goes out. According to Mandiant, attackers were present on a victim's network an average of 205 days before being discovered (a drop of only 24 days from 229 in 2013 and an additional 14 from 243 in 2012). One attacker was in a network for six years and three months.[35]

Even if aware of a hack, companies have few incentives to go public with the knowledge. According to a *Bloomberg News* report, in March 2009 the FBI informed Coca-Cola that it had been hacked. The attackers stole sensitive files related to the planned $2.4 billion acquisition of China Huiyuan Juice Group. The deal collapsed, and Coca-Cola never publicly disclosed the loss of information. While Coca-Cola's reticence may have been China specific, driven by fear that that the Chinese government would punish the company for going public, most CEOs are allergic to disclosures that can damage stock prices or reputations.[36]

Unlike hacks involving credit cards, Social Security numbers, and other personal data, which companies must report under state breach laws, commercial firms face few legal requirements to disclose the theft of intellectual property. Federal securities law requires companies to report "material" risks that could affect investment decisions, but the term is vague enough that many do not know how to relate it to cyber threats or simply choose not to report. One study found that nearly 40 percent of Fortune 500 companies failed to disclose cyberattacks in their public filings. In October 2011, in order to create more transparency, the Securities and Exchange Commission issued new guidelines on how and when publicly traded companies should report hacking incidents and cybersecurity threats, but a Reuters investigation of 2,000 filings found that most companies adopted "boilerplate" language to describe the events and risks, and some hacked companies did not even do that.[37]

Even with this reluctance to disclose, the list of US companies reportedly hacked is long: Adobe, Boston Scientific, ConocoPhillips, Disney, Dow Chemical, DuPont, ExxonMobil, General Dynamics, General Electric, Google, Intel, Johnson & Johnson, Juniper Networks, Marathon Oil, Sony, Symantec, and Yahoo, to name just a few. Hackers looking for corporate secrets, business strategies, and intellectual property have also targeted small, tech-driven start-ups and law firms.

China-based hackers are not interested only in American technology. The intelligence services of Germany and Britain warned businesses in their respective countries of the threat of Chinese hacking. Stefan Kaller, head of the department in charge of cybersecurity at the German Interior Ministry, told a meeting of European law enforcement agencies, "Seventy percent of all major German companies are threatened or affected" by cyberattacks. The British internal intelligence service, MI5, reportedly warned of PLA and Ministry of Public Security officers socializing with British business people at conferences and trade fairs and giving them cameras and thumb drives containing malware that could enable remote access to the recipients' computers.[38]

WHAT IT ALL COSTS

The strategic impact of cyber espionage on US (or German or British) competitiveness is unknown, and assessments have varied widely. Or as ONCIX has put it, estimates from the academic literature on the losses "range so widely as to be meaningless—from $2 billion to $400 billion or more a year." When he called such theft the "greatest transfer of wealth in history," former NSA head General Keith Alexander estimated the actual cost to US companies at $250 billion in stolen information and another $114 billion in related expenses. A 2013 private commission, chaired by Dennis Blair, former director of national intelligence, and Jon Huntsman, former ambassador to China and Republican presidential candidate, argued that the annual "losses are likely to be comparable to the current annual level of U.S. exports to Asia—over $300 billion." A study by the Center for Strategic and

International Studies and cybersecurity firm McAfee estimates the cost to the entire global economy of all cyber theft, including the theft of intellectual property and crimes like bank fraud and credit card scams, to be over $400 billion annually. The same study estimated costs to the US economy to be around 0.64 percent of gross domestic product.[39]

The failure of companies to report breaches makes it difficult to develop a clear metric of what the costs really are. Much of the data on intrusions comes from surveys with the victims self-reporting the degree of damage. Damage might mean the cost of developing the stolen information or loss of future revenues and profits. Security firms that benefit from the perception of hacking as a widespread and serious problem often conduct these same surveys. In addition, it is extremely difficult to estimate the value of stolen intellectual property. Should it be valued based on the investment in R&D or the product's potential market share?[40]

There is also a question of how important the theft is to Chinese innovation. What is China doing with all of the intellectual property it is stealing, and should we not start to see it paying off in more competitive Chinese companies? It is not obvious how much of the stolen information Chinese firms will actually be able to use. Converting it into a finished product and economic gain often requires a great deal of tacit knowledge not contained in a blueprint or database.

The one public case in which a firm seems to have suffered irrevocable damage is the hacking of telecommunications equipment manufacturer Nortel, which may have spanned ten years. Hackers stole the passwords of top executives, including the chief executive, and exfiltrated R&D reports, business plans, and employee e-mails. Brian Shields, former senior systems security adviser at Nortel, told the Canadian Broadcasting Company that Chinese hacking was a "considerable factor" in the company's collapse. "When they see what your business plans are, that's a huge advantage. It's unfair business practices that really bring down a company of this size." At the same time, Nortel's problems predated the hacking. It first missed sales targets in November 2000, and by 2002 half of the company's 90,000 workers had been laid off.[41]

It is also important to consider how much technology is already lost through legitimate technology transfers, indigenous innovation, and other policies designed to force technology transfer, and China's failure to protect intellectual property rights. Is the damage from cyber espionage significantly greater? GE reportedly lost technology to China-based hackers, but whether it was worth more or less than the technology GE voluntarily transferred to the Chinese state-owned enterprise involved in an avionics joint venture is unclear.

NAMING AND SHAMING

Fully measuring the costs of the theft may be difficult, but policy-makers and business officials take it seriously all the same, especially when it infringes on the potential for innovation. For years, the targeting of Canada's energy and natural resource companies, including PotashCorp and Telvent, was an open secret. Canadian officials said little. But in July 2014, Corinne Charette, Canada's chief information officer, announced that a "highly sophisticated Chinese state-sponsored actor" managed to hack into the computer systems at Canada's National Research Council, the government's premier science and technology research organization. Foreign Affairs Minister John Baird had a "full and frank" discussion about the issue with his Chinese counterpart, Wang Yi. The July announcement was the first time the Canadian government explicitly accused China of cyber theft.[42]

Naming and shaming became the center of the US response to Chinese cyber espionage. Until 2013, Washington had been reluctant to name China directly. The sequence of events went something like this: The media would report the hacking of a US company and then quote an unnamed official who would say that the sophistication of the attack suggested nation-state backing. The official would not speculate on the record which state it might be, and so the reporter would call me or one of my colleagues at another think tank, and we would say, "It was China."

The hesitancy of US officials to name China directly in part stemmed from an unwillingness to risk the larger bilateral relationship. Washington needed (and continues to require) Beijing's cooperation to deal with numerous difficult challenges, including climate change, the global recession, and North Korea's and Iran's nuclear programs. Some also may have hoped that an overall good working relationship would be useful in convincing Beijing to ratchet down the pace of attacks.

More to the point, however, the United States feared that it could not provide proof of Chinese cyber espionage without disclosing its own capabilities. In September 2011, at a lunch with a senior US government official working on China, I asked why the United States did not respond more vocally and visibly to Chinese attacks. Obviously annoyed by the suggestion that Washington was making cyber issues less of a priority compared to the pursuit of other goals, he argued that it was difficult to present evidence of Chinese hacking without revealing American capabilities. He also told me I had no idea of the types of signal intelligence he was privy to on China. The implication was that the United States got as much as, if not more, from hacking China as the Chinese did from hacking the United States.

A 2011 report released by Snowden states that the NSA is able to "tap into Chinese SIGINT [signals intelligence, the intelligence gathered from electronic signals transmitted from communications systems, radars, and weapons systems] collection," and another report showed the NSA infiltrating the computer of a high-ranking Chinese military official and accessing information regarding targets in the US government. One slide described the NSA exploiting five computers used by Chinese hackers and even tracked a bill for renting websites and other hacking infrastructure to the Third Department of the PLA's General Staff Department, a unit responsible for SIGINT operations.[43]

Sometime in 2013, however, the calculus on public disclosure changed, and I, along with the other think tankers, was cut out of the loop. Government officials began calling out the Chinese government and military. In February 2013, cybersecurity firm Mandiant released a report contending that Unit 61398 of the PLA was behind attacks on 141 companies, including 115 in the United States. Around the same time, the Department of Homeland Security provided Internet service providers with the Internet addresses of hacking groups in China. In March 2013, National Security Advisor Tom Donilon spoke of the "serious concerns about sophisticated, targeted theft of confidential business information and proprietary technologies through cyber intrusions emanating from China on an unprecedented scale." Two months later, the Defense Department went further and, in a sharp break from the past, ascribed blame for cyberattacks to the Chinese government and military, saying, "Numerous computer systems around the world, including those owned by the U.S. government, continued to be targeted for intrusions, some of which appear to be attributable directly to the Chinese government and military."[44]

When President Barack Obama and President Xi Jinping met for a two-day "shirt sleeve" summit in California in June 2013, in his public comments President Obama spoke diplomatically, noting that cyber espionage was not unique to the US-Chinese relationship. Privately, Obama was more forceful, warning Xi that the hacking could severely damage the bilateral relationship.[45]

Naming and shaming put cyber on the summit agenda but had little effect on Beijing. Not surprisingly, the Chinese denied responsibility for cyber espionage. President Xi suggested the presence of cybersecurity on the agenda resulted in part from "increased media coverage" and noted that China was also a victim. In response to US claims, Chinese sources listed the Internet protocol addresses for the attacks against China, with the majority originating from Japan, the United States, and South Korea.

Soon after the summit ended, Snowden revealed himself in Hong Kong as the source of the NSA leaks. He also told the local press that the NSA had hacked mainland Chinese targets, including universities and telecommunications companies. The Chinese press quickly jumped on the allegations, highlighting the perceived hypocrisy of the US government's claims about China. By the end of the year, state-owned media were referring to the United States as "the real hacking empire" and the "matrix." Much of the air went out of the US campaign. While Treasury Secretary Jack Lew and National Security Advisor Susan Rice mentioned cyber espionage in some public speeches, there was little doubt that the revelations had, at least temporarily, vitiated the diplomatic pressure on Beijing.

Even as the naming and shaming was happening, many wondered what the US government would do if (and when) the strategy proved ineffective. After being named responsible for the *New York Times* hack in February 2013, Unit 61398 temporarily curtailed its activities. Yet other groups seemed to pick up the slack, and the overall level of cyber espionage stayed the same. The Chinese government kept up a steady stream of denials, counteraccusations, and claims of victimhood. Moreover, by September, Unit 61398 was back in the game again, hacking at its previous rate. Throughout these months, members of Congress searched for ways to raise the cost to China by pursuing a trade case in the World Trade Organization, levying economic sanctions and travel restrictions on individuals or entities suspected of conducting cyber espionage, and blocking Chinese companies that benefited from espionage from US markets.

The Obama administration's next step was the indictment of Ugly-Gorilla and the other PLA hackers. The wanted posters printed by the Justice Department may have looked good on TV, and the indictment may have signaled to Beijing that Washington still took the issue seriously, but the gestures were merely symbolic. The hackers will never see the inside of a US courtroom, and Beijing will certainly never cooperate in the investigation. An editorial in the *Wall Street Journal*, arguing that the indictments will accomplish little, called them "useful as a way to educate the public about the growing espionage threat."[46]

A larger sense of futility with the US effort stems from the problem of definitions. The United States wants to stop attacks on private industry resulting in intellectual property theft but leave the NSA free to conduct political and military espionage. President Obama, for example, distinguished between good and bad hacking: "Every country in the world, large and small, engages in intelligence gathering. . . . There is a big difference between China wanting to figure out how can they find out what my talking points are when I'm meeting with the Japanese which is standard . . . and a hacker directly connected with the Chinese government or the Chinese military breaking into Apple's software systems to see if they can obtain the designs for the latest Apple product. That's theft. And we can't tolerate that." In essence, the United States would like to limit Chinese pilfering of intellectual property from American companies but is not particularly interested in any discussions that might constrain US intelligence gathering in cyberspace. As General Michael Hayden, former director of the CIA and NSA, put it: "'You spy, we spy, but you just steal the wrong stuff.' That's a hard conversation."[47]

This distinction raises at least two problems. First, others are unlikely to believe that the United States does not spy for economic reasons. Snowden asserted that the United States was spying on Swiss banks, Chinese telecoms, European trade negotiators, and Petrobras, the Brazilian energy company. WikiLeaks posted documents in June 2015 alleging that the NSA intercepted the communications of French corporations for deals over $200 million in telecommunications, electrical generation, gas, oil, nuclear and renewable energy, and environmental and health-care technologies. Officials have admitted that the United States might spy on trade negotiators for national economic interest. They distinguish between gathering strategic economic intelligence for policymakers and giving intelligence to a private firm. In a public statement, Director of National Intelligence James Clapper insisted that these types of activities were designed to enhance security and protect national interests; the intelligence community does not steal "trade secrets of foreign companies on behalf of—or give intelligence we collect to—U.S. companies." The line between national interest and helping companies in the aggregate, on the one hand, and stealing trade secrets for specific companies, on the other, looks pretty thin to the rest of the world.[48]

Second, many states, especially those like China that have developed a form of state capitalism at home, do not see a difference between public and private actors. Chinese firms are part of an effort to modernize the country and build comprehensive power, no matter whether they are private or state owned. Stealing for their benefit is for the benefit of the nation.

The fallout from the indictments has come to look like a digital trade war. Chinese policymakers have long believed that US technology products have backdoors that allow the United States to bypass security protections and directly access data. In 2003, to assuage security concerns, Microsoft shared part of the Windows source code with China and fifty-nine other countries, and China has promoted Linux products over Microsoft ones for at least a decade to promote local competitors and boost security. Linux is open-source, which means the code is available to all.

In 2008, Microsoft unintentionally heightened Chinese distrust when it created a program that temporarily blackened computer screens on detecting a pirated version of Windows. The blackout screen could be turned off but returned every hour with a reminder to buy legitimate products. The intrusion incensed Chinese users, and many Chinese policymakers suddenly faced the unpleasant truth that a US company was controlling computers inside their country. Writing several years after the screens had gone black, Tang Lan, an information security expert at the China Institute of Contemporary International Relations, argued that the incident "exposed China's online vulnerability to high-tech intrusion from overseas."[49]

According to an April 2012 article in *Outlook Weekly*, 90 percent of China's microchips, components, network equipment, communications standards, and protocols, as well as 65 percent of firewalls, encryption technologies, and ten other types of information security products, rely on imported technology. Foreign producers also dominate the market for programmable logic controllers—devices used to control manufacturing and other industrial processes. As a result, an article in the military newspaper *China Defense* asserted, "all core technologies are basically in the hands of U.S. companies, and this provides perfect conditions for the U.S. military to carry out cyber warfare and cyber deterrence."[50]

In the wake of the Snowden revelations and the PLA indictments, Beijing increased its focus on the security of the products it purchased from Microsoft and others. *China Economic Weekly*, owned by the Communist Party's official newspaper, *People's Daily*, ran the headline "He's Watching You" under the image of a helmeted head from a World War II–era US propaganda poster but inscribed with the NSA logo. The article warned of "eight guardian warriors"—Cisco, IBM, Microsoft, Oracle, Intel, Qualcomm, Apple, and Google—that "have seamlessly infiltrated China."[51]

Many of these companies would soon find Chinese policymakers throwing up new barriers to doing business in China. Banks were encouraged to swap out IBM servers for Inspur, a local brand, and government workers in a northeastern city replaced Microsoft Windows with NeoKylin, a China-developed operating system. Chinese officials in Shanghai and other cities were told to ditch their Apple iPhones for Huawei phones. After photos circulated on the web of Peng Liyuan, China's First Lady, taking pictures with an iPhone 5 on a trip to Mexico, she was seen a year later with a Nubia, a handset made by the Chinese firm ZTE.[52]

Along with the push for local technology alternatives came aggressive investigations of Qualcomm and Microsoft by Chinese regulators.

The National Development and Reform Commission scrutinized Qualcomm for over a year for allegedly abusing its market position and overcharging local handset manufacturers for use of its patents. In July and August 2014, roughly one hundred regulators from the State Administration for Industry and Commerce raided Microsoft's offices in Beijing, Shanghai, Guangzhou, Chengdu, Liaoning, Fujian, and Hubei. Despite the relatively small size of its official business in China, Microsoft was charged with violating antitrust regulations for bundling its Windows operating software with Microsoft Office and for incompatibility issues with other software.[53]

Just in case the investigations did not send the message clearly enough, China began hacking foreign companies. During the rollout of the new iPhone 6 in October 2014, Chinese consumers who thought they were using iCloud, Apple's online storage service, confronted what is known as a man-in-the-middle attack; attackers managed to decrypt the communication between the user and the iCloud server and put themselves between two parties who believed they were talking to each other over an encrypted channel. Because the attack came from servers that only the government or state-owned telecommunications companies could access, the Chinese authorities were widely believed to be involved. The hack probably signaled China's displeasure with the iPhone's new encryption methods, which would make data on the phone unreadable to anyone but the user, including Apple and the government.

Then, in January 2015, things got even worse. The seemingly individual response of specific ministries and local governments became a blanket threat to foreign companies doing business in China. Beijing circulated regulations that would force foreign technology companies supplying Chinese banks and other critical sectors to turn over secret source code, submit to invasive audits, and build backdoors into hardware and software. According to the draft, 75 percent of technology products used by banks had to be classified as "secure and controllable" by 2019, and the end result would be a "cybersecurity review regime" to assess all Internet and information technology products across the economy. Alarm among US technology firms ran so high that eighteen business associations sent a letter to Xi Jinping and members of the Central Leading Group for Cyberspace Affairs, arguing that only "commitment to an open market and global trade" could achieve the technological innovation needed to protect against bad actors. The banking regulations were suspended, but on July 1, 2015, the National People's Congress passed a new law calling for a national security review of the technology industry and foreign investment.[54]

Chinese officials justified the acceleration and intensification of pressure on US firms by pointing to the Snowden revelations and to what they saw as the similar actions of the US government in blocking market access to Chinese companies. Most of the US efforts and the Chinese pique have centered on Huawei, the largest telecommunications equipment manufacturer in the world. While it has built up a fairly robust business in second-tier markets, supplying providers like LEAP Wireless and Clearwire, it has been blocked from a number of larger deals in the United States that would have opened America's Internet backbone up to Huawei products. Bill Bishop, an American observer of Chinese technology and social media, calls what the Chinese government has done to US technology companies "being Huawei'd"—that is, being cast as suspicious and shut out of the market. As one senior Chinese Foreign Ministry official told me, "If you do this to Huawei, what do you expect us to do?"[55]

For some Chinese policymakers, the issue is not just tit for tat. The United States' apprehension about the alleged security threat posed by Huawei in itself proves that foreign companies are a danger. The United States was so far ahead of China, the thinking went, that if Washington was hesitant to have foreign suppliers in their computer and telecommunication networks, then there must really be something to worry about.

Ren Zhengfei, a PLA engineer who had been demobilized, founded Huawei in Shenzhen in 1987. The company originally sold equipment imported from Hong Kong and, excluded from coastal markets reserved for more connected companies, sold its own products in the poorer, more rugged Chinese interior. It applied this strategy of "using the countryside to encircle the cities," borrowed from Mao Tse-tung's strategy of guerrilla war, in developing markets as well. In Africa, for example, Huawei sold products for 5 to 15 percent less than Ericsson and Nokia Siemens and supplied all of the services—engineering, tower and base construction, and networks supplies—that telecoms demanded. The company slowly moved into more developed markets in Europe. Huawei has filed for over 49,000 patents and employs more than 120,000 people; total revenues topped $38 billion in 2013. In order to remain technologically competitive, it has established twenty R&D centers around the world, including in Bangalore, Dallas, and Santa Clara.[56]

Other controversies have surrounded the company. Cisco and Motorola sued the company for allegedly stealing software designs and infringing on patents. The company claims it has no connections to the Chinese government, but it has participated in numerous government infrastructure plans and received R&D and financial support from policy banks like the China Development Bank. The security angle, however, has been the darkest cloud hanging over the company. Huawei has vociferously denied colluding with the Chinese government. As the company's US spokesman Bill Plummer said in 2012, "Huawei is a $32 billion independent multinational that would not jeopardize its success or the integrity of its customers' networks for any government or third party. Ever." Asked if the Chinese government had ever requested assistance in intelligence gathering, Ren responded, "There is no way we can penetrate into other people's systems, and we have never been asked to do so." "Why would I want to take someone's data?" Ren asked. "Who would give me money for it?"[57]

A widely quoted 2005 study by RAND scholars, however, argued that Huawei had links to the Chinese military. According to the report, Huawei helped the PLA replace its antiquated analog communication system with digital communications via fiber-optic cable, satellite, microwave, and encrypted high-frequency radio. A 2012 congressional study came to a similar, if heavily qualified and circumstantial, conclusion: "The combination of recent infusions of cash, regular appearances at PLA defense industry events, and working relationship with various government research institutes on projects with dual use applications suggests that an ongoing relationship between Huawei and the Chinese military and Chinese political leadership may exist." Repeated assurances from Ren and other executives of the company's independence have landed on deaf ears. I was once at a conference of Chinese and American experts on Chinese technology development at which every American was as confident that Huawei some had connections to the PLA as every Chinese was sure that it did not. Other US security analysts worry that even if Huawei is an independent, private company, once it gained access to strategic networks through commercial bidding, it would not be able to refuse demands from the PLA or the Ministry of State Security for access to the communication infrastructure.[58]

The lack of trust in Huawei has limited its business opportunities in the United States. Government officials opposed a bid from Huawei and Bain Capital to buy 3Com, a computer equipment maker, in 2008. A year later US objections derailed Huawei's efforts to buy patents and hire employees from a computer-services company, 3Leaf. In 2010 then commerce secretary Gary Locke called the head of Sprint Nextel to express "deep concerns" that Huawei might win a contract to upgrade the mobile phone carrier's network. Sprint Nextel instead awarded the contract to companies from France, Sweden, and South Korea.[59]

Suspicion of Huawei ran so high that the NSA reportedly created backdoors into the company's equipment. A project code-named "SHOTGIANT" attempted not only to find connections between the company and the PLA but also to conduct surveillance on countries that normally avoid buying US technology products, according to documents released by Snowden and published by the *New York Times* and *Der Spiegel*. "If we can determine the company's plans and intentions," an analyst wrote, "we hope that this will lead us back to the plans and intentions of the PRC." It is unknown what the NSA discovered.[60]

Huawei's problems were not limited to the United States. The Indian Department of Telecom told mobile operators not to import Huawei equipment, and Australia blocked its participation in a national broadband network. After senior British intelligence officials expressed concern about Huawei gear in the national network, the company established a unit in 2010, overseen by a former head of GCHQ, to inspect equipment before installation. Situated outside Banbury, Oxfordshire, the Cyber Security Evaluation Center is staffed and funded by Huawei. In 2013, after a parliamentary committee raised concerns about the independence of the center, the government announced that it would increase GCHQ oversight and that the intelligence agency would direct all senior appointments. A follow-up report, issued in March 2015, found the evaluations to be consistently of high quality and that the center operated with "sufficient independence from Huawei headquarters and any other body."[61]

In November 2011, the US House Select Intelligence Committee, chaired by Mike Rogers, started an investigation of the threat posed to US cybersecurity by Huawei and ZTE, another Chinese telecommunications company headquartered in Shenzhen. Huawei executives, including Ren Zhengfei, traveled to Hong Kong to answer questions from the committee. The final report was thin on details and filled with complaints about the Chinese firms' refusal to answer the committee's questions or their contradictory and confusing responses. Huawei did not do itself any favors in its testimony. During one hearing, for example, Charles Ding, corporate senior vice president and Huawei's representative to the United States, claimed he had no knowledge of the term "national champion," which describes companies given financial and other support by the government because of their strategic importance to the economy. Since Huawei itself had earlier provided a slide using the term, the committee did not find Ding credible.[62]

While the Select Intelligence Committee referred to a classified annex that "provides significantly more information," the actual report provided no direct evidence of spying. Most of the security vulnerabilities it highlighted about Huawei applied also to Cisco, Juniper, or any other company that manufactures in China. Still, the report concluded that Huawei and ZTE "cannot be trusted to be free of foreign state influence" and must be blocked from "acquisitions, takeovers, or mergers" in the United States.

States rarely attack in cyberspace, but they almost always spy. Espionage is as pernicious as it is pervasive. In pursuit of information for political, strategic, and economic gain, states are more than willing to undermine the trust required for the Internet to function.

Spying used to have a relatively low impact on foreign relations. Moscow, London, and Washington followed a set of unstated rules on how to treat each other's intelligence agents, sometimes expelling diplomats after a dramatic incident or when spying reached unacceptable levels. In September 1971, for example, after a defector revealed plans for a sabotage campaign in the United Kingdom, Britain expelled ninety Soviet diplomats and did not allow fifteen already outside the country to return. London announced that it would not prepare for the European Security Conference proposed by the Soviet Union until the crisis was resolved. But this type of diplomatic break was the exception; espionage was kept out of the public eye.

The idea of PNG'ing a person—declaring a diplomat persona non grata—and sweeping the fallout from espionage under the rug looks quaint today. By the time President Obama welcomed President Xi to the White House for a state dinner in September 2015, cyber espionage was at the top of the diplomatic agenda. In the weeks before the meeting, officials suggested that the United States would sanction Chinese individuals or entities that benefited from cyber theft, and a number of presidential hopefuls called for Obama to cancel the summit or downgrade it to a working meeting.

The threat of sanction appeared to rattle China. At the conclusion of the summit, the United States claimed that the two sides had agreed that "neither country's government will conduct or knowingly support cyber-enabled theft of intellectual property, including trade secrets or other confidential business information, with the intent of providing competitive advantages to companies or commercial sectors." It remains to be seen if China will follow up on the agreement or if it will rely more on hacking groups, criminals, and other proxies that allow it to deny that it "knowingly supported" cyber espionage. Only days after President Xi had left Washington, Director of National Intelligence James Clapper, asked by Senator John McCain whether he was optimistic about the agreement, responded, "I personally am somewhat of a skeptic. It will be our responsibility to look for the presence or absence of their purloining of intellectual property and other information."[63]

Cyber espionage is unavoidable at a diplomatic level because the scale of the spying is so much larger, gathering up the data of millions of people and the intellectual property of thousands of companies. And you cannot expel someone sitting at a computer in another country. Moreover, spillovers created by responding to uncovered espionage can no longer be contained. Even if a nation-state does not confront the presumed attacker and limits itself to improving cybersecurity at home, policy decisions inevitably have an impact on the competitiveness of the private sector and the rights and responsibilities of individual users. This intertwining of espionage, trade, and privacy characterizes the hacked world order and has come into view most clearly in Germany.

Chapter 6

THE BATTLE OVER DATA
SECURITY, PRIVACY, AND TRADE POWER

. . . .

I n the hacked world order, disclosures of espionage may have as much of an impact on trade as they do on diplomatic relations. Driven by a potent mix of ideology, strategic necessity, economic competition, and historical memory, Berlin's responses to Edward Snowden's revelations demonstrate this most clearly. German policymakers have alternatively been shocked by what they see as a breach of trust by the National Security Agency (NSA) and clear-eyed about the importance of the alliance with Washington and their dependence on US intelligence capabilities. A strong vein of economic interest also runs through Berlin's pronouncements. Officials have suggested new trade and data-collection policies in a principled defense of privacy as a human right and have also been willing to exploit the outrage about the disclosures to punish US companies and promote German commercial interests.

When the news broke, in the summer of 2013, that the NSA and the Government Communications Headquarters (GCHQ) had been collecting the phone and e-mail metadata of millions of European users, the initial official reaction was fairly muted. Governments throughout the continent suggested that the surveillance had been fairly narrow and constrained by legal limits. Ronald Pofalla, then minister of the Chancellery and Angela Merkel's coordinator for the oversight of German intelligence agencies, tried to calm the public by stating that there had not been "million-fold violations of basic liberties in

Germany." Berlin had written assurances from the US and UK governments that the collection procedures were "within rights and law in Germany." Cooperation and coordination between intelligence agencies in Europe and the United States were close, and the metadata and other information shared constituted an essential pillar of transatlantic security.[1]

As the revelations continued, however, this public insouciance began to melt, especially in Germany. Many of the programs suggested the United States was spying on European officials for reasons that had little to do with antiterrorism. Surveillance threatened to become an election issue. The opposition Social Democrats questioned whether Merkel's government could truly be ignorant of the extent of NSA and GCHQ programs. After *Der Spiegel* published allegations that the Bundesnachrichtendienst (BND), the German foreign intelligence agency, had exchanged information with the NSA, Peer Steinbrück, the Social Democratic candidate for chancellor, called on Merkel to "lay all her cards on the table." Forced to act but clearly not seeing the issue as a major irritant, Merkel sent German intelligence and interior ministry officials to meet with their US counterparts in search of greater clarification.[2]

In October, new revelations surfaced that the NSA had tapped the phones of Chancellor Merkel, her aides, and other political elites. (In June 2015, WikiLeaks posted documents purporting to show that the NSA had monitored the communications of high-level French officials, including Presidents François Hollande, Nicolas Sarkozy, and Jacques Chirac.) This time the outrage among the political class was markedly higher, and the scandal became known as Handygate. *Handy* is German for cell phone, and Merkel, an early adopter of mobile phones and texting, was known in the German media as "Handy-Kanzlerin," or "mobile phone chancellor." Moreover, born in the former East Germany, Merkel was extremely sensitive to privacy issues. Merkel phoned President Barack Obama and reportedly told him, "This is just like the Stasi," the East German internal state security and surveillance service. The White House assured Berlin, "The United States is not monitoring and will not monitor the communications of Chancellor Merkel." German commentators quickly noted that the guarantee did not extend into the past.[3]

These pledges did not placate Merkel, and while she continued to push the issue bilaterally, Germany internationalized its grievance against US surveillance. Merkel found a partner in another victim of NSA snooping: Brazilian president Dilma Rousseff. A little more than a week after the mobile phone revelations, Brazil and Germany introduced a UN General Assembly resolution calling for the right to privacy in the digital age. The draft of the resolution did not name a specific country, but called illegal mass collection of data a potential human rights abuse and a violation of freedom that might threaten the foundations of democratic society. It called on member states "to review their procedures, practices, and legislation on the surveillance of communications, their interception and collection of personal data, including mass surveillance."[4]

As he presented the draft, Permanent Representative of Germany to the United Nations Peter Witting highlighted the German and Brazilian argument that in pursuit of security, the United States and its intelligence partners had gone too far. "There seem to be hardly any technical limitations for accessing, storing, or combining personal data," Witting said, then asked, "But should everything that is technically feasible also be allowed? Where do we draw the line between legitimate security concerns and the individual right to privacy? And how do we ensure that human rights are effectively protected both offline and online?"[5]

The United States, United Kingdom, and Australia worked to dilute the language of the draft, especially around the rights of noncitizens to immunity from foreign intelligence gathering. The draft spoke of deep apprehension about the negative impact of "extraterritorial surveillance and/or interception of communications." The United States and its partners argued that online privacy was an internal issue, one violated by a citizen's own government, not by foreign surveillance. The world should worry about China or Russia spying on dissidents, not NSA bulk collection. Moreover, the United States could argue that it had never engaged in illegal surveillance; its programs were authorized by law, overseen by Congress, and reviewed by the courts. As a compromise, Germany and Brazil dropped a phrase linking mass surveillance to human rights violations. The United States ultimately signed the resolution, the first UN General Assembly privacy resolution voted on since 1988.

Brazil and Germany would cooperate to push another resolution in 2015 creating a special rapporteur on privacy in the digital age. The appointment of the first investigator, whose responsibility is to report on privacy violations wherever they occur, became another opportunity for a German official to demonstrate his pique with Washington. A consultative group ranked an Estonian, Katrin Nyman-Metcalf, first for the post, but Joachim Ruecker, permanent representative of Germany to the United Nations in Geneva and president of the Human Rights Council, blocked the nomination, reportedly because she was too pro-American and not "activist enough."[6]

In November 2013, fifty writers, actors, and other public figures published an appeal to grant Edward Snowden asylum in Germany. Heiner Geissler, former general secretary of Angela Merkel's Christian Democrats, wrote, "Snowden has done the western world a great service. It is now up to us to help him." The Merkel government, however, seemed close to signing a "no-spy" agreement with the United States. Media reports suggested that the NSA would agree to respect German law and the rights of German citizens in any surveillance activities conducted in Germany. The deal would also prohibit any economic espionage against German companies. Public leaks further suggested that Germany would rise almost to the level of the Five Eyes, the information sharing agreement among Australia, Canada, New Zealand, the United Kingdom, and the United States.[7]

At the time there was a sense that Washington was sympathetic to some sort of deal. NSA head General Keith Alexander said in an interview, "Partnering with countries may be more important than collecting on them." As one former senior intelligence official told me, "It [spying on Merkel's phone] was stupid. Anything we needed to know about Merkel we could get through human intelligence. We have known her for a long time. We could ask people." Yet, as early as January 2014, confidence in an arrangement looked misplaced, and by June the agreement was dead. National Security Advisor Susan Rice told her counterpart, Christoph Heusgen, that such a deal would set a precedent, and every European ally, along with South Korea and Japan, would demand a similar arrangement. John Podesta, serving as counselor to the president and in charge of the review of surveillance practices, told *Der Spiegel*, "We don't have no-spy agreements with any country, including the U.K."[8]

The German government responded with public anger. Berlin claimed that the idea of the "no-spy" agreement had come from Washington. Podesta suggested the tiff was the result of German misunderstanding, "a little bit of a lack of clarity as to what the US was offering." The end result was a "structured dialogue" to discuss principles that would guide future cooperation, but the issue continued to roil bilateral relations. On several occasions, including a visit to the NSA, German officials submitted lists of questions to the US government about the scope, target, and location of surveillance. A parliamentary investigative committee was established. Germany's chief public prosecutor initiated an investigation into the NSA and its monitoring of the chancellor's cell phone.[9]

The strength of German feeling about bulk data collection and surveillance was hard to ignore. German history and the widespread internal spying conducted by the Nazi and East German regimes in particular have made the public extremely sensitive to surveillance. In one poll conducted by the German Marshall Fund, 70 percent of Germans opposed their own government's conducting domestic surveillance for national security reasons, while 54 percent of Americans opposed the US government's efforts; 72 percent of Germans said governments should not collect phone and Internet data on citizens of allied countries, while only 44 percent of Americans felt the same.[10]

Data protection laws were essentially born in Germany. In 1977, Germany introduced the Bundesdatenschutzgesetz (BDSG), Germany's federal data protection act. Designed to protect personal data from misuse in storage, transmission, modification, or deletion, the act essentially forbade the processing of personal data unless allowed by the BDSG or another law or if the individual granted consent. In 1983, the German Supreme Court recognized a constitutional right to "informational self-determination"—the fundamental right of each individual to determine the circulation and the use of his or her own personal data.

Moreover, the European public viewed the struggle against terrorists differently, at least before the January 2015 attack on the satirical magazine *Charlie Hebdo* in Paris. For Washington and London, the terrorist threat was massive and amorphous. It collapsed the boundary between foreign and domestic and required bulk data collection to connect disparate dots. Most Europeans, by contrast, were likely to view the terrorist threat as a criminal matter, allowing the maintenance of individual privacy. In 2005, in the wake of bombings in Madrid and London, the European Union passed its data retention directive, which required communication providers to store data about their customers for up to two years. The European Court of Justice, however, declared that this directive violated EU privacy rights.

Within European intelligence agencies, however, there was a movement toward the American view. European and US intelligence collaborated closely, and in several instances, German, French, and other European security officials sidestepped privacy protections and sidelined privacy advocates. Snowden documents analyzed by *Der Spiegel*, for example, focused on the G-10 law, which establishes conditions under which surveillance of German citizens is permissible. One document in a section titled "Success Stories" reads, "The German government modifies its interpretation of the G-10 privacy law . . . to afford the BND more flexibility in sharing protected information with foreign partners."[11]

If the Snowden revelations had only been about bulk collection, political elites may have been able to contain the damage. Many policymakers in Germany seem to have assumed this was the case, which may explain why Merkel's first public reaction was relatively low-key. But once it came out that the NSA was also spying on Merkel and other German politicians, much of the political will in Berlin to limit the fallout dissolved. As several members of the German Foreign Ministry told me, the spying felt like a personal betrayal and generated a level of distrust that eclipsed the bad feelings many felt toward President George W. Bush and the war in Iraq. "The United States had helped get rid of the Stasi and helped unify the country," one senior German official told me, "but now we find out our big brother is spying on us." Pro-American German conservatives felt this loss of trust even more keenly; having argued that the intelligence relationship benefited both sides, they now felt like second-class allies. Or as the political scientist Henry Farrell wrote, "The centrists who argued that Europeans could trust the United States to respect their privacy have been hung out to dry."[12]

While some policymakers in Washington acknowledged German feelings, irritation with the intensity and obstinacy of Berlin's response was widespread. Some ascribed it to a political need to assuage the German public and to a reflexive anti-Americanism held by German leftists. Some saw it as naiveté. Given German relations with Russia and Iran and the perennial complexity and uncertainty of foreign relations, of course the United States would continue spying. Or as Rolf Mowatt-Larssen, former chief of the CIA's Europe Division, wrote, "No serious intelligence organization can rely exclusively on cooperation with other states, even close allies, to fulfill its mission. Often, crucial information cannot be acquired through established channels for intelligence cooperation."[13]

Still others saw pretense and ingratitude. As one senior intelligence official said, "There is huge hypocrisy here. Allies spy on each other—that's not exactly news. And Germany makes huge use of what we provide them from our infrastructure in Europe and around the world." News reports then revealed that the BND had spied on Turkey, a NATO ally, and tapped the phones of Secretaries of State John Kerry and Hillary Clinton. The collection was said to be inadvertent and the recordings destroyed quickly, but the public damage to the German position had been done.[14]

During a conversation in Berlin in the spring of 2013, a German academic speculated that it would take no more than two years for the US-German relationship to recover from the NSA revelations. His estimate now seems prescient, though tensions would worsen before they got better. In July 2014, Berlin expelled the CIA head in Berlin after the agency paid a German intelligence officer for information gathered by a parliamentary committee on NSA activities. In December 2014, the parliamentary committee investigating the tapping of Merkel's phone reported there was no public evidence that it had actually happened. "The document presented in public as proof of an authentic tapping of the mobile is," according to the committee, "not an authentic surveillance order by the NSA. There is no proof right now that could lead to charges that Chancellor Merkel's phone connection data was collected or her calls tapped." The failure to find a specific document was a useful legalistic finding that would allow Berlin and Washington to begin to repair the damage in relations.[15]

Moreover, the continuing chaos in the Middle East, particularly the rise of the Islamic State in Iraq and Syria (ISIS), heightened the sense of interdependence with the United States. Thousands of French and German citizens have traveled to Iraq, Syria, and Yemen. The real fear that that they would return and commit acts of violence played out when two brothers armed with assault rifles burst into the Paris offices of *Charlie Hebdo,* killing eleven and injuring twelve. During a February 2015 visit to the White House, after President Obama asked the German people to trust the United States not to abuse its surveillance powers, Chancellor Merkel emphasized Germany's dependence on Washington's ability to gather intelligence. "The institutions of the United States of America still continue to provide us with a lot of very significant information," she said, "and we don't want to do without this."[16]

Even at the zenith of the public backlash, cooperation between the US and German intelligence agencies never stopped. As *Der Spiegel* notes, "No other country in Europe plays host to a secret NSA surveillance architecture comparable to the one in Germany." More than five hundred Germans have traveled to Iraq and Syria, and Berlin has relied on US ability to track e-mails, cell phones, and social media accounts to see if any have joined ISIS and whether they have returned home. Only the United States has the capacity to create a comprehensive database of all foreign fighters entering Syria. Former BND chief August Hanning told the *Washington Post* in 2014 that the NSA "has better technical means, far more capacity, [and] better software to deal with more data." In the spring of 2015, a scandal broke in Germany with revelations that the BND had been helping the NSA spy on European officials and companies for at least ten years, forcing Merkel again to fall back on the argument that the battle against terrorism required US help. The BND's "ability to carry out its duties in the face of international terrorism threats is done in cooperation with other intelligence agencies," said the chancellor, "and that includes first and foremost the NSA."[17]

If not railing against what they saw as German hypocrisy at the outrage over surveillance, then policymakers were suggesting that new privacy provisions really reflected ulterior commercial motives. In response to a question put to him by the tech website Re/code about the European investigation of Google and Facebook, President

Obama answered, "We have owned the Internet. Our companies have created it, expanded it, perfected it in ways that they can't compete. And oftentimes what is portrayed as high-minded positions on issues sometimes is just designed to carve out some of their commercial interests." "There are some countries like Germany, given its history with the Stasi, that are very sensitive to these issues," Obama continued. "Sometimes their vendors, their service providers who can't compete with ours are essentially trying to set up some roadblocks for our companies to operate effectively."[18]

This is not exactly right. President Obama was struggling with the intermingled motivations and rationales that swirl around the question of access to data in the hacked world order. The divide between Europe and the United States on privacy is real, and it would be a mistake to characterize the impulse to protect government secrets and the data of citizens against espionage and foreign surveillance simply as a mask for European protectionism. The idea of privacy as a human right is a basic European principle. The investigation of Google and Facebook for privacy violations that Obama was commenting on predated both the Snowden revelations and the subsequent efforts to leverage outrage over the disclosures in order to build European competitors to US technology companies.

But President Obama's argument was also not completely wrong. It is true that some German business leaders and policymakers have used the Snowden revelations and the battles over privacy as an excuse to build their own national champions, domestic digital industries that can compete in the global market. These policymakers and their counterparts in Beijing, Moscow, Brasilia, and elsewhere question whether the open, global Internet is an indisputable good for everyone or an undeniable good for US technology companies.

The US government and American technology companies have consistently advocated for the free flow of information and data across national borders, with the requisite framework for respecting intellectual property rights and the privacy of individuals. In May 2015 Deputy US Trade Representative Robert Holleyman warned that rising "digital protectionism" was battering existing trade agreements. Data localization, censorship of information, and other types of "data nationalism" have the potential, according to Holleyman, "to hit at the heart of the digital economy." In response, the United States developed the "Dirty Dozen," twelve principles for digital trade that US negotiators worked to incorporate into the Trans-Pacific Partnership, a trade agreement with eleven other countries in the Asia-Pacific region. The principles include keeping the Internet free and open so that consumers can access online services and preventing countries from requiring companies to transfer technology or localize their computing services.[19]

The argument that the Internet has had a positive impact on the economy is not controversial. In 2014, the Boston Consulting Group suggested that the Internet contributes between 5 and 9 percent to total gross domestic product (GDP) in developed markets and that the total value of the Internet economy would reach $4.2 trillion in the Group of Twenty economies by 2016. For the US economy, online sales of products and services in "digitally intensive" sectors totaled $935.2 billion, or 6.3 percent of GDP in 2012. It is estimated that for every 10 percent increase in broadband penetration, global GDP increases by an average of 1.3 percent. A Deloitte report, sponsored by Facebook, argued that increased Internet access could lead to productivity gains of 31 percent in India, 29 and 26 percent in Africa and South and East Asia, respectively, and 13 percent in Latin America, as well as add close to 140 million jobs.[20]

The negative impact of cutting off the Internet is also widely accepted. During the protests against President Hosni Mubarak in Cairo in January 2011, the Egyptian government shut off the Internet for five days. The Organization for Economic Cooperation and Development estimated that this break resulted in direct losses of $90 million to the economy, with indirect social and economic effects perhaps reaching an additional $100 million.[21]

Even if a country does not go so far as to cut itself off from the Internet, it can still harm itself. The Boston Consulting Group report identifies fifty-five sources of "e-friction," differences in infrastructure access, speed, and price, as well as quality of talent, banking services, and intellectual property protection, "that can prevent consumers, companies, and countries from realizing the benefits of the online economy." Ranking sixty-five countries, the report finds that low-friction countries have Internet economies twice as big, as a percentage of GDP, as high-friction countries. For comparison to "real-world" trade, the World Economic Forum found that improvements in border administration and communication and transportation infrastructure would boost GDP growth in Southeast Asian nations by 9.3 percent, in South Asia by 8 percent, and in sub-Saharan Africa by 12 percent.[22]

Countries that pass data localization, retention, and other policies that interrupt the free flow of information also appear to be inflicting self-harm. Research by the European Centre for International Political Economy describes how domestic communication, finance, and insurance industries in China, the European Union, Korea, and Vietnam suffer under data regulations. In July 2013, for example, Vietnam introduced Decree 72, which required social media, websites, and other companies to maintain at least one server in the country. The decree, if fully enforced, could cost the country 1.7 percent of GDP and drop domestic and foreign investment by 3.1 percent. Estimates of the damage of laws requiring all data to be stored locally would be markedly higher.[23]

While we think of filtering and censorship as motivated by political goals, they also have potential economic effects. Given China's growth rate over the last decade, it is hard to argue that the Great Firewall has been a huge negative drag on the Chinese economy. But it clearly affects foreign businesses operating in China. In a February 2015 survey by the American Chamber of Commerce in Beijing of 477 businesses operating in China, 80 percent of respondents said that Internet blocking and censorship hurt their business. In a similar survey conducted by the EU Chamber of Commerce, 86 percent responded that their business had been hurt.[24]

The censorship slows China's efforts to become an innovative economy. The journal *Nature* surveyed 784 Chinese scientists on how the blockage of Google products affected their work; 84 percent said not having access to Google Search hampered their research "somewhat or significantly," and 78 percent said that if Google Docs and Google Scholar were also blocked it would "somewhat or significantly" affect international collaboration. During a crackdown in the first months of 2015 on virtual private networks, a tool used to get around filters, a number of Chinese academics, technologists, and media analysts went on Weibo to complain that Internet sovereignty was reducing creativity and productivity.[25]

In 2013, Tim Berners-Lee, inventor of the World Wide Web, argued that self-interest would lead Beijing to relax control: "The agility of a country which allows full access to the web is just greater; it will be a stronger country economically as well." Not surprisingly, the Chinese have a different view of their interests. There is a difference between accepting that the Internet will benefit a national economy and embracing the idea that the Internet must be completely without borders. Domestic stability trumps potential economic gains, and leaders are often willing to sacrifice material benefits for important political objectives.[26]

Even if one recognizes that all might be better off with the free flow of information across national borders, states often care as much about relative gains as about absolute ones, if not more. A widespread view holds that the United States and US technology companies have disproportionately captured the economic benefits of the global Internet. What Washington and Silicon Valley see as efforts to "fragment" the web, policymakers in Brazil, Brunei, China, South Korea, Switzerland, and Vietnam see as "de-Americanizing" it.

E-MAIL MADE IN GERMANY

Germany has been the leading voice of a wider European effort to rebalance the economics of cyberspace, shrink the market share for American firms, and support European competitors. Just weeks after the *Guardian* published some of the first stories on the NSA surveillance program code-named "PRISM," German interior minister Hans-Peter Friedrich argued, "Whoever fears their communication is being intercepted in any way should use services that don't go through American servers." The country's 2014 Digital Agenda is explicit, calling urgently for the expansion of "Germany's autonomy and authority over information and telecommunication technology."[27]

The tools used to transform angry rhetoric into real outcomes have been technical and political. In an effort to offer local alternatives to services such as Gmail, Deutsche Telekom, the largest telecommunications organization in the European Union, launched an "E-mail Made in Germany" initiative, and other German e-mail providers began seeing significant increases in users (though how many canceled their

Gmail and Yahoo accounts was unclear). Freenet, a telecommunications provider promising strong anonymity protection, saw an 80 percent increase in new users over three weeks. Posteo, another company
providing e-mail encryption, tripled its number of subscribers to more
than 30,000. Deutsche Telekom began not only offering Secure Sock-
ets Layer encryption, which establishes an encrypted link between a
website and a server or between a mail client and an e-mail program,
but also ensuring that e-mail traveling between three of its e-mail services never left local servers. The actual security benefits to users of
these services are minimal, however, especially against national intelligence agencies. Most of the companies did not promise to store the
e-mails encrypted, making them vulnerable to snooping, though Posteo now does.[28]

In June 2014, the German government ended a contract with Verizon and announced that it would phase out all of its remaining business with the company by 2015. Berlin had seen Verizon as tarnished
ever since the first set of Snowden documents in June 2013 named it
as having passed US users' data to the NSA. The Interior Ministry was
quoted as saying, "The relationships between foreign intelligence agencies and companies revealed in the course of the NSA affair show that
especially high demands must be made of federal government communications infrastructure that is critical for security." Deutsche Telekom
picked up the contract.[29]

At the end of 2014, the German parliament began debating a bill
that would keep US technology companies out of certain parts of the
German economy. Companies selling to the government or to parts of
the private sector deemed critical would have to undergo additional
inspections and certifications. Deutsche Telekom has also raised the
idea of creating "Schengen-area routing." The Schengen area includes
twenty-six European countries that have removed passport controls
at their borders. With Schengen-area routing, data would stay within
Europe, not crossing the Atlantic unless necessary. Since the area does
not include the United Kingdom, it would also theoretically avoid the
prying eyes of the GCHQ, the UK signals intelligence agency. Deutsche Telekom had a clear economic interest in the plan, as did the
German government itself, which owns a 32 percent stake in the company. Telecoms generally engage in peering, an agreement whereby

neither side pays for the exchange of traffic, but Deutsche Telekom does not swap traffic on a no-payment basis. The creation of such a routing scheme would create more opportunities to bill for access to German users.[30]

The idea of a Schengen or Europe-wide cloud complemented the notion of Schengen-area routing. Data would not only travel through Europe but be stored there. As Estonian president Toomas Hendrik Ilves argued, "It is very important for Europe to create its own data clouds, operating under EU law and completely safe for users." "I think it is an opportunity for us," Ilves continued, "and we must use this opportunity instead of beating our breast, saying 'oh, how terrible that United States is following everything we do.'" A report commissioned by the European Parliament advocated for "a full industrial policy for development of an autonomous European Cloud computing capacity based on free/open-source software."[31]

For now, the plan for a European cloud remains simply that. But US firms have already lost business to European competitors because of sensitivity to US government requests for user data. The Information Technology and Innovation Foundation estimates that US cloud companies could lose $35 billion by 2016, or up to 20 percent of the foreign market, because of European security concerns. Companies like SAP, Hewlett-Packard, Microsoft, and Oracle now offer local cloud solutions. In October 2014, Amazon's cloud computing business, known as Amazon Web Services, announced plans to build data centers in Germany; previously the data of German customers might be held in Ireland or nine other centers outside the European Union.[32]

Microsoft began advertising that it was expanding local cloud services in Europe in order to address privacy fears and, in a much bolder, bigger move, began a legal case against the US government. The Department of Justice wants Microsoft to hand over data from an Outlook e-mail account belonging to a suspect in a narcotics case. Microsoft has refused to comply, saying the data, stored in Ireland, is outside US jurisdiction and that requests for the information should go to the Irish government. A magistrate and federal district judge ruled against the software giant, and in December 2014 Microsoft filed with the US Court of Appeals. More than thirty tech companies, as well as several trade associations and thirty-five computer scientists, filed a supporting brief arguing that the search warrant for the data in Dublin would set a dangerous precedent and "damage American businesses economically." The brief continued, "It will upset our international agreements and undermine international cooperation. And it will spur retaliation by foreign governments, which will threaten the privacy of Americans and non-Americans alike."[33]

REVISING THE DATA PROTECTION DIRECTIVE

The biggest shift in the marketplace could result from the revisions to the EU Data Protection Directive. The original directive went into effect in 1995 and mandated that every member of the European Union create national privacy regulations and a Data Protection Authority to protect citizens' privacy. The directive requires that companies ask for permission before they gather private information and gives users the right to review the data and correct inaccuracies. Companies cannot share personal information with each other or across borders without express permission from users. Any company that collects information must register its activities with the government.

The rapid expansion of digital technologies and a growing patchwork of national regulations meant the directive needed updating. The European Commission, the European Union's executive arm, has estimated that the revisions could save businesses throughout Europe €2.3 billion by creating a simple standard. This would also dovetail with a larger effort to create a digital single market across the European Union, which would include standardization of copyright protections, simplification of e-commerce, and a boost in skills and education.

A draft of proposed revisions, published by the European Commission in January 2012, has become the most lobbied piece of European legislation in history, receiving over 4,000 comments. The draft introduced new controls on what companies could do with data and new limits on how long they could keep it, along with new tools for individuals to control how their information can be used. It also introduced portability—users will be able to move their data from one site to another. And it offered eye-popping fines for transgressing companies: up to 5 percent of annual worldwide revenue, or €100 million, whichever is greater.[34]

The revision of the directive took place at the same time as some in Europe were questioning the continued viability of the Safe Harbor agreement. Safe Harbor, developed by the Department of Commerce and the European Commission in 2000, allows US firms to repatriate data as long as they subscribe to and follow European principles. The Federal Trade Commission (FTC) can investigate and fine companies that fail in their responsibilities. In 2011, for example, the FTC reached an agreement with Facebook that prohibited the company from overriding privacy preferences without user consent, along with other actions, and established a twenty-year process of independent third-party auditing of privacy policies.

Despite periodic complaints about US companies violating privacy promises and a perceived lack of stringency in FTC enforcement, the agreement generally worked. In the wake of the Snowden disclosures, however, Europe threatened to suspend Safe Harbor. EU vice president Viviane Reding announced a full review of Safe Harbor, calling PRISM a "wake-up call." In her statement, Reding concluded that Safe Harbor "may not be so safe after all," which seemed both a description and a threat.[35]

In November 2013, the European Union sent a list of thirteen demands that the United States needed to meet to keep the agreement in place. At the time, more than 3,500 US companies and European companies with operations in the United States were covered by the agreement (the number reached over 4,400 in September 2015). By November 2014, eleven of the demands had been satisfied; the remaining two touched on how the government could use data in defense of national security, and the central sticking point was a requirement for the United States to invoke the national security exception in the Safe Harbor agreement only "to an extent that is strictly necessary or proportionate." In particular, Europe did not want the United States conducting bulk data collection.[36]

A lawsuit brought against Facebook in the European Court of Justice by an Austrian law student, Max Schrems, aimed squarely at the question of whether US companies could keep European data safe. Schrems's team of lawyers argued that programs like PRISM ensured that Safe Harbor could not work as designed. There was no way for US technology companies to provide an "adequate level of protection." In

October 2015 the European Court of Justice agreed with Schrems's lawyers and ruled Safe Harbor invalid. In expectation of the ruling, most big companies, including Facebook, worked out side deals with individual European countries or inserted clauses in their user agreements allowing them to continue to transfer data.[37]

The ruling will empower governments to place more restrictions on all companies and hobble small companies with fewer legal resources to respond to data authorities' demands. Big companies may also decide to store data locally in country. But the ruling will do little to increase the privacy of European users. Data stored in the United States is under more legal protection than data located on European servers. If the NSA wants access to data in the United States, it needs the permission of the Foreign Intelligence Surveillance Court. Foreign user data in Europe can be collected without a court order. Moreover, the British, French, and German intelligence agencies do not require a court order for national surveillance.[38]

GOOGLEPHOBIA

Sometimes data sovereignty is about European privacy. Sometimes it is about market power. The Snowden revelations fanned and reinforced a growing unease in Europe with the size and dominance of US technology companies reflected in the acronym "GAFA"—Google, Apple, Facebook, and Amazon—often deployed by French critics. While perhaps simply euphonic, Google's primary position in the acronym also highlights the discomfort of Europe's relationship with the search giant, which mirrors the reaction some in Europe had to Coca-Cola, McDonald's, Disney, and the spread of "American cultural hegemony" in the 1970s. Like those earlier battles, the struggle over Google stems from a cultural clash and a worry that local industries will not be able to compete with global multinationals.[39]

The search engine giant has about 68 percent of the market in the United States, but 90 percent in Europe. Its online advertising revenues are about four times those of its nearest competitor, Facebook. Moreover, Google has businesses that upset book publishers (Google Books), media (YouTube and Google News), and car manufacturers (driverless cars). The European Commission launched an antimonopoly investigation in 2010, and in 2012 Joaquín Almunia, then vice president of the European Commission responsible for competition policy, highlighted four practices as suspect: Google prioritizes links to its own services, like Google Shopping and YouTube, over rival links; it takes content from rivals and uses it on its own services; it shuts out competitors who offer advertising on search engines from its own results; and it makes it hard for businesses that use AdWords, Google's auction-based advertising platform, to move to other services.[40]

Wanting to avoid formal charges, a fine of nearly $6 billion or 10 percent of global annual sales, and the possibility of legal restrictions on its business, Google put several concessions on the table, offering, for example, to give greater prominence to results from competitors in specialized searches for travel or restaurants. By July 2013, the two sides appeared to have reached an agreement, but an announcement of the potential for a deal provoked a backlash from a coalition of European tech companies and prominent politicians. French economy minister Arnaud Montebourg told an audience outside Paris, "France will not accept 'a minimal' deal with Google. What's at stake is our sovereignty itself." Even if meant as a bargaining strategy, the hyperbolic invocation of a threat to sovereignty was remarkable.[41]

Google brought significant resources to the fight. The company reportedly tripled the amount it spent on lobbying, reaching €2 million in 2014, and hired political insiders with experience in European Commission agencies. In an October 2014 speech in Berlin, Eric Schmidt, Google's chairman and former CEO, argued that users "have choices, and they are exercising them all the time. Google operates in a competitive landscape, which is changing constantly." Moreover, Schmidt continued, since barriers to entry are low, Google could fail to seize the next market opportunity. "No one is stuck using Google."[42]

Negotiations continued, and in November 2014 the European Parliament voted to separate search from other services, like maps or docs, essentially voting to break up Google (though without explicitly naming it). The resolution carried no legal weight but was another sign of the widening antipathy to the company. The *Economist* called the move, designed to increase pressure on the European Commission's new antitrust chief to act, "the latest and most dramatic outbreak of Googlephobia in Europe."[43]

The European Parliament resolution was an ominous warning of what might come, but the ruling on the "right to be forgotten"—the right of individuals to remove potentially harmful or embarrassing online data—was a tectonic shift for Google. It is very hard to escape the past in the digital age. Every video, blog post, or tweet lives forever. In 1998, a Spanish newspaper published a thirty-six-word article saying Mario Costeja González's home was being repossessed to repay debts. Almost ten years later, *La Vanguardia* digitized its archives, making the article accessible to web crawlers, programs that automatically scour the Internet for data. At some point, Costeja, now a lawyer with a consultancy practice, googled himself, as we all do occasionally, and found the repossession story higher in his search results than he wanted. He contacted the newspaper and asked it to take the article down. *La Vanguardia* said it could not, since the Spanish Ministry of Labor and Social Affairs had ordered that the original announcement be published in order to attract more bids on the house.

Costeja asked Google to take down links to the article. After the company refused, Costeja turned to the Spanish Data Protection Agency, responsible for overseeing compliance with data regulations. Eventually the case ended up in front of Europe's highest court, the European Court of Justice in Luxembourg. In May 2014, the court found for Costeja. Google could be forced to remove links "even when the publication in itself of those pages is lawful." Users should have the right to be forgotten by having links erased, unless there are "particular reasons" to keep them. But the court argued that the right to privacy should in most cases have precedence over the public's right to know.

TWO CULTURES OF PRIVACY

Although a shock to Google and other US technology companies, the finding emerged from two major cultural differences between the United States and Europe. The first has to do with different ideas about regulation. As we have seen, privacy is a human right in Europe, and government is expected to actively regulate technology companies to protect it. In the United States, the cliché goes that users do not care about privacy. This is not the case. In a 2015 Pew survey, 93 percent of respondents said controlling who has access to their information is important, and 90 percent said control over what information gets shared is also important. But for Americans, privacy protection is in large part the responsibility of the user. I am expected to be aware of and accept the risks of using technology services, even if understanding privacy policies buried in complicated, lengthy documents is close to impossible. There is an expectation that companies will self-regulate and that Silicon Valley will innovate first and reassess later. Companies rush new products or services to market, expecting users to provide feedback to help improve version 2.0. If things go badly, they apologize and move on. If things go really pear-shaped, the government steps in.

When Google introduced Buzz in 2011, for example, the new social media platform harvested contact information from users' Gmail accounts, exposing connections and sharing private data. The FTC found that the company had used deceptive tactics and violated its own privacy policies. In the settlement, Google agreed to independent privacy audits for twenty years. In 2012, the Obama administration introduced a report pushing for a Consumer Privacy Bill of Rights that, while still envisioning a very light government touch, represented a small step away from self-regulation. It urged the tech industry to work with the Department of Commerce to develop an enforceable code of conduct and Congress to enact comprehensive privacy legislation. The blueprint for legislation desired by the White House included some controls over private data.[44]

After almost three years of inactivity on the project, President Obama proposed such a bill of rights in 2015. Exhorting the technology industry to develop its own regulations, the draft empowered the FTC to make sure they met certain standards: that users be told clearly how their data will be used, that data not be reused for different purposes, and that consumers be given greater control over their information "in proportion to the privacy risk." Not surprisingly, the bill attracted criticism for opposite reasons. Privacy advocates argued that industry would define a lax standard of risk. Business groups saw the proposed regulations as too restrictive and the sanctions as too steep. Nobody expected any progress on the bill in Congress through the end of the Obama administration, given the polarization on and complexity of the issue.

The second cultural distinction centers on a fundamentally different set of understandings about privacy. Yale law professor James Whitman identifies two Western cultures of privacy, "unmistakable differences in sensibilities about what ought to be kept private." In Whitman's framing, European protections are about dignity, personal respect, and honor. They include the right to control a public image, to shield it from embarrassment. The right to be forgotten emerges from *le droit à l'oubli*—or the "right of oblivion"—found in French law. Even criminals who have served their time can have information about their conviction and incarceration removed as it affects their dignity and place in society. By contrast, the American right to privacy is rooted in liberty and a distrust of the police and state power; it entails the right to freedom from an intrusive state, especially in one's own home. Or as defined by Louis Brandeis and Samuel Warren at the end of the nineteenth century, the right to privacy is "the right to be left alone." Once that is assured, the First Amendment protects information already in the public domain, including criminal history.[45]

These differing philosophies, as expressed in the European Court ruling, created a real morass for Google. How was the company supposed to balance the right to privacy with the public good? Should negative information about a person be accessible for a specific period and then made to disappear? Do the criteria for removal differ if the individual is famous? For those who wanted their information removed, Google provided an online request form; the company also created an advisory council to help weigh an "individual's right to be forgotten with the public's right to information." Yahoo and Bing also began removing links.[46]

In the first year after the ruling, Google received more than 250,000 requests covering more than 920,000 links. Google removed 35 percent of the links submitted and declined to remove 50 percent, with 15 percent still under review. For example, at an Italian woman's request the company took down a link to a decade-old article about the murder of her husband that mentioned her name. It did not remove twenty links to articles about the arrest of an Italian man for financial crimes committed in a professional capacity. This certainly looks burdensome on the company, but in comparison Google received requests to remove over 34 million URLs in one month for copyright violations.[47]

In November 2014, Europe's privacy regulators argued that the right to be forgotten should go global. Google was removing links from the local versions of Google in France (www.google.fr) and Germany (www.google.de) but not from the primary Google site (www.google.com). This allowed both users and Google to sidestep the question of censorship. If you were in France, you could always search for and find information on the global site. But data protection agencies insisted their authority was global. In the words of Isabelle Falque-Pierrotin, who heads the French data protection authority, "For Google, the answer is worldwide. If people have the right to be delisted from search results, then that should happen worldwide."[48]

Extension of the right to be forgotten would allow European judges and policymakers to decide what people in other parts of the world see. Typically, Europe's influence has been much more indirect if no less pervasive. European Union standards already have a global reach, and privacy standards are only the latest regulations to migrate from Brussels to the rest of the world. Or as Peter Fleischer, Google's global privacy counsel, argues, "On the global stage, Europe is convincing many countries around the world to implement privacy laws that follow the European model. The facts speak for themselves: in the last year alone, a dozen countries in Latin America and Asia have adopted European-style privacy laws. Not a single country, anywhere, has followed the U.S. model." Fleischer argues that Uruguay, for example, looked to Spain and not the United States because the American model is an opaque, confusing patchwork of state and federal laws, multiple regulators, from attorneys general to the FTC, and class action lawyers. Europe has a single identifiable regulator and laws that are "general, aspirational, horizontal and concise."[49]

Looking across the Atlantic, US policymakers have long had to adapt to competing visions of privacy, regulation, and security. Prior to Edward Snowden's revelations, fissures between the two sides endured, but everyone involved knew their contours and where cooperation was possible. The Snowden disclosures, however, pushed these differences to the front and splintered the often implicit understandings that made cooperation possible. As new revelations came to light week after week, the United States struggled to accomplish three rather gargantuan tasks.

First, the Obama administration had to publicly defend the security benefits of NSA activities against fears of eroding privacy. Two weeks after the revelations began, for example, President Obama said in Germany, "We know of at least fifty threats that have been averted because of this information not just in the United States, but, in some cases, threats here in Germany. So lives have been saved." While the initial claim that collecting the entire haystack helped prevent fifty terrorist attacks did not hold up to public scrutiny, the White House continued to defend the NSA collection program with some minor qualifications. Second, Washington tried to repair the rupture in relations with Berlin as well as to restore its credibility with the rest of the world. Finally, the White House had to develop a strategy to respond to regulations in China, Europe, and elsewhere that could otherwise result in significant economic disruption for US tech firms. In essence, for at least a decade security goals had overwhelmed diplomatic and economic interests; now it was time to swing the pendulum away from the NSA's headquarters in Fort Meade, Maryland, toward Silicon Valley.[50]

In December 2013, the President's Review Group on Intelligence and Communications Technologies provided a potential playbook to rebalance competing interests. The group, appointed by the president and made up of five lawyers and national security experts—including Richard Clarke, who served as special adviser to President George W. Bush for cybersecurity—worked from the premise that Washington must pursue multiple, often competing goals at home and abroad. These include the need to defend national security, promote other foreign policy goals, encourage an open Internet, strengthen alliances, and protect privacy, civil liberties, and the rule of law. The group produced a long list of forty-six recommendations on how to reform surveillance, including terminating government storage of bulk telephony metadata and having it held by the telecoms or another private third party, which would force the NSA to request permission to access it. The USA Freedom Act, passed by the House and Senate in June 2015 and signed by the president, essentially takes this position.[51]

In trying to control the diplomatic fallout, the group recommended curtailing unnecessary surveillance of non-US persons. In the early days of the revelations, US government officials had the unfortunate habit of justifying certain programs by saying they were directed at non-US citizens—at foreigners. "What I can say unequivocally," said President Obama to Charlie Rose, "is that, if you are a U.S. person, the N.S.A. cannot listen to your telephone calls, and the N.S.A. cannot target your e-mails." This may have made sense legally but was terrible public relations, alienating billions of non-US persons in important diplomatic partners such as Brazil, the European Union, India, Indonesia, and South Africa.[52]

The intelligence review group suggested that spying on foreign citizens should be "directed exclusively at protecting the national security interests of the United States and our allies." Moreover, the United States should not share information irrelevant to that goal either within the US government or with other governments. This would have resulted in a significant narrowing of collection, since under the 2008 revision of Section 702 of the Foreign Intelligence Surveillance Act (FISA), the NSA could collect all types of information from foreigners as long as it "relates to . . . the conduct of the foreign affairs of the United States," a relatively expansive category.[53]

The reforms did not go far enough for most Europeans. In January 2014 the president announced that the NSA and others must consider the privacy of foreigners when disseminating intelligence, and the White House released Presidential Policy Directive (PPD) 28 on signals intelligence activities. Among other changes, PPD 28 reaffirmed the uses of intelligence collected in bulk to respond to threats in only six categories: espionage, terrorism, proliferation of weapons of mass destruction, cybersecurity, attacks on US or allied armed forces, and transnational criminal threats. In addition, it banned intelligence agencies from distributing information collected on foreign citizens with GCHQ, BND, or other foreign intelligence agencies without considering "the privacy interests of non-U.S. persons." Information collected on non-US persons must be deleted after five years, unless there is a valid foreign intelligence requirement to keep it. "No country on the planet has gone this far to improve the treatment of non-citizens in government surveillance," said David Medine, chairman of the Privacy and Civil Liberties Oversight Board, an independent oversight agency established after 9/11.[54]

The problem for many in Europe, however, was still bulk collection, not just distribution. They wanted mass collection to stop. Given the low levels of trust and the high opacity of the NSA's activities, few were willing to accept the agency's assurances at face value. Moreover, most European privacy advocates found little comfort in hearing that Europeans would be treated just like Americans, since they deemed the protections afforded US citizens themselves inadequate.

WHOM DO YOU TRUST LESS?

The potential damage to US economic interests hangs over the review group's report. The authors feared that surveillance would harm US businesses as distrust in their ability to protect the privacy of international users spread. The review group also noted the importance of encryption to the economy and urged the US government not to "in any way subvert, undermine, weaken, or make vulnerable generally available commercial software."

The technology sector's response to the revelations has been a sustained howl about the threat to their businesses and customers around the world. During an interview at a technology conference in September 2013, Mark Zuckerberg said, "Frankly I think the government blew it" and did a bad job of balancing privacy and security. "The government response was, 'Oh don't worry, we're not spying on any Americans,'" continued Zuckerberg. "Oh, wonderful: that's really helpful to companies trying to serve people around the world, and that's really going to inspire confidence in American Internet companies." Reports that an NSA project code-named "MUSCULAR" had hacked into cables carrying data traffic among Google's servers in different locations, as well as into the same system run by Yahoo, garnered a more profane response: "Fuck these guys," posted Brandon Downey, a security engineer with Google.[55]

The companies also resented the linking of mass surveillance with the data collection central to their business models. In his speech laying out the process and principles of PPD 28, President Obama reminded the companies that they were in the same boat, implicitly asking the audience whom they trusted less: the companies or the government. The "challenges to our privacy do not come from government alone," said the president. "Corporations of all shapes and sizes track what you buy, store and analyze your data, and use it for commercial purposes."[56]

Seeing no remedy coming from the White House, Apple, Facebook, Google, and others attempted to distance themselves from the surveillance programs. Initial reporting on the PRISM, for example, suggested not a legal framework for demanding information but "direct access," a tap into the companies' servers. The companies claimed that they had never heard of PRISM before and, as it became clear that mentions of the program in NSA documents referred to FISA requests, began demanding greater transparency to explain to the public how the legal process worked. In early 2014, Apple, Facebook, Google, Microsoft, Yahoo, and others sued Attorney General Eric Holder and the FBI for permission to publish the number of national security requests, including FISA disclosures, each company received. After weeks of negotiations, the government conceded that the companies could disclose the number of requests but with limitations. The transparency reports the companies now publish reveal how many requests they receive within ranges of 1,000; so, for example, between January and June 2013, Microsoft revealed that it received between 0 and 999 FISA requests that impacted between 18,000 and 18,999 accounts.

The companies and their business associations have thrown their weight behind new legislation. AOL, Apple, Facebook, Google, Microsoft, and Yahoo supported the USA Freedom Act and other legislative efforts to end bulk metadata collection of US phone and data records, require disclosure of important rulings by the secret FISA Court, and permit greater company reporting on surveillance orders received. In addition, the same companies started a public campaign demanding "sensible limitations" on the ability of government agencies to compel tech companies to disclose user data. The companies argued, "Governments should limit surveillance to specific known users for lawful purposes, and should not undertake bulk data collection of Internet communications."[57]

The technology companies have tried to align themselves rhetorically with the security and resilience of the global Internet in opposition to what they see as the willingness of the US government to weaken the security of all users for national security interests. In

December 2013, Brad Smith, general counsel and executive vice president at Microsoft, likened government surveillance to the advanced persistent threat, the term of art for Chinese, Russian, and other state-sponsored hackers. In other words, Smith equated the actions of the NSA with those of the People's Liberation Army's Unit 61398. To raise the costs to those who want to collect data, the company would implement a series of measures "to ensure governments use legal process rather than technological brute force to access customer data."[58]

One of those steps, encryption, has become the tech sector's trump card. It appears the NSA has successfully weakened the implementation of encryption, but done properly, cryptographic systems still deliver a measure of protection from criminals and state-backed hackers, including US law enforcement and intelligence agencies. Snowden has said, "Properly implemented strong crypto systems are one of the few things that you can rely on."[59]

Microsoft, along with Google, Yahoo, and others, began encrypting data not only as it moved between the companies and users but also as it traveled on internal servers. In September 2014, Apple announced that its new iPhone operating system (iOS) would encrypt data by default. While the FBI and others would be able to reach data backed up to the cloud, stored by many apps, or held by the wireless provider, the company would have no access to the encryption keys and so could not respond to a government request to unlock a phone. In an additional step to make encryption a daily practice, not just something available to security specialists and computer geeks, Yahoo introduced a browser extension in March 2015 that allows e-mail users to encrypt their messages simply by clicking a button. A determined state actor can still break into computers, but these measures do make it harder to engage in bulk collection.

DÉJÀ VU ALL OVER AGAIN

Many parts of the government reacted to these announcements with alarm. FBI director James Comey argued that law enforcement was "going dark"—authorities could no longer access the data needed to protect the country and prosecute crime when they had a court-approved search warrant. "Perhaps it's time to suggest," Comey said in a speech at the Brookings Institution, "that the post-Snowden pendulum has swung too far in one direction—in a direction of fear and mistrust [of the government]." He expressed surprise that Apple would "market something expressly to allow people to place themselves beyond the law." To prevent criminals from taking advantage of this blinding, Comey suggested that US technology companies build in "front doors" on cell phones and smartphones that would allow the FBI access.[60]

For many in the technology community, the call for "front doors" created an unwelcome sense of déjà vu. Front doors, also known as backdoors, are keys or vulnerabilities that allow third-party access, and law enforcement and information technology companies faced off over the same issue during the "crypto wars" of the early 1990s. At the time, then FBI director Louis Freeh made a similar plea: "We're in favor of strong encryption, robust encryption. The country needs it, industry needs it. We just want to make sure we have a trap door and key under some judge's authority where we can get there if somebody is planning a crime." The solution offered at the time was the clipper chip, which would have kept decryption keys with intelligence and police agencies. The problem then, as now, is that there is no way to build in front- or backdoor access for law enforcement that is not also available to a bad actor. Attempts to add such doors introduce new security flaws. In 2005, for example, a still unknown group hacked a backdoor placed on Greek cell phones by law enforcement. Another group did the same thing in Italy in 2006.[61]

The technology and privacy communities also argue that there really is no risk of the law enforcement and intelligence agencies going dark because we are in fact entering a "golden age" of surveillance. The FBI and others now have the ability to access texts, e-mails, social networking sites, and other data stored in the cloud. Even with encrypted phones, they can obtain more information on potential suspects than ever before. Peter Swire, a Georgia Tech law professor and a member of President Obama's Review Group on Intelligence and Communications Technologies, argues that "the availability of such powerful tools for collecting information means that there is no emergency to justify the built-in surveillance backdoors (or front doors) that FBI Director James Comey, and others in the US government, are pushing for." In addition, the FBI can access information by hacking into devices.[62]

The call for backdoors also has an international ripple effect. At a February 2015 conference, Alex Stamos, formerly Yahoo's chief information security officer and now at Facebook, asked NSA director Michael Rogers, "Should [Yahoo] be building defects into the encryption in our products so that the U.S. government can decrypt?" He then wondered how this would affect Yahoo's operations abroad. "If we're going to build defects/backdoors or golden master keys for the U.S. government, do you believe we should do so—we have about 1.3 billion users around the world—should we do for the Chinese government, the Russian government, the Saudi Arabian government, the Israeli government, the French government?"[63]

Stamos's unease made sense. Just a few weeks later, the Chinese government proposed new antiterrorism laws that would have required foreign companies to hand over encryption keys and install security backdoors. Fu Ying, spokesperson for the National People's Congress, warned the United States not to criticize the policies and demonstrate a double standard: "It is common for the Western countries, such as the United States and Britain, to request tech firms to disclose encryption methods."[64]

By July 2015, the US government and the tech sector had reached a stalemate. Asked by a reporter in April whether he could name a technologist who thought it was possible to build a secure system to which a third party held the key, White House cybersecurity policy coordinator Michael Daniel answered, "I don't have any off the top of my head." He added that if any place could come up with a technological solution, it was the "enormously creative" Silicon Valley. Yet thirteen eminent cryptographers, computer scientists, and security experts published a report three months later arguing that there was no way to provide backdoors without endangering the security of users. Introducing technical access points, the report noted, "will open doors through which criminals and malicious nation-states can attack the very individuals law enforcement seeks to defend. The costs would be substantial, the damage to innovation severe, and the consequences to economic growth hard to predict. The costs to the developed countries' soft power and to our moral authority would also be considerable."[65]

In October 2015, the White House decided that it would not seek legislation to compel technology companies to create backdoors. Policymakers instead would rely on persuasion: "We are actively engaged with private companies to ensure they understand the public safety and national security risks that result from malicious actors' use of their encrypted products and services," said a National Security Council spokesman. The National Security Agency is better placed to deal with the encryption; it can gain access through other measures. The FBI and local police enforcement will face greater technical barriers.[66]

The problem with the encryption standoff, as Stanford University research scientist Herb Lin has pointed out, is that neither side in the debate can prove whether backdoors will make us safer or create a whole new set of vulnerabilities. No one has tried, yet, to build the type of system the FBI would like, and as a result we "see a theological clash of absolutes." Who should build and test this system also remains at issue. In the view of security experts, computer scientists, and technology company managers, the government wants the access, so it should put forward a system for evaluation. From the FBI's and the NSA's perspective, once the government describes what it needs, Silicon Valley should develop the system.

The DNA of US cyber power is a double helix of military strength entwined with the technological prowess of Silicon Valley. The Snowden revelations have, however, set off reactions, at home and abroad, that are cutting the strands and shuffling their components. No matter how the strands get reassembled, Washington needs the relationship repaired. The Department of Defense's research and development budget has shrunk by more than 20 percent since 2010, whereas the tech giants have money and talent. As the White House and the tech companies were waiting to see who would blink first over encryption, Defense Secretary Ashton Carter was out at Stanford announcing that the Pentagon was establishing a new innovation center not far from Google and seeking advice from Facebook on managing high-tech talent. Carter recognized that many software engineers were deeply hostile to military culture and to the DoD's NSA connections, but they were needed to fill out the military's cyber ranks, creating a "force . . . equipped with bold new technology and new ideas."

Carter told reporters, "To be relevant in today's world, you have to have a coolness factor. We want that."[67]

The demands nation-states make on the technology companies are ever expanding. Not only do these companies innovate, commercialize technologies, and provide new services, but they also defend against cyberattacks, uncover espionage campaigns, and help the Pentagon become cooler. And now, US and European governments expect tech companies to help them deliver their diplomatic messages and disrupt those of extremists, jihadists, and rogue states. In an interview before he traveled to Silicon Valley, after the January 2015 terrorist attacks in Paris, French interior minister Bernard Cazeneuve said, "We are facing a new threat. We need tech companies to realize that they have an important role to play." In the hacked world order, partnerships with the private sector are a major sinew of cyber power.[68]

Chapter 7

LET SLIP THE TWITTER
FOLLOWERS OF WAR
INFORMATION, IDEAS, AND LEGITIMACY

● ●

n June 2008, Egypt brokered a six-month "lull" in fighting between Israel and Hamas. The cease-fire agreement had no official text, but the terms included Hamas ending rocket and mortar attacks and Israel easing the embargo on Gaza and ending military raids into the strip. The truce, after a faltering start, dramatically reduced the violence between the two sides. A month before its expected end, on November 4, Israel launched a raid into Gaza, reportedly to destroy a Hamas tunnel. Mortar and rocket fire picked up again and by the end of the month were at pre-truce levels.[1]

During the first weeks of December, as attacks across the border continued in both directions, the two sides laid out the conditions under which they were willing to extend the truce. Late on the morning of December 27, Israel launched airstrikes that hit one hundred targets in less than four minutes. Operation Cast Lead had begun.[2]

During the war, which lasted for three weeks, Israel kept foreign media out of Gaza. Instead the Israel Defense Forces (IDF) introduced their own YouTube channel and provided news updates on Twitter. The channel showed videos of attacks on targets in the Gaza Strip in an effort to illustrate Israeli restraint. In the words of IDF spokeswoman Major Avital Leibovich, the videos demonstrated that "Israel is a moral army with nothing to hide." Many of the videos, filmed from the point of view of the attacker, were grainy, black-and-white shots with targets circled and missiles entering the screen and then exploding. In one video, a helicopter pilot changes the course of a missile when civilians enter the target area; in another, Israeli soldiers visit a mosque located next door to the house of a Hamas leader and discover an antiaircraft cannon and rockets. The IDF also provided early access and briefings to established (and sympathetic) bloggers.[3]

Niv Calderon, a wearable-technology entrepreneur and social media activist, helped organize a parallel media effort called "Help Us Win." Funded by a US advocacy group, Calderon held training courses at the Interdisciplinary Center Herzliya for twenty volunteers, speakers of Dutch, English, French, German, Russian, and Spanish, and armed them with talking points for responding to Israel's critics on Facebook, Twitter, and the group's website, HelpUsWin.org. They also created a Qassam Counter for Facebook; users would "donate" their statuses— short descriptions of where they were, what they were doing, or how they were feeling—which the counter replaced with automatic updates showing when a Qassam rocket had landed in Israel. At its peak, 75,000 users from 150 countries were enrolled. In the immediate months after the conflict, the Israeli Foreign Ministry recruited teams to post positive comments on blogs and news stories and to upload thousands of pictures of solar panel farms, female IDF soldiers, religious sites, and other positive images so that Google searches for the word "Gaza" would be less likely to turn up images of devastation and destruction.

While the social media campaign impressed many at the time— some of the YouTube videos of Israeli airstrikes had over 2 million views—it was ad hoc and failed to exploit the full potential of the new tools. Social media accounts were set up immediately prior to the invasion of Gaza, making them look more like propaganda organs than legitimate sources of information. In addition, many of the YouTube videos featured a spokesperson standing in a room with an Israeli flag to the side. The scene did not have the air of a casual conversation in a more informal setting. Twitter updates were filled with military jargon. Most importantly, none of the channels engaged the audiences. The IDF did not respond to viewers or others on Twitter, and the account went quiet for 179 days once the cease-fire went into effect.[4]

If social media platforms were new fields in a battle for world opinion in 2008, then Operation Cast Lead raised serious questions about what Israeli engagement could hope to achieve. The IDF's tweets and YouTube posts aimed to explain the morality of the war, but they did not have the same power as pictures of the destruction in Gaza. The high number of civilian casualties led to renewed efforts to isolate Israel internationally. Most damaging was the 2009 UN Fact-Finding Mission on the Gaza Conflict, also known as the Goldstone Report, which accused the IDF and Hamas of war crimes and claimed it was Israeli policy to target civilians.[5]

Seeing the need to further sharpen its engagement, at the end of 2009 the IDF announced a plan to draft computer and media experts into a new social media unit, the IDF New Media Desk. The unit, led by American-born First Lieutenant Aliza Landes and staffed by approximately ten social media experts, immediately began preparing for the next conflict. Or as one senior member of the new team put it, "We gather Twitter followers in times of peace, so that they are ready to disseminate our message when we are at war."[6]

Soon after it was established, the New Media Desk confronted the difficulty of controlling the narrative. In May 2010, international activists organized the "Freedom Flotilla" aimed at breaking Israel's blockade of Gaza. The organizers provided updates on Facebook, Twitter, YouTube, and other social media sites; they plotted the progress of the ships with blue dots on Google Maps. As the flotilla sailed from Cyprus to Gaza, the Israeli navy tried to jam communications, but organizers managed to continue to get their message to supporters. A quarter million people watched the live stream.[7]

At 4 a.m. on May 31, commandos raided the Turkish ship *Mavi Marmara*, the lead vessel in the convoy, in international waters, killing nine people and detaining several hundred others in the Israeli city of Ashdod. Israeli forces quickly confiscated media equipment as they boarded the ship and stopped the live streaming, but news of the raid spread rapidly, and information continued to leak throughout the day. Israel did not respond until noon, by which point negative stories and images had flooded social media.

As with the Gaza conflict, Israel tried to counter the story that it had acted excessively or irresponsibly, that it had massacred peaceful activists on a humanitarian mission. Using video shot by the commandos and seized from the activists and journalists on the ship, the IDF posted more than twenty clips to YouTube showing what it described as commandos being attacked as they landed on the deck, activists throwing stun grenades, and a collection of knives, slingshots, rocks, and smoke bombs found on board. As with Operation Cast Lead, action videos were the most popular; clips of commandos rappelling from the helicopter to the deck racked up 1.2 million views in a day.[8]

But the incident was a diplomatic disaster. In the hours after the raid, at the United Nations, Turkey's foreign minister Ahmet Devutoğlu called the Israeli raid "tantamount to banditry and piracy. It is murder conducted by a state." Turkey recalled its ambassador from Israel and canceled three joint military exercises. Pro-Palestinian activists quickly countered the IDF on social media, purporting to show how the IDF manipulated images and misleadingly captioned videos. Several months after the actual raid, a group posted a mashup video titled "Internet Killed Israeli PR," mocking Israeli spokesmen and the New Media Desk by interspersing footage from Israeli coverage of the conflict with images of cats, Barbra Streisand, and other Internet memes, set to reworked lyrics sung along to the music of "Video Killed the Radio Star."[9]

Within Israel, the sense pervaded that the IDF had completely lost the media war. Amir Mizroch, executive editor of the *Jerusalem Post*, wrote, "For a country so technologically advanced, and with such acute public diplomacy challenges, to fail so miserably at preparing a communications offensive over new media is a failure of strategic proportions." An official investigation found the IDF slow to release images of the raid. It did not post videos said to show passengers beating the commandos until 10 p.m. on May 31. In spreading its message, the prime minister's office failed to differentiate between domestic and international audiences. There was, moreover, little Arabic-language outreach in the period preceding and following the *Marmara* raid.[10]

Even with the clear democratizing and destabilizing potential of social media, it is important to note that Israeli videos are often viewed in vastly larger numbers than those produced by others with alternate views, and still Israeli analysts see the IDF as having lost the conflict. By August 2014, viewers had watched "Internet Killed Israeli PR" slightly more than 42,000 times. A pro-Israel, antiactivist video, "Flotilla Choir Presents: We Con the World," had more than 2.6 million views. The first video is more Internet savvy. The Israeli video—set to the tune of "We Are the World" and featuring Israelis dressed as Arabs and activists waving weapons—is more than a little cringe inducing; the Israeli government eventually apologized for distributing it. Page views were not enough to counter the reality that social media were primarily reaching those already sympathetic to Israel and that the Jewish state's international standing was falling precipitously.[11]

GAZA: THE FIRST TWITTER WAR

By the time of the 2012 and 2014 Gaza conflicts, Israel had expanded the reach and resources of the social media units within the IDF and Foreign Ministry, but it still struggled to engage audiences in cyberspace. Israel used Twitter to announce that it had launched a "widespread campaign on terror sites & operatives in the #GazaStrip, chief among them #Hamas & Islamic Jihad targets," and the 2012 conflict was quickly tagged the first "Twitter war." The IDF's New Media Desk also posted photos to Flickr and updated Facebook pages, and in numerous interviews with US and British media outlets, unit members reinforced the conflation of social media and military conflict inherent in the term "Twitter war." IDF media spokespeople referred constantly to wars of ideas, campaigns, deployments, and rules of engagement.[12]

The IDF and Hamas, under the handles @IDFspokesman and @AlQassambrigade, both tweeted approximately twenty times a day, though they could reach ninety tweets in a day during the 2012 conflict. The IDF ran a running tally of rockets launched from Gaza and introduced a series of graphics of missiles raining down on the Eiffel Tower, Statue of Liberty, and Big Ben, with the tagline "What Would You Do?" While the IDF frequently linked to external news sources, Hamas made greater use of photos; about 20 percent more of its tweets contained images, often of destroyed buildings and people killed in airstrikes. By the end of the conflict, followers of @IDFspokesman had increased by 146,000, or about three times; of @AlQassambrigade, by 39,000, or twelve times.[13]

After a cease-fire went into effect in the third week of November, representatives of the two sides continued the conflict in cyberspace. In response to the assassination of Hamas military chief Ahmed al-Jabari, Anonymous launched its #OpIsrael Campaign, attacking websites belonging to the Israel Defense Forces, the prime minister's office, Israeli banks, and airlines. Although Israeli businesses, the Shin Bet, and military cyber forces defeated most of the attacks, they continued for weeks.

Both sides tried to mobilize international support in cyberspace across Facebook, Google, Pinterest, and Tumblr. Israel encouraged supporters to retweet its messages under the hashtag #IsraelUnderFire or #PillarOfDefense, the official name of the operation. Palestinians deployed the hashtags #GazaUnderSiege and #GazaUnderAttack, which reached a peak of 170,000 mentions in a single day, compared to only 25,000 mentions for #IsraelUnderFire. There was little contact or cross communication, with less than 10 percent overlap in conversations, and 94 percent of the discussion took place outside Israel and Gaza.

Much of the social media played to the base, appealing to supporters and doing little to convince the other side or to sway neutral or uncommitted observers. This may make sense given the high degree of homophily demonstrated on social media. As many have pointed out, social networks demonstrate the principle that similar individuals tend to group together, and people choose their Facebook friends and whom to follow on Twitter based on their worldviews. So supporters of Israel "friend" other supporters of Israel and are unlikely to follow the bloggers of Electronic Intifada. The algorithms Facebook and other social media firms use to determine which news people should see can reinforce this homophily: the more you engage with a certain type of news story, the more similar content is made available to you.

But if Israel was trying to reach third-party observers, its message missed. Many found Israel's boasting about the technological sophistication of its airstrikes callous in the face of civilian casualties. Hussein Ibish, a senior fellow at the American Task Force on Palestine and a moderate voice committed to a two-state solution to the decades-old conflict, tweeted, "This is extremely damning. IDF cheerily live-tweets infanticide."[14]

While al-Jabari, the Islamic Jihad leader assassinated at the beginning of the conflict, posed a clear terrorist threat, tweeting his picture emblazoned with the word "ELIMINATED" was likely to negatively influence those skeptical of Israeli actions. As Michael Koplow of the Israel Institute wrote, European publics and others were already inclined to "cast a wary eye on Israeli militarism and martial behavior, and crowing about killing anyone or glorifying Israeli operations in Gaza is a bad public relations strategy insofar as it feeds directly into the fear of Israel run amok with no regard for the collateral damage being caused." Writing in the left-leaning newspaper *Haaretz*, Anshel Pfeffer argued that you can "cut and polish diamonds, but there's no way to transform a bombed-out house with its residents still inside and dead babies being dug out of the rubble into a PR coup." The best Israel could hope for was a "tie."[15]

Operation Protective Edge, the 2014 conflict in Gaza, repeated most of the battlefield and social media events of its predecessor. Israeli attacks killed more than 2,100, including about 500 children, and left more than 100,000 homeless. Hamas fired over 4,500 rockets into Israel, killing six civilians. Sixty-seven soldiers died during the wars. After fifty days of fighting, the two sides agreed to a cease-fire that changed almost nothing on the ground.

Again Israel strove to demonstrate that it was acting responsibly. The New Media Desk and IDF spokesmen tweeted images of weapons stores in mosques and UN schools and rockets being fired from highly populated areas, providing evidence of what the IDF described as not just Hamas's indifference to civilian casualties but, in fact, its conscious effort to produce, in Prime Minister Benjamin Netanyahu's infelicitous phrase, "telegenically dead Palestinians."[16]

Using the hashtags #GazaUnderAttack, #Gaza, #StopIsrael, and #PrayForGaza, Hamas defended its actions and stressed the plight of Palestinian civilians. For Palestinian supporters, social media offered an important way to sidestep what they saw as pro-Israel bias in the mainstream media. In a few instances, the two sides directly addressed each other. Hamas posted a music video, sung in Hebrew and Arabic, showing rockets being transported and fired at Israel, perhaps in an effort to undermine morale and support for the government.

Despite all the money invested over the decade and the increasingly sophisticated graphics and apps, it was hard to say Israel was gaining any ground in the social media war. From July 26 until August 25, the hashtag promoted by Israel's supporters, #IsraelUnderFire, was tweeted over 320,000 times; the hashtag of supporters of Palestine,

#GazaUnderAttack, got over 3.6 million tweets. Compared to 2010 and 2012, the stakes seemed larger on Twitter. This in part reflected the growing importance of Twitter as a platform—the service now had a 100 million more users than it did in 2012.

More importantly, Twitter had become an essential tool for journalists on the ground. Many witnessed the destruction firsthand, and some were present as children died. Their tweets had an immediacy and emotional punch often edited out in their formal reporting. *New York Times* reporter Anne Barnard tweeted of the death of a girl, "In ER, girl, 9?, lies still, staring. No relative w/her. Docs gently check pulse, again & again, until it's time. A white sheet & she's gone." But as author and journalist Gal Beckerman notes, newspapers strive for balance and impartiality, and the article Barnard eventually wrote described the girl's death in much less detail, in several paragraphs near the end, after providing much more context about the fighting. No narrative Israel could provide on social media would counter these directly felt emotions delivered through Twitter.[17]

Israel's international standing suffered everywhere, except perhaps the United States. The White House publicly declared it was "appalled" by the "disgraceful" shelling of a UN school, but the American public continued to show strong support for Israel during the conflict. Polls showed Israel losing sympathy in Europe, and a number of governments warned citizens against doing business with Israeli companies located in settlements in the West Bank. Prominent American, European, and Israeli liberal Zionists—supporters of the project of building a Jewish homeland and a separate Palestinian state in the occupied West Bank—despaired of the war and the future. The immediacy of social media did not cause this alienation, but it highlighted an inescapable characteristic of the asymmetric conflict in Gaza: the majority of casualties would be Palestinian citizens.

TROLLS FOR CHINA AND RUSSIA

If social media campaigns have indirect if marginal effects on opinion during high-stakes, high-intensity conflicts, they can redirect and obfuscate during longer-term campaigns. The goal is often to have bad information crowd out the good. In March 2012, if you attempted

to tweet about Tibet or retweet a story about Tibetans setting themselves on fire, you would have been drowned out on Twitter. Several
hundred bots (automated programs that generate content) flooded
discussions using the hashtags #Tibet and #freetibet with meaningless
tweets and spam. A sea of garbage swamped discussion by real Tibetans and experts. Twitter eventually shut down the bots and slowed the
spam to a drip.[18]

Two years later, if you were still interested in Tibet, you might have
decided to follow Tom Hugo. His profile photo displayed an attractive
man showing off his washboard abs on a beach. Tom tweeted videos
of happy Tibetans singing and dancing on Chinese state-run television and linked to stories about bumper harvests in Tibet. Tom was
a fake, as were hundreds of other attractive people tweeting Potem-
kin village–like stories about Tibet. The profile photo was actually
of a Brazilian model named Felipe Berto, and every story and video
tweeted came from a Chinese propaganda website. One account even
used a photograph of Syd Barrett, the late Pink Floyd vocalist, to push
out pro-government messages.[19]

As with all hacking and activism, it is hard to say with any certainty
who is behind these actions. We do not know the Internet protocol (IP)
addresses of the people who set up the Twitter bots, and even if we did,
they can mask their true location with proxies. But China has a clear
motive to shape the discussion about Tibet and other sensitive issues
globally. In addition, China's active policy of "Internet public opinion
guidance" attempts to steer public discussion on the web at home. The
use of fake Twitter accounts echoes the efforts of the so-called Fifty
Cent Party, a collective of Internet commenters reportedly paid 0.5
renminbi (about 8 US cents) per comment on stories in an effort to
sway domestic public opinion on politically sensitive issues. The Chinese government pays an estimated 250,000 to 300,000 people in the
"party" to cultivate anti-American and pro–Chinese Communist Party
sentiment. One fifty-center described receiving an e-mail every morning from the local Internet office telling him what news stories to focus
on that day.[20]

These actions reflect both how serious the Chinese leadership
takes the Internet and China's lack of soft power. As a September
2013 *Beijing Daily* article explained, "The Internet has become a main

battlefield in today's ideological war. . . . If we don't seize control of [it], someone else will." The official response to the wave of Tibetan self-immolations, which began in 2011 and was still occurring in 2015, sounded ham-handed and insensitive to Western ears, especially given the popularity of the Dalai Lama, Tibet's exiled spiritual leader. As the Western media sympathetically reported on the Tibetan protests, the Chinese press and government officials doubled down on their vilification of the Dalai Lama for "inciting splittism," calling him a "jackal" and a "wolf in sheep's clothing." The self-immolators were "criminals." Within China the authorities responded with harassment of activists and mass arrests.[21]

The Kremlin's theory of influence also relies greatly on mass disinformation. Russia has mobilized an army of trolls, part of a larger information war to legitimize its actions and divide, distract, and disturb its opponents in and out of Russia. Internet trolls post inflammatory or off-topic comments in a deliberate attempt to provoke or distract opponents. During the conflict in Ukraine, Russian television ceaselessly portrayed Kiev as fascist and neo-Nazi, playing up the threat to the Russian-speaking minority in the east of the country. Russian media repeated fake news stories. The goal, according to author and producer Peter Pomerantsev, "seems [to have been] less to establish alternative truths than to spread confusion about the status of truth."[22]

At the same time, the Kremlin reportedly paid English-speaking Russians to post pro-Putin and pro-Moscow comments on the websites of US and UK media outlets. A moderator who vets comments on the *Guardian*'s websites said, "Zealous pro-separatist comments in broken English claiming to be from Western countries are very common, and there's a list of tropes we've learned to look out for." Even more aggressively, Russian trolls are thought to be responsible for the online rumors in the United States of an Ebola outbreak in Atlanta, a chemical leak in Louisiana, and the lethal shooting of an unarmed black woman by police in the wake of the shooting in Ferguson, Missouri.[23]

Hacked e-mails and documents released to *BuzzFeed* revealed Moscow's hand in some of these posts. According to the e-mails, the Internet Research Agency, based in St. Petersburg, managed a strategy to influence the discussion of the crisis in Ukraine on behalf of the Kremlin. The documents detail the workload demanded of each

Internet troll based on anxiety that the foreign press was forming negative views of Russia and that "in the foreign Internet community, the ratio of supporters and opponents of Russia is about 20/80 respectively." The Internet Research Agency expected trolls to maintain six Facebook accounts and ten Twitter accounts, tweeting fifty times a day. The documents also described how posters should comment on the websites of Fox, *Politico*, and the *Huffington Post*. It is hard to imagine that any of the posts had any effect on Western opinions of Russia or Vladimir Putin, as they were often laughably macho or sophomoric. The goal, as with most trolling, was to make reasonable, rational conversation impossible.[24]

(The trolling was taken all the way to the top. Dmitry Rogozin, deputy prime minister of Russia and special envoy of the president, tweeted a photo with side-by-side images of Putin and Barack Obama. Putin, seated, wearing jeans and a black jacket, cuddles with a leopard. Obama, standing in a suit, holds a fluffy white dog. The caption reads, "We have different values and allies.")[25]

China and Russia have often used a torrent of noise to drown out competing messages. Social media amplify their propaganda, and anonymity obscures the ulterior motives of those spreading content. Reality becomes increasingly indistinguishable from simulacra of it. By contrast, the United States has faltered in efforts to create an alternative message for those potentially tempted to go down the road of extremist violence. After the Islamic State in Iraq and Syria (ISIS), also known as the Islamic State in Iraq and the Levant, managed to take over almost a third of Syria in 2013 and the Iraqi city of Fallujah in January 2014, it burst into the conscience of the wider American public in June 2014. ISIS forces swept into Mosul and advanced within sixty miles of Baghdad, drawing the United States back into conflict in Iraq.

ISIS conquests on the ground were accompanied by an information campaign so slick that the online magazine *Vice* called the group "total social media pros." As ISIS approached the Iraqi capital, users who searched for "Baghdad" in Arabic on Twitter found the top image showed ISIS's black flag flying over Baghdad and the warning "Baghdad, we're coming." According to J. M. Berger, an analyst of online jihadism, ISIS tweeted almost 40,000 times in one day; ISIS followers and others around the world then retweeted those tweets. ISIS also developed its own app for the web and Android phones called The Dawn of Glad Tidings. Supporters who downloaded the app gave ISIS authority to post from their Twitter accounts, which allowed the group to use hundreds of accounts to coordinate campaigns and get its own hashtags trending.[26]

Brutality and barbarism, packaged with sophisticated production techniques, became integral to ISIS's social media campaigns, which are broadcast in at least twenty-three languages. The ISIS media unit produced the videos of the beheadings of American journalists James Wright Foley and Steven Sotloff. It also tweeted photos of massacres of Iraqi and Syrian prisoners and crucifixions of Christians and members of the minority Yazidi faith. Yet the campaign also worked to portray ISIS fighters as "normal people who love to goof around with each other," in the words of one tweet. Militants posted pictures of kittens, sunset shots framed with guns in the foreground, and comrades holding jars of Nutella in grocery stores.[27]

ISIS is, of course, not the first to exploit the Internet. Terrorist organizations have for two decades relied on the web for training and recruitment, radicalization, and fund-raising. In a 2002 letter to Mullah Omar, head of the Taliban, Osama bin Laden wrote, "It is obvious that the media war in this century is one of the strongest methods; in fact, its ratio may reach 90 percent of the total preparation for the battles." Websites and social media allow groups to reach out to geographically dispersed individuals, make them feel part of a larger community, and over time radicalize their views. The late Anwar Al-Awlaki, the Yemen-based US-born cleric, used e-mails, blogs, discussions, chat rooms, videos, and the English-language online magazine *Inspire* to publicize al-Qaeda's cause and to recruit new members.[28]

According to Gabriel Weimann, professor of communications at the University of Haifa, the number of websites run by terrorists climbed from a dozen in 1998, to nearly 5,000 in mid-2006, to over 9,800 in 2014. Deprived of physical spaces and training camps by the invasion of Afghanistan and drone attacks in Pakistan, Yemen, and elsewhere, terrorists moved to the Internet to post audios and videos of attacks, as well as technical instructions: how to build pressure cooker or car bombs, make high-quality forgeries, encrypt documents, and use the web under the radar of Western intelligence.[29]

By the mid-2000s, wanting to target younger audiences, al-Qaeda and other terrorist groups migrated much of their content from static websites to Facebook, Instagram, Twitter, YouTube, and other social media networks. Terrorists also moved to social media as Western law and intelligence agencies monitored and attacked their websites. Constant hacking and removal by Western counterterrorist agencies, for example, made it necessary for al-Qaeda to use Twitter to direct followers to new sites to find content. In one attack, the United Kingdom's Government Communications Headquarters scrambled the online content of *Inspire*, replacing an article titled "How to Build a Bomb in the Kitchen of Your Mom" with cupcake recipes. In response, terrorists cycled through different media for different purposes, using YouTube to attract new recruits and instant messaging to develop closer contact and further indoctrination, eventually moving to a point where the relationship had grown close enough to start planning attacks.[30]

In another advantage, social media pushes out information rapidly. Twitter in particular gives terrorist groups a tool to distribute information in real time. During a September 2013 attack on the Westgate Mall in Nairobi, Kenya, a location popular with Westerners and middle-class Kenyans, the Somalia-based al-Shabaab tweeted live updates glorifying the militants and taunting the Kenyan government. "The Mujahideen entered Westgate mall today at around noon and they are still inside the mall, fighting the Kenyan *kuffar* [nonbelievers] inside their own turf," tweeted the account @HSM_Press-Shabaab. The feeds were tailored to different audiences, and each time Twitter closed an account tied to the group, a new one popped up in its place.[31]

The fact that the Western mainstream media is often not on the ground magnifies the impact of these tweets and thus the political impact of al-Shabaab, ISIS, and others. Financial cutbacks have reduced foreign bureaus, and the battlegrounds are often too dangerous for journalists. As a result, reporters turn to Twitter as a news source. Some of the tweets flesh out the reporting, giving it an on-the-ground feel, but in some instances unverified or false information gets repeated, hyping the importance of a group or an event that may in fact be marginal.

While completely abhorrent to most, ISIS's social media usage has a strategic logic. As Berger writes, "Fear and brutality are a crucial part of its strategy to win on the ground, by amplifying fear and demoralizing those who might stand up to it." Of great importance to ISIS is proving that it has superseded al-Qaeda and should receive the support of Sunnis sympathetic to jihad against Europe and the United States. Or as one American official told the *New York Times*, "ISIS is able to hold itself up as the true jihad." Another set of messages—about ISIS providing social services and fighters distributing food—bolsters the group's identity as an insurgent militia intent on seizing territory and serves as evidence that it can govern Sunni areas justly and efficiently.[32]

The social messaging helped ISIS force its way into the consciousness of the American public. The beheading videos, in particular, played a large role in shifting the political ground. President Barack Obama, who had earlier called the Islamic State al-Qaeda's "jayvee team," gave a prime-time address explaining the threat the group posed to the nation. In an October 2014 NBC/*Wall Street Journal* poll, 94 percent of Americans said they were following the news of the journalists' beheadings, an astounding number considering the traditional lack of awareness of foreign affairs among the American public (in the same poll, less than 40 percent knew who the prime minister of Israel was). ISIS's brutality also managed to accomplish what nothing else has: to unite Egypt, the Gulf States, Iran, Iraq, the Kurds, Saudi Arabia, Syria, Turkey, and the United States in destroying a common enemy. Although not a strategy for long-term viability, the brutality serves the Islamic State's goal of provoking a region-wide war or, if you believe that ISIS is an apocalyptic group, an "end of days" battle.[33]

ISIS's messaging draws a surprising number of American and European recruits. In 2014, the Soufan Group, a strategic security consulting company, found that about 3,000 Westerners were fighting in Syria for various groups opposing the Bashar al-Assad regime, and US intelligence officials estimate that close to a dozen Americans have joined ISIS. By September 2015, intelligence and law officials estimated there were 4,500 Westerners, including 250 Americans, who had entered Iraq and Syria to join ISIS. Radicalization is a complex process, however, and the consumption of extremist videos and tweets is only one factor in the decision to become a jihadi. While a growing body of research has begun to identify a few general trends, it is still impossible to predict who will become radicalized regardless of the social media consumed. Moreover, much of the attraction of the Islamic State has derived from its success on the battlefield and ability to seize territory, not from tweets about fighters finding Nutella in grocery stores.[34]

The US and European governments have vacillated between blocking ISIS and other groups from using Internet platforms to radicalize, recruit, and motivate and disrupting or competing with the Islamic State's narrative. For liberal democracies, taking down content and accounts raises obvious sensitivities about free speech rights, which Islamic State supporters often exploit by skating near but not crossing the line of protected speech. Twitter, which once identified itself as "the free speech wing of the free speech party," has had to balance an aversion to censoring material with a strong desire not to be associated with or held responsible for brutal images and words.

It is nearly impossible for social media corporations to prevent terrorists from posting content on their sites. Too much information gets uploaded at any one time; one hundred hours of video, for instance, were uploaded to YouTube every minute in 2014. Companies do take down accounts for violating terms of service that prohibit the promotion of violence, but historically they do this only after other users complain, not after conducting an active search for such material. Twitter, for example, removed an image of Jim Foley being murdered and suspended accounts only after users flagged the content as inappropriate. Even then, the image continued to circulate for several days after Twitter announced that it was suspending accounts, as Islamic State supporters moved quickly to register new accounts.

While the companies rely on users to flag offensive content, tech company employees are not equipped to distinguish between free speech content and tweets, posts, or videos that promote terrorist violence. Liberal societies do not want to delegate these types of decisions to private businesses and so have searched for ways to involve the government in takedown decisions. In March 2015, the European Union proposed the creation of an Internet Referral Unit that, as part of the law enforcement agency Europol, would remove extremist material from the Internet. This model is based on the Counter Terrorism Internet Referral Unit (CTIRU) set up by the UK government in 2010. The CTIRU cooperates with technology companies in identifying content to be removed. Counterterrorism officers have special privileges that allow them to flag online content for instant moderation by Google and other services. By March 2015, CTIRU had removed 75,000 pieces of online extremist material.[35]

Under pressure from governments and the public, Twitter has become proactive on suspension. On one day in April 2015, the company suspended 10,000 accounts in response to violent threats directed at activists. People like to use the "whack-a mole" image to suggest that new accounts will spring up as soon as old ones are taken down, but research conducted by J. M. Berger demonstrates that taking accounts offline does hurt. At the least, new accounts have to build up new follower lists, which is time-consuming and can take several months. Between July and October 2014, when Twitter actively removed ISIS accounts, the number of retweets by ISIS users went down, and the quality of interactions declined. The takedowns also limited ISIS's ability to broadcast its message beyond its core supporters. Berger's research suggests that, given Twitter's massive computing resources and rapid access to user data, the company could deny use of the platform to ISIS, reducing its ranks "to as few as a couple hundred hyper-committed supporters with negligible influence." That ISIS began threatening Twitter employees with assassination suggests the suspensions were causing the group some pain.[36]

Having Islamic State fighters maintain a limited presence on social media has benefits for intelligence collection. Through tweets and videos, intelligence agencies have learned a great deal about how ISIS operates, the structure of the organization, and its partners. Despite warnings from ISIS social media units, many fighters failed to turn off the geolocation markers in their Twitter feeds, allowing counterterrorism officials to locate them. Moreover, intelligence agencies are likely to have approached Twitter and Facebook for information about individual accounts, such as the IP addresses or e-mails used to open them. In June 2015, General Hawk Carlisle, commander of the US Air Combat Command, announced that the air force had launched three bombs at an ISIS headquarters. Intelligence officers were combing "through social media and they see some moron standing at this command," Carlisle said. "So they do some work," the general continued. "Long story short, about twenty-two hours later through that very building, three JDAMs [Joint Direct Attack Munitions] take that entire building out. Through social media. It was a post on social media. Bombs on target in 22 hours."[37]

The US government has not been of one mind about whether to keep extremists online. In 2008, the CIA and the Saudi government were running a honeypot for extremists, a fake forum covertly monitored for information on possible attacks in Iraq and other countries in the region. This enabled Saudi police to round up a number of potential attackers early in their preparations. US Cyber Command wanted to take the site offline, and it did, over CIA protests, ending the counterterrorism operation and inadvertently disrupting more than three hundred servers in Germany, Saudi Arabia, and Texas.[38]

THE LAST THREE FEET

The US struggle to develop public diplomacy that balances competing interests and delivers an effective message through social media stems in part from neglect. Public diplomacy usually involves efforts to communicate a country's polices and values to the people of another nation. The objective is influence—to shape the perception of foreign audiences in order to advance foreign policy goals. During the Cold War, the United States accomplished this by beaming Voice of America and Radio Free Europe messages to audiences in Eastern Europe. This was a broadcasting model, a discussion in one direction from the few to the many.

With the advent of social media, foreign ministries began to believe that they could traverse what journalist Edward R. Murrow called the "last three feet": "The real crucial link in the international exchange is the last three feet, which is bridged by personal contact, one person talking to another." A network-based and horizontal model of interaction that would build direct relationships with national audiences, civil society groups, and even individuals would span this gap. Interactive discussions would replace broadcasting.

Social media and Twitter diplomacy have been especially useful for small states with clearly defined agendas. Two of the most skillful users of social media are Carl Bildt and Toomas Hendrik Ilves. Bildt, whose Twitter handle reads, "Entrepreneur in future and peace. Before that most other things," was formerly Sweden's prime minister and foreign minister. Bildt uses his platform to promote online freedom and shape Europe's response to Russian encroachment into Ukraine. On November 19, 2014, for example, Bildt tweeted a picture of a Russian T-72BM tank, with timelines of its sighting in east Ukraine, commenting, "President Putin still denies that his army is in Ukraine. He must believe we are complete fools."[39]

While Hillary Clinton had almost 13 million Facebook fans, 2 million Twitter followers, and more than 16 million video views as secretary of state, these numbers could not hide the fact that the US government's public diplomacy capabilities had atrophied after at least a decade of disregard. With the 1999 merger of the US Information Agency with the State Department, the number of public diplomacy officers fell, and funding was cut for Radio Free Europe. New efforts like Radio Sawa and Alhurra television failed to attract audiences in the Arab world, and some evidence suggests that attitudes toward American foreign policy actually became worse after people listened to and watched these stations.[40]

Facebook, Tumblr, Twitter, YouTube, and others provided new platforms and opportunities. In her confirmation hearing, Judith McHale, former president and CEO of Discovery Communications and President Obama's first undersecretary of state for public diplomacy and public affairs, spoke of social media as providing "the opportunity to move from an old paradigm in which our government speaks as one to many, to a new model of engaging interactively and collaboratively across lines that might otherwise divide us from people around the world."[41]

Due to social media's privileging of networks over hierarchies, what many called public diplomacy 2.0 required cultural and organizational changes. Or as James K. Glassman, undersecretary for public diplomacy and public affairs in the George W. Bush administration, put it in 2008, "PD 2.0 is an approach, not a technology." Historically, embassies prefer to say as little as possible publicly, and when they do communicate, they prefer the more controlled mechanism of print. Most diplomats are risk averse; a poorly chosen statement to the media or an inept post on social media can end a career. Even as US embassies moved more content online, their sites tended to be boring and uninformative. In 2005, Pakistan suffered a devastating earthquake that killed more than 70,000 people and destroyed more than 600,000 homes. The United States provided $200 million in relief. US military helicopters flew more than 4,600 missions, and medical teams treated approximately 35,000 patients. Yet a survey of US embassy websites in countries where Muslims are a majority or constitute a significant portion of the population revealed that most had not put anything up about US aid relief to Pakistan.[42]

A change in presentation and style could address these deficits in part, but the larger problem, according to Glassman, and a major source of animosity toward the United States was the perception, especially among the young, that the United States did not "respect their opinions, that we do not actively listen and understand." The response should be "not to lecture them or tell them what to think or how wonderful we are." Rather a US diplomat should act as "a facilitator or convener," in order for the United States to have its ideas heard and be seen as "a society that itself hears and respects the views of others."[43]

The move to public diplomacy 2.0 began under the Bush administration and accelerated under President Obama. It became personalized in Alex Ross and Jared Cohen, two young, tech-savvy State Department advisers with hundreds of thousands of followers on Twitter, whom the *New York Times Sunday Magazine* profiled. Countless news stories showed Ross, the first senior adviser for innovation to the secretary of state, and Cohen, who served on the policy planning staffs of Condoleezza Rice and Hillary Clinton, tweeting current events and pop culture, visiting the Googleplex, leading tech delegations to Iraq, Russia, and Mexico, and discussing how to remake US embassies online.[44]

The inaugural event for these efforts was Obama's Cairo speech in June 2009. The president's call for better relations with the Arab world was webcast live, and translated versions of the speech were available on Facebook, MySpace, and YouTube, as well as on the popular South Asian networking site Orkut. Portions of the speech were transmitted by text message to mobile phones in more than 170 countries.

If Cairo became synonymous with a high point of digital diplomacy, the metropolis also became associated with how it could go off the rails. On September 11, 2012, as outrage spread across the Muslim world over an anti-Mohammed video posted on YouTube, US embassy officials posted and tweeted a statement saying, "We firmly reject the actions by those who abuse the universal right of free speech to hurt the religious beliefs of others." A little after midnight on September 12, after a day of protests and demonstrators breaching the embassy's gates, officials tweeted, "This morning's condemnation (issued before protests began) still stands. As does condemnation of unjustified breach of the Embassy." Republicans quickly seized on the tweets as proof of President Obama's willingness to cave to the demands of Islamists, and the Mitt Romney campaign called them "shameful." Many who were not looking to use the missteps in a political campaign were still dismayed by the embassy's initial failure to defend the principle that even offensive speech deserves protection.[45]

The Obama administration distanced itself from the statement; the tweets were deleted and the public affairs officer recalled to Washington. In the wake of the controversy, the State Department reportedly considered a two-day review for all tweets. To succeed, a tweet must be speedy and often personal and witty. A two-day delay would have completely enfeebled US diplomats' efforts to use social media. So while State Department tweets are often reviewed, the process does not take forty-eight hours.[46]

US efforts to engage the Muslim world have swung from gentle conversation to something more like trolling. The State Department's Digital Outreach Team, made up of Arabic, Punjabi, Somali, and Urdu speakers, tried to reach "swing voters," Muslims, and others on BBC, Al Jazeera, and Arabic-language forums who might sympathize with al-Qaeda and other terrorist organizations, yet remain open to information about US government policy. Unlike the Internet trolls paid by the Chinese and Russian governments who operate in the shadows, members of the digital team identified themselves as State Department representatives. This was part of an effort to educate and persuade, to tell America's story and undercut the attraction of violent extremism. The outreach however, at least according to one study, did little to moderate anti-Americanism, and only 4 percent of those surveyed expressed positive views of the content the team posted.[47]

In 2011, the president and the secretary of state established the Center for Strategic Counterterrorism Communications (CSCC) as part of the National Strategy for Counterterrorism. The strategy recognized that "the Internet has become an increasingly potent element in radicalization to violence" and committed to developing "a separate, more comprehensive strategy for countering and preventing violent extremist online radicalization." The comprehensive strategy was never released, but in the CSCC gentle argument evolved for a while into a sharper-edged engagement. As the group's director, Alberto Fernandez, said in an interview, CSCC began "contesting a space" that had "previously been conceded to the enemy." "Our goal is not to make people love the U.S. Our goal is to make al-Qaeda look bad." CSCC began challenging extremists and sympathizers directly, exposing what it saw as hypocrisy and stupidity. The tone turned negative and combative.[48]

In targeting the Islamic State, CSCC used the hashtag #thinkagainturnaway and promised to deliver "some truths about terrorism." It tweeted stories about people arrested while making their way to fight for ISIS and about Kurdish and Lebanese forces making gains against the militia, as well as arguments that ISIS killings violated Islamic law. CSCC spoke directly to ISIS supporters and sympathizers, telling one who compared the United States and its allies to the Crusaders that ISIS in fact consisted of "modern-day conquerors—they invade, kill Muslims, take land, loot & steal, terrorize & enslave #Shameful." When Abu Bakr al-Baghdadi declared a new caliphate ruled by ISIS, the State Department questioned whether he was wearing a luxury watch, calling out the incongruity between the expensive timepiece and his self-portrayed humility and modesty.[49]

Outside media specialists have questioned whether a bureaucracy like the State Department is flexible, adaptable, and essentially cool enough to have an impact on the Twitter dialogue. Writer Jacob Silverman likened CSCC's tweets to "someone's dad showing up at a college party" and criticized the center's verbal style and use of graphics and fonts. To succeed, CSCC would need more leeway to fail, which is unlikely in a highly partisan environment. Moreover, there is a question of resources. The center's budget is small—in the realm of $10 million—and the CSCC does not have the capacity to generate the volume of content to disrupt Islamic State messaging. CSCC did create a video, called "Welcome to ISIS Land," that went viral in the summer of 2014. Using footage shot by the Islamic State of severed heads, executions, and crucifixions, the video amassed more than 850,000 views.[50]

But the video also drew criticism from the White House and other parts of the State Department, which saw it as embracing the Islamic State's tactics and counterproductive to US goals. The extreme violence garnered attention but was not off-putting to Islamic State supporters. Fernandez lost his job, and the CSCC was told to stop trolling ISIS. The strategy would return to a more factual, counternarrative approach. "When amplified properly, we believe the facts speak for themselves," said Rashad Hussain, the new director.[51]

The government, of course, is not the only actor and, in fact, is probably not going to be the dominant voice in countering ISIS online. Local Syrians and Iraqis active on Twitter and Facebook provide counternarratives and mock ISIS fighters. In February 2015, for example, Syrians living in the ISIS-occupied towns of Raqqah and Abu Kamal harassed and heckled fighters and documented the brutal conditions. Several activist groups actively report Islamic State accounts for closure and promote competing messages; Anonymous claimed responsibility for taking down nearly eight hundred Twitter accounts, twelve Facebook pages, and more than fifty e-mail addresses linked to ISIS. Facebook, Google, Twitter, and YouTube are also offering social media training and advice to American Muslims and nongovernmental organizations to help them more effectively communicate. Additionally, despite skepticism about collaborating with the Obama administration because of the Edward Snowden hangover, social media companies participated in the February 2015 White House Summit on Countering Violent Extremism. At the conclusion of that event, President Obama announced a number of new initiatives, including the creation of "technology camps" where executives, government officials, and civil society and religious leaders will develop digital content that discredits violent extremist narratives.[52]

MICROTARGETED DIPLOMACY

It is too early to tell if a mixed strategy of State Department–crafted counternarratives, company takedowns and suspensions, and activist networking and messaging will work. While intelligence collection in Syria and Iraq, as well as in London, Paris, and Minneapolis, gives some sense of how effective the messaging is, developing a metric for something that does not happen—a young Muslim does not become radicalized—is difficult. But the early news is not good, and as long as ISIS continues to succeed on the battlefield, we can expect it to attract new recruits.[53]

In addition to exploiting social media platforms to spread their messages, nation-states will also deploy the tools of big data to shift perceptions and influence opinions and sentiments. The term "big data" describes data sets too large or complex for traditional methods of analysis and processing. The technology research and consulting company Gartner used a widely repeated "3V" model to describe the challenges and opportunities of big data: big data is high-volume, high-variety, and high-velocity information. Data, once scarce, is now abundant. Walmart, for example, processes 1 million transactions an hour, and Instagram hosts over 30 billion photographs. The sources of data have also expanded. Data comes from multiple sources—photo, audio, video, web, GPS, documents, industrial sensors and logs, cell phones—and as new programs and applications are introduced, new data comes to life. The speed with which it is produced and analyzed has also changed. Previously, companies and individuals analyzed data in a batch process: researchers submitted a chunk of data to a server and then waited for results. Now data can stream to the server almost continuously, and analysis can happen in close to real time.

We have seen the application of big data to influence behaviors most clearly in the marketplace and in domestic political campaigns. In June 2014, for example, Facebook and the dating site OkCupid announced that they had conducted experiments on their users. Facebook manipulated the feeds of 689,003 people to see if it could alter users' emotions and induce them to post more positive or negative content. For a week, users' feeds omitted certain types of content. Users who saw more positive content in turn posted more positive updates, and when negativity was reduced, they also reduced their own negativity. This was a public announcement of research results, but as technology scholar Zeynep Tufekci notes, Internet platforms conduct A/B tests (does a user prefer option A or B) every day, which gives them new insights to model personalities, alter behaviors, and predict which social groups will stick together.[54]

Even when the companies are not experimenting, algorithms decide what stories appear in users' newsfeeds. During protests over the killing of Michael Brown, an unarmed black youth, by a Ferguson, Missouri, police officer, stories on the demonstrations did not show up immediately in Facebook feeds, whereas on Twitter, discussion exploded. This resulted from a characteristic of Facebook's complex and secret calculations that decide what shows up in a feed, and in this case, current events did not surface in a timely manner. A study done by Facebook itself found that feeds occasionally hid posts that readers were likely to disagree with. If a user self-identified as conservative, one in twenty links to contrary opinions disappeared. For self-identified liberal users, one in thirteen links vanished. In addition, companies, organizations, and individuals can pay to have their stories show up in newsfeeds. *New York Times* tech writer Nick Bilton paid $7 to have a post promoted and saw a 1,000 percent increase in interactions, with 130 likes and thirty shares within an hour.[55]

The collection of data and the development of algorithms and other computational methods that draw inferences and correlations from disparate sources of data have allowed businesses and political campaigns to move beyond influence based on groups and to develop approaches targeting individuals. Before, companies and campaigns worked on large but limited amounts of data, and the connections inferred were highly probabilistic. Magazine subscriptions plus financial and real estate records, educational attainment, and survey responses gave a rather fuzzy picture of what individuals might buy or how they might vote. Two individuals labeled "urban creative" might have very different attitudes.

The amount of data available today is much vaster and more closely linked to the individual. Commercial databases can match IP addresses to voter names for the majority of Americans. The Obama campaign, for example, could do more than view a voter as a white, Southern, middle-class teacher. Massive cross-referenced data sets and randomized experiments allowed strategists to fill in details from these very broad brushstrokes to create a much clearer portrait of individual citizens whom they could measure and assess. With this data, the campaign could focus on mobilizing voters who were already likely to vote for Obama and avoid wasting resources on citizens who were very unlikely to visit the ballot box.[56]

Not surprisingly, intelligence agencies are hoping to develop and exploit the same types of capabilities. Both Google and In-Q-Tel, the CIA's venture capital firm, have invested in Recorded Future, a company that uses websites, blogs, and Twitter accounts to map the relationships among hacker groups and among individuals and institutions. The company looks at when events happen and the tone of posts. The Defense Department has tested software, called Dynamic Twitter Network Analysis, that sorts data from the public Twitter feed by phrases, keywords, or hashtags, mapping the data to its users and giving intelligence officers insight into people's moods and feelings to help them understand, for example, what Pakistani users think about US airstrikes against ISIS. The State Department awarded a $142,000 contract to InTTENSITY, a social media analysis company based in Catonsville, Maryland, for a "social media command center" in order "to better understand foreign populations and what they really think."[57]

Despite grandiose claims, there are still limits to what big data can tell. Much depends on the quality of the data collected, and people lie, omit, and misdirect when they are online. A political organization can identify lots of likes and opinions and still fail to motivate a voter. If this is true of American politics, where there is a huge amount of data and a shared political and cultural background, it is even more likely the case with efforts to influence foreign audiences. Focused messages may come across as distractions and annoyances instead of generating awareness and influencing attitudes.

In addition, sociologist Duncan Watts, discussing the spread of musical taste, finds that social networks magnify the impact of early random or chance events, making it very difficult to predict which cultural trends will catch fire and which will burn out quickly or never ignite at all. Some political ideas will spread quickly, shaping domestic politics and relations between states, but it will be very hard for intelligence agencies to predict which.

People's antennas go up when they interact with official social media. They look for authenticity—a congruence of values, words, and deeds—which is a rare characteristic for states. The rhetorical commitment to democracy, free speech, and the open, global Internet of the United States and its European allies often withers under the harsh light of realpolitik, especially in the wake of the Snowden revelations. Power shapes credibility, deeds are frequently divorced from words, and the past hangs heavily over current promises. As Richard Stengel, undersecretary of state for public diplomacy and public affairs, argues with regard to US engagement with the Middle East, "We're not always the best messenger for our message."[58]

There may also be a fundamental mismatch between the message and the medium. Social media is difficult terrain for a strategy of competing in the "marketplace of ideas" through alternative narratives. It favors the easily digestible and shareable. Content that is shocking, conspiratorial, or false often crowds out the reasonable, rational, and measured. Liberal democracies are in theory expected to operate within legal constraints. Public messaging is supposed to be transparent, and the organizations that conduct information operations do so under the supervision of other branches of the government and public scrutiny. Though they need to disseminate high volumes of content rapidly, they operate under budget constraints. In contrast, China and Russia do not face critique from partisan publics, and they mobilize hundreds and thousands of trolls operating at a relentless pace.

This struggle for influence takes place before our eyes in the tweets and comments that scroll across our screens. But another battle for influence is happening at obscure meetings in Brasilia, Busan, Dubai, and Geneva. These conflicts are highly technical and involve a bewildering array of actors and acronyms—ICANN, WSIS, IANA, IGF, IETF, WCIT, ITU, and DNS, among others. These battles determine the architecture and governance of the Internet.

Chapter 8

GEOPOLITICS
STRIKES BACK

NATION-STATES AND THE POLITICS
OF INTERNET GOVERNANCE

● ●

Jonas Marr moved from Brazil to Silicon Valley in the 1980s to develop a low-cost computer. Despite rumors that Marr was illegally hacking into competitors' networks in the 1990s, his Marra Corporation developed a global presence, and Marr married Pamela Parker, a part-time actress and heir to a media company. After two decades of growth, the company plateaued, and Marr faced a revolt from his board. Rather than retire gracefully, he suddenly moved the company's headquarters back to Brazil.

In order to revitalize the company, and perhaps find his successor, Marr sponsored a hacking competition called "Recife Digital." Contestants were asked to develop and popularize new smartphone apps. An early standout in the competition and its eventual winner was Davi Reis. Reis had been working at a nongovernmental organization that taught programming skills to children in low-income communities. Reis and his partner, Manuela Yannes, were eventually named as the next generation of leadership at Marra Corporation. It soon came out that Reis was in fact Marr's son, the child of a short affair.

You have probably never heard of Marr or his legendary low-cost computer, Bro, unless you are a fan of Brazilian television. Marr, Parker, Reis, Yannes, and many, many others were fictional characters on the *telenovela Geração Brasil* (Generation Brazil), also written

G3R4Ç4O BR4S1L. My brief summary does nowhere near justice to the twists and turns of the story, which involves countless affairs, marriages and divorces, kidnappings, duplicitous business deals, and media scandals. And this does not even include the story line of a new-age spiritualist named Brian, a genius who attends Harvard at age ten, succeeds in Silicon Valley, and later returns to Brazil to write a book titled *Love Mystery*, which tells of the insights revealed to him in front of a secluded waterfall. The story of Jonas Marr was, in the minds of its creators, not only good entertainment but also a call to arms for the Brazilian public to engage in a vibrant domestic Internet culture and for Brazil to have a larger voice on the international stage.

For policymakers in Brasilia, Internet governance is a sweet spot, bringing together three foreign policy concerns: technological development, promotion of Brazil as a leader on the world stage, and checks on US power. Over the almost three decades between the fictional Marr's starting his company and moving to Recife, Brazil would gradually evolve from a leading advocate for a greater government role in the Internet into an active promoter of a more bottom-up, private-sector-led model of governance. As we have seen, cyber espionage, cyberattacks, and digital trade are disrupting geopolitics; Brazil's diplomatic efforts to shape Internet governance, like those of China, Estonia, India, Russia, the United States, and others, are signs that geopolitics are striking back. So far, the impact of this new form of realpolitik on the workings of the web has been relatively minimal. But the contest could become more consequential and disrupt cyberspace.[1]

It is hard to overstate the importance of shows like *Geração Brasil* within Brazilian culture. Their entertainment value aside, the serialized soap operas have always had an educational purpose and broad political impact. This was especially true during the 1970s through the 1990s, when the spread of televisions outpaced access to education. The *telenovelas* highlighted the conflict between the old and the new, between rural traditions and modern mores, and helped ease the process of urbanization. As Brazil moved away from military rule and toward democracy, the stories reflected both pride in the change and skepticism in the efficacy of the new government.

The *telenovelas* do more than mirror what is on Brazilians' minds: they help shape behavior. These shows often criticize traditional values and at their center tell stories of female empowerment; women undergo profound heartbreak but also have careers and make their own choices. One study by the Inter-American Bank found a strong correlation between the arrival of television and rising divorce rates in Brazil. As the *telenovelas* spread, divorce rates rose from 3.3 divorces per 100 marriages in 1984 to 17.7 in 2002, influenced in part by the new role models on TV. In addition, the main characters in these stories often have small families, and so the *telenovelas* have been one factor contributing to the falling birthrate in Brazil, not only among the urban wealthy but also in rural areas and favelas.[2]

Broadcast during prime-time evening hours, the *telenovelas* change frequently, running for a few months. *Geração Brasil* aired for 155 episodes, six days a week at 7:00 p.m., from May 5 to October 31, 2014. The soaps can attract huge audiences; *Avenida Brasil*, about the lives of the middle class in the suburbs of Rio rather than the wealthy elite, who are usually the focus of the programs, attracted an average of 46 million viewers a night and 80 million for the finale. Broadcasts of the show reportedly forced President Dilma Rousseff to adjust her work schedule.[3]

Geração Brasil focuses on a new social transformation: the rapid adoption of information and communication technologies in Brazil. As the first episode opens, Davi participates in a street protest and holds a sign reading "Information is Power." A voiceover tells the audience: "The future has already arrived. We live in a technological revolution. In front of us, the super programmers, these visionary geniuses that are changing the world with their programming, and of course, the youth." Later, the narrator tells viewers that Brazilians are positioned to take advantage of the Internet age: "Today's Brazilian youth was born in the Internet era, has the entire world one click away, is connected collectively, wants to share experience, wants to become an entrepreneur."

The show did not exaggerate in describing Brazilians as young and collectively connected. In 2000, Brazil had only about 5 million Internet users, amounting to a little less than 3 percent of the population. By 2014, the number had exploded to 107 million, more than 50 percent, and half of Brazil's Internet population is under age thirty. In the past, landline telephones were limited to the wealthy; by 2014, there were more mobile phones—over 270 million—than people in the country. Brazilians embrace social media widely and, like outside observers, do not hesitate to invoke the cliché of a warm, outgoing social culture to explain it. In the words of John Perry Barlow, political activist and cofounder of the Electronic Frontier Foundation, "Brazil was the Internet before the Internet existed." Brazil is now the second-largest market for Facebook, Tumblr, and Twitter after the United States, and Brazilians spend twice as much time as any other nationality on social media and more time online than watching television.[4]

As in other parts of the developing world, activists and entrepreneurs developed social media, apps, and websites to address government transparency and accountability. Seventeen-year-old Rene Silva used social media to tell residents what was happening as the Brazilian military mobilized to rout Comando Vermelho and Terceiro Comando, two powerful drug gangs that controlled Alameo, a Rio favela. At eleven years old, Silva, his brother, and a few friends had started a community paper called *Voz da Comunidade*, and he eventually moved online, using Facebook, Twitter, and YouTube. On November 28, 2010, thousands of military police rushed into Alameo behind three tanks. Fighting was so intense that journalists from the large outlets remained outside the favela. Silva live-tweeted the operations and became the main source of information on the ground.[5]

Social media also played a large role in demonstrations that sprang up across the country in June 2013. Angered by rising bus fares and the government's investment of at least $25 billion in stadiums and other sport facilities for the World Cup and Olympics—funding that failed to better the lives of average citizens—protestors took to the streets. A violent response from riot police swelled the demonstrations, and tens of thousands marched for months in over one hundred cities, posting images and organizing on Facebook and Twitter around the hashtags #itsnotjust20cents (referring to the twenty-cent increase in bus fare), #VemPraRua (come to the streets), and #MudaBrasil (change Brazil).

I first heard of *Geração Brasil* at a dinner in Rio with Carlos Affonso Souza and Ronaldo Lemos, directors of the Institute for Technology and Society. Young, cosmopolitan, and highly accomplished, Souza and Lemos are influential technology thinkers. Lemos writes a weekly column in *Folha de S. Paulo*, the country's largest national newspaper, and hosts a weekly TV show, *Navegador*, focused on technology issues. Souza and Lemos were advisers to *Geração Brasil* and had a hand in some of the stories that involved privacy, encryption, and geolocation. They told me they had also wanted to rescue the idea of hacking from its negative reputation as malicious behavior, as breaking things for no reason. While the hackers in the show tangle with the FBI and the Brazilian Federal Police, they are also a force for good. One hacker, for example, breaks into university computers and exposes a professor who has systematically been giving black students lower grades.

Geração Brasil's writers, producers, and advisers wanted viewers to engage with and take pride in Brazilian Internet culture. This vibrant domestic culture in turn has energized activists, entrepreneurs, and diplomats who have argued that Brazil deserves a voice in shaping the international governance of the Internet not only because it has a large population of web users but also because the country has a unique democratic process for Internet policy.

Brazil's governance model grew up along with the Internet itself. The Internet first arrived in Brazil in 1987, but until 1995 it was used primarily by academic institutions. The year 1995 saw both the expansion of the Internet to commercial enterprises and the founding of the Brazilian Internet Steering Committee (CGI.br). Structurally the committee is meant to reflect the interests of users, regulators, academics, and business. Of the twenty-one members, nine are from the federal government, four are from the corporate sector, four are from civil society, three are scientists and technologists, and one is an "Internet expert." Demi Getschko, a member of the Internet Hall of Fame who helped establish Brazil's Internet connection, currently holds the Internet expert position. In 2009, CGI.br adopted ten principles for the governance and use of the Internet related, among other things, to privacy and human rights, collaborative governance, and network neutrality.[6]

The structure of CGI.br was innovative, but Brazilians have taken even greater satisfaction in passing the world's first Internet bill of rights, the Marco Civil da Internet. The bill actually had its origin in concerns over crime and intellectual property theft. In 2007, Congressman Eduardo Azeredo introduced new text for the Bill on Cybercrime, which had been in limbo since 1999. Many feared the new bill would result in severe punishment, up to four years in jail, for illegally down-loading music. At least 50 percent of Brazilians download movies and a third download music from the Internet, and much of the content is pirated; a 2011 study cited piracy rates of 56 percent for software, 22 percent for movies, 48 percent for music, and 91 percent for games.[7]

Ronaldo Lemos, at the time a law professor at Fundação Getulio Vargas (FGV), a research institute in Rio, wrote a widely read opinion piece arguing that the proposed bill had its priorities wrong. Brazil did not need greater criminalization of the Internet; rather, especially to promote online innovation, a civil regulatory framework was required that "defined the rules and responsibilities of users, companies and other institutions accessing the network." Criticism of the crime bill mounted as three others, two academics and a digital activist, orga-nized an online petition emphasizing the importance of an open Internet for Brazil's economic and social development. Over 160,000 Brazilians signed the petition.[8]

Activists maintained pressure against the bill over the next year and a half. In June 2009, President Luiz Inácio Lula da Silva, widely known as Lula, jumped into the fray, making a speech while attend-ing a free software forum. Responding to the pressure from civil soci-ety groups, President Lula linked the crime bill to censorship. "What we need," he said, "is to make the people who work with the digital issues, with the Internet, responsible. We need to create responsibil-ity but not to forbid or punish." After the speech, the Ministry of Jus-tice contracted the FGV to organize the debate around a new Internet framework.[9]

The drafting of the Marco Civil was crowdsourced. Thousands commented through a website sponsored by the Ministry of Culture. The draft bill also incorporated opinions expressed in tweets, blogs, and newspaper articles. Divided into five chapters, the bill introduced users' rights and some general regulatory principles before moving on to issues such as liability for Internet service providers and net neutral-ity. In August 2011, Lula's successor, President Dilma Rousseff, sent the bill to the Brazilian Congress, where it languished for a little less than three years.

Two issues held the bill up: net neutrality and copyright protections. Net neutrality means that all data is treated identically and sent to its destination at the same speed. Brazilian operators restricted connection speeds for users downloading videos and movies and strongly opposed the provision in the bill that proposed treating all data the same way. In addition, media companies demanded that Internet service providers remove pirated materials without a court order or be subject to civil damages. The Internet companies argued that this obligation to remove material would be too burdensome and limit innovation.

Edward Snowden would help break the logjam. He would also galvanize Brazil in its efforts to shape the governance of the Internet at the global level.

REALPOLITIK MEETS THE INTERNET

An obscure issue that affects us all, Internet governance is the domain of geeks, utopians, and, increasingly, foreign policy realists. For many of the Internet's progenitors, any discussion of global governance was misguided, if not undesirable. But as the Internet became central to economics, politics, and society, states increasingly exerted sovereignty. Discussion of "who runs the Internet" became unavoidable.

Before the global Internet existed, there was the ARPANET, a computer network supported by the Defense Advanced Research Projects Agency, a funder of high-risk research at the frontiers of technology with the goal of reaching beyond immediate military needs. While the search for survivable communications during a nuclear attack in part catalyzed the creation of the network, the idea of packet switching—breaking data into chunks, having each take its own path to a destination, and reassembling the data at the endpoint—was also developed to allow research scientists in different parts of the country to access supercomputers. Researchers made decisions on the technologies and processes that would undergird the Internet with little oversight and with little thought about security, since almost all the users were known to each other. They valued collegiality and the open flow of information. As Vint Cerf, one of the Internet's founders, described it, "We were just rank amateurs, and we were expecting that some authority would finally come along and say, 'Here's how we are going to do it.' And nobody ever came along, so we were sort of tentatively feeling our way into how we could go about getting the software up and running."[10]

The institutions that managed and coordinated the Internet's development and growth mirrored the web's early ethos. They operated at a distance from, if not under the radar of, government authority. They were often informal, with a legitimacy based in technical expertise. Formed in 1986 to coordinate standards setting, for example, the Internet Engineering Task Force (IETF) has no board of directors, members, or dues. Its guiding principles state that it believes in "rough consensus and running code." Attendees at meetings hum in approval of motions rather than voting.

One bearded, long-haired, sandal-wearing man, Jon Postel, from the Information Science Institute at the University of Southern California (USC), created a central hub for the coordination of the Internet. For the ARPANET to function, each computer on the system had to have an address. Postel invented the numerical system used, the Internet protocol (IP) address, and the domain name system (DNS), which translated that number into a spelled-out address: 75.101.137.229 became www.cfr.org. He was also responsible for the introduction and distribution of top-level domain (TLD) names, the designations .com, .gov, .org, and others, and country-code top-level domain (ccTLD) names, generally reserved for countries, sovereign states, or dependent territories—for example, .br for Brazil. With few computers connected at the time, Postel did this by hand, on scraps of paper. The system became known as the Internet Assigned Numbers Authority (IANA), and the US government eventually signed a contract with USC's Information Science Institute to run IANA.

As the Internet grew, however, the US government began to worry about the stability of the networks. A global network could not be run on scraps of paper. Postel himself recognized the need for change and began searching for a home for his IANA responsibilities. After one failed experiment, USC signed a memorandum of understanding with the Internet Society and the United Nations' International Telecommunications Union (ITU). The US government opposed the plan, and in a letter that set the tone of the official attitude toward UN and ITU involvement in the Internet for at least a decade and a half, then secretary of state Madeleine Albright criticized ITU secretary-general Pekka Tarjanne for exceeding his mandate. Geopolitics intervened, and the agreement collapsed.[11]

In July 1997, the United States published a green paper asking for proposals for a private, nonprofit corporation that would take over the domain name system. The new body, which came to be known as the Internet Corporation for Assigned Names and Numbers (ICANN), was incorporated under California law in 1998. The Department of Commerce signed the IANA contract with ICANN and authorized ICANN to allocate IP addresses and edit the root zone file, the master list of all top-level domain names. The Department of Commerce would approve any changes in the root zone file.

From its inception, the idea of giving a private organization, with a board in California and a contract with the US government, control over what was becoming a global resource was both experimental and controversial. Even Washington's friends in Europe thought the plan too US-centric. The solution to this tension was to make ICANN truly international and independent. The Bill Clinton administration, recognizing that "an increasing percentage of Internet users reside outside of the U.S., and those stakeholders want to participate in Internet coordination," declared its intention to internationalize ICANN by 2000.

Realization of this plan was much more complicated. As ICANN stumbled over some difficult choices, such as the introduction of new top-level domain names that would join the original .com, .edu, .gov, and others, the transition was delayed. Two years stretched to seventeen plus.

Realpolitik pushed aside development concerns during preparations for the first World Summit on the Information Society (WSIS), a UN process created to promote access to information and communication technologies. The summit took place in two stages, a preparatory meeting in Geneva in December 2003 and a final conference in Tunis in 2005. While the original intent of the preparatory meeting had been to narrow the digital divide—the inequality of access to information and communication technologies between developed and developing economies—conflict over Internet governance, particularly the United States' relationship with ICANN, dominated the agenda. As Talal Abu-Ghazaleh, vice chairman of the UN Information and Communication Technology Task Force, said at the time, "The world should be grateful to Uncle Sam for creating the Internet," but the system of governance needed to be democratized.[12]

Brazil was one of the most outspoken proponents of international-ization, arguing that the Internet was a global public good, states were the legitimate authorities, and international organizations should make Internet policy. China was even more direct. Beijing proposed an International Internet Treaty and the formation of an Intergovern-mental Internet Organization. Even the European Union expressed its discomfort with the IANA contract and the US role in the Internet. Not surprisingly for a large, complicated international conference, the Geneva meeting ended with a broad statement of principles and an agreement that the issue needed more research. A UN working group was formed to study how to achieve greater international involvement in ICANN.

The UN working group released its findings before the second meeting convened in Tunisia in 2005. The group concluded that no single government should have a preeminent role in Internet gover-nance and suggested four paths forward for ICANN, three of which supplanted ICANN with, or held it accountable to, a multilateral organization. The US government would have expected a UN work-ing group to be unfriendly, but it was caught off guard when Europe, thought to be in its court, appeared to wobble. A month before Tunis, the European Union proposed a new intergovernmental body to over-see ICANN. Viviane Reding, the European commissioner for media and information society, told the *Wall Street Journal*, "Today, in a glo-balized world in which the Internet has become a global resource for freedom of expression and for economic exchange, this monopolistic oversight of the Internet by one government is no longer a politically tenable solution."[13]

The US government lobbied furiously against any changes in ICANN's status. In a letter to UK foreign minister Jack Straw, then EU president, Secretary of State Condoleezza Rice and Commerce Sec-retary Carlos Gutierrez stressed, "The governance structure and con-tinued stability and sustainability of the Internet are of paramount importance to the United States." The current structure, includ-ing "the historical US role in authorizing changes or modifications" to the root zone file, needed to be maintained. Rice and Gutierrez expressed "regret" that the European Union proposed a new structure of intergovernmental control over the Internet, a harsh reprimand in diplomatic jargon. American technology companies came out with even stronger language. "In advocating greater government involvement in governance of the Internet, the European Union has pleased countries like China, Iran, Syria, and Cuba, but left the U.S., Canada, Japan, and other democratic countries agog," said Harris Miller, president of the Information Technology Association of America, an industry trade group.[14]

The lobbying had its intended effect. The European Union did not push for a competing model. The Tunis session concluded, having done little to strengthen the United Nations' and ITU's Internet roles. The final text of the meeting recognized the multistakeholder model and approved of the "private sector taking the lead." There was no plan to reform ICANN, but the parties agreed to a compromise, creation of the Internet Governance Forum (IGF), under the auspices of the United Nations. The IGF became a place for governments to hold nonbinding discussions on Internet governance and little else.[15]

INTERNET YALTA

WSIS was the first "battle for the soul of the Internet," one of the rare occasions when the conflict between worldviews on how the Internet should be governed exploded onto the pages of the *New York Times* and *Wall Street Journal*. Soon after, the political wrangling retreated to the institutions where management and coordination happen day to day, out of the public eye and below the radar of most policymakers and politicians.[16]

Then, in 2012, the dispute came back with a vengeance at the ITU's World Conference on International Telecommunications (WCIT) in Dubai. When the meeting ended, analysts and pundits screamed that it marked the dawn of a "digital cold war" or represented an "Internet Yalta," the beginning of a long conflict between liberal democracies and authoritarian states over the openness of cyberspace.

The purpose of the conference was to review the International Telecommunication Regulations (ITRs), a 1988 treaty designed to foster "global interconnection and interoperability" of telecommunication. In the run-up to the meeting, the United States and its allies argued that the Internet fell outside the ITU's mandate, which has historically been radio spectrum, satellite orbits, telecommunications, and technical standards. The United States even used arguments about capitalization to make the point. In 2003, the *Economist* magazine stopped capitalizing "Internet," arguing that it was now part of everyday life, not a separate entity. The ITU suggested use of the lowercase spelling in 2006, but David Gross, US coordinator for international communications and information policy at the State Department, opposed the move, which he felt would diminish the separateness of the Internet and justify the ITU's treating it like another telecom system belonging within its jurisdiction.

Washington's argument did not get much traction with the majority of member states at Dubai. Not only did they remain skeptical of the United States' influence over the Internet, but real economic interests were now at stake. Traditional telecom operators had no business model that took advantage of the open Internet. In their view, they were carrying traffic for Facebook and Google but seeing little profit. Moreover, new services, like the voice-over-Internet phone calls provided by companies like Skype, Viber, or WeChat, were threatening their traditional business.

At the meeting, the US delegation fought a rearguard action against a number of resolutions that appeared to threaten the multistakeholder model of the Internet and provide cover to states that wanted to increase their surveillance of the web. A provision on controlling spam, unsolicited bulk electronic messages, reflected the distance between Washington and some developing economies. Spam is more than just a nuisance for a number of African countries, where it can clog already slow networks. The United States feared that countries would use the antispam regulations to prevent the free flow of information; the US State Department representative to the meeting argued that spam was a "form of content and that regulating it inevitably opens the door to regulation of other forms of content, including political and cultural speech." In effect, one man's junk mail spammer could be another's democracy activist.[17]

Many states in Africa and Latin America also lacked cybersecurity or other technical expertise, had a long history of dealing with the ITU, and saw it as a credible partner. For them, the ITU was not some bogeyman threatening Internet freedom. It seemed like a good place to find help in stemming the unwanted deluge of messages. As one Brazilian diplomat told me, "The United States is always trying to portray discussions at the ITU as 'good guy' versus 'bad guy.' But once you cast it as 'good' versus 'bad,' disputes become impossible to resolve. It is a question of differing interests between developed and developing economies."[18]

The meeting ended dramatically and divisively in a bit of procedural irregularity. The ITU resolution process was supposed to be consensus driven. States introduced resolutions, and if they could not find a consensus on a controversial issue, the resolution went to an ad hoc group, which tried to find common ground. If the ad hoc group failed, it returned a draft with any controversial language in brackets. But late in the evening of the tenth day of the meeting, ITU secretary-general Hamadoun Touré announced that he would ask for the "feel of the room" on a controversial draft resolution allowing countries to discuss Internet-related technical and public-policy issues. States were asked to hold their voting boards up, and Touré proclaimed the majority to be with the resolution. The next moments were confused, as everyone tried to figure out if a vote had just occurred.

The next day, Ambassador Terry Kramer, head of the US delegation, told the meeting, "I do need to say that it's with a heavy heart and a sense of missed opportunities that the U.S. must communicate that it's not able to sign the agreement in the current form." Fifty-four other countries joined the United States in refusing to sign the agreement. Eighty-nine signed the new ITRs.[19]

WCIT was a clear marker of the differing views on Internet governance, but the divisions were not new. Various nations—including China, Iran, Pakistan, Russia, and Saudi Arabia—had been pushing for a more state-centric system to manage the Internet long before the WCIT. The "digital cold war" analogy caught some of what was at stake but was overstated. The ITRs only bind those who sign them, and many of the developing states see themselves not as part of one camp or the other but rather as in search of technical help. Moreover, much of the discussion about the WCIT overplayed the importance, influence, and power of the ITU. As Georgia Tech University professor and Internet analyst Milton Mueller noted at the time, the ITU has none of the "institutional mechanisms to regulate, restrict, surveil, censor and license Internet suppliers and users." Only national governments have those capabilities.[20]

An uneasy status quo reigned until the summer of 2013, followed by a flurry of activity. In July, a month after Edward Snowden boarded a flight from Hong Kong to Moscow, Glenn Greenwald published a piece in *O Globo* claiming that Brazil was under National Security Agency (NSA) surveillance: "The NSA has for years systematically tapped into the Brazilian telecommunications network and indiscriminately intercepted, collected, and stored the mail and telephone records of millions of Brazilians." US justifications of the mass surveillance as required to prevent terrorism and protect national security rang hollow. Brazil saw itself as a friend of the United States and had no known experience with al-Qaeda or other international terrorist networks. The surveillance also provoked memories of the military dictatorship, which had jailed and tortured dissidents (including President Rousseff) and received occasional US support. The Brazilian Senate announced an investigation of the United States, and the Brazilian Foreign Ministry said that it would pursue UN action to "guarantee cybersecurity that protects the rights of citizens."[21]

New accusations in September pushed Brazil's umbrage even higher. In a television broadcast, Greenwald alleged that the NSA had intercepted Rousseff's e-mails and telephone calls, along with those of Mexican president Enrique Peña Nieto. Greenwald also revealed that US intelligence agencies had targeted Petrobras, the state petroleum company. Outraged, Rousseff used her address to the UN General Assembly that month to demand an international response to espionage. "Tampering in such a manner in the affairs of other countries is a breach of international law," she told the General Assembly, "and is an affront of the principles that must guide the relations among them, especially among friendly nations." Drawing on her personal history, Rousseff continued, "As many other Latin Americans, I fought against authoritarianism and censorship, and I cannot but defend, in a uncompromising fashion, the right to privacy of individuals and the sovereignty of my country."[22]

Unfamiliar with the organizations that manage the Internet's technical protocols, President Rousseff reportedly asked her aides "who was in charge" of the Internet after she heard Greenwald's accusations.

She invited all members of the Brazilian Internet Steering Committee to confer with her before she traveled to New York. She used her UN speech to warn, "Information and communication technologies cannot be the new battlefield between States." After calling for the United Nations to play a leading role in regulating these technologies, Rousseff announced that Brazil would develop proposals for establishment of a "civilian multilateral framework for the governance and use of the Internet."[23]

Washington and Brasilia tried to contain the damage. Conversations about the surveillance programs took place between the Brazilian foreign minister Luiz Alberto Figueiredo Machado and National Security Advisor Susan Rice, as well as between the two presidents. Rousseff was not assured. "I want to know everything they have regarding Brazil," she said. "The word 'everything' is very comprehensive. It means all. Every bit. In English, 'everything.'" The White House expressed regret. In the face of an "unacceptable invasion" of sovereignty, Rousseff canceled her state visit to Washington planned for October, the first by a Brazilian leader in two decades. An intended symbol of warming relations between the Western Hemisphere's two largest powers instead became a political embarrassment for the Barack Obama administration.[24]

The NSA documents spurred technical moves to reduce dependence on US companies and Internet infrastructure. In search of a substitute for Microsoft Outlook, Brazil announced deployment of a national encrypted mail service to be provided by Correios, the equivalent of the US Postal Service. In order to keep more data inside the country, Brasilia announced the building of more Internet exchange points, which allow networks to connect directly. Since the vast majority of Latin America's Internet traffic was being routed through a single building in Miami known as the Network Access Point of the Americas, the government pushed forward plans for a new high-capacity fiber-optic cable connecting the Brazilian city of Fortaleza to Lisbon, Portugal.[25]

The government also asked that a provision be added to the Marco Civil requiring Facebook, Google, Microsoft, Twitter, and other foreign companies to store Brazilian users' data within the country. Proponents of the measure argued that it would make Brazilian users safer and make it easier for the Brazilian police to access data for criminal investigations. The local offices of Facebook, Google, and most other American companies, engaged primarily in advertising and maybe some research and development, claimed they were not operating within the country. In fact, the data of Brazilian Facebook users would likely be stored in several places outside Brazil; data from games, messaging, and wall posts were distributed among global centers to improve efficiency, limiting Facebook's local presence. If a Brazilian judge wanted to see what a suspect in a murder case had posted to Facebook before a crime was committed, he or she had to go through a slow and cumbersome diplomatic process called a multilateral assistance treaty. The United States might then decide not to hand the information over. This was, in the words of a representative of an American technology company based in Brasilia, "humiliating to the Brazilian judge. They are the local authority, and they have to submit to a foreign process."

Foreign companies complained that data localization was expensive and impractical. In a 2012 survey, Brazil had ranked last in a list of thirty countries in terms of favorability for locating data centers, due primarily to high energy costs and low education levels. And, as one representative of the Brazilian tech industry put to me, "Brazil is the country of taxes." Costs for Brazilian users would go up. Several Brazilian tech writers pointed out that the idea did little to increase user security. One Brazilian lawyer framed it this way: "The question is not where the data is stored but who controls it." Data localization would make it easier for Brazilian police and intelligence agencies to access the data, but there was no reason to think the NSA could not break into the same servers in Brazil.[26]

The Snowden disclosures also stirred action on the Marco Civil. Brazilian policymakers saw passage of the bill as a rebuke to US surveillance programs and a booster shot to Brazil's efforts to shape global Internet governance. Soon after the July revelations, Communications Minister Paulo Bernardo proclaimed passing the bill critical. On September 11, 2013, after it had languished for years, Rousseff deemed the bill a constitutional urgency, meaning that Congress could not vote on any other issues until it passed the Internet legislation. On March 25, 2014, the Chamber of Deputies voted on the bill, and the Senate passed the Marco Civil unanimously on April 22, 2014. The final copy of the bill included net neutrality but not data localization. By passing the bill, Brazil, according to Tim Berners-Lee, would "unleash a new era—in which the rights of citizens in all countries are protected by a Digital Rights Charter."[27]

Brazilian diplomacy went into high gear. One senior Foreign Ministry official told me that the NSA disclosures "paved the way forward. Before, people said there was one group defending privacy and openness, another group that was a threat. Now we see the lines are blurred and Brazil can help the two sides face each other. We need to develop principles of Internet governance."[28]

Brazil soon had an opening to promote its agenda internationally. On October 7, 2013, the directors of the major Internet organizations—ICANN, the IETF, the Internet Architecture Board, the World Wide Web Consortium, the Internet Society, and all five regional Internet registries—distanced themselves from the US government. Meeting in Montevideo, Uruguay, the groups issued a joint statement calling for "accelerating the globalization of ICANN and IANA functions, towards an environment in which all stakeholders, including all governments, participate on an equal footing."

The day after the Montevideo Statement, Fadi Chehadé, the smooth, charismatic chief executive of ICANN, flew to Brasilia with no assurance that he would meet with Rousseff. Chehadé, a Beirut-born engineer and businessman appointed CEO in 2012, had been working to internationalize the organization. This meant opening regional "engagement centers" in Montevideo and Beijing, in addition to other small details. One Brazilian who participated in ICANN meetings noted approvingly that ICANN was now hiring people who spoke more than one language.

Chehadé had identified Brazil as central to the conflict over Internet governance and would have noted that, in her September UN speech, Rousseff had used the phrase "multilateral framework for the governance and use of the Internet," which in the Brazilian view has traditionally referred to intergovernmental meetings. Coming to some détente with Brasilia was critical. Brazil was large, democratic, and historically skeptical, if not hostile, to the role of the US government in ICANN. A Brazilian diplomat explained to me, "Of course Fadi would identify us as pivotal. We are always at the center of these issues. The two sides are so rigid in their positions. And Brazil is in a better position to offer new ideas. We have a very interesting domestic model to offer."

Once in the room with Rousseff, he suggested Brazil host an international conference on Internet governance. After the October 9 meeting, President Rousseff announced via Twitter, "Brazil will host in April 2014 an international summit of government, industry, civil society, and academia."[29]

The US government initially approached the April meeting with wariness. In September 2011, Brazil, along with India and South Africa, had called for a "new global body," "located within the UN system," to "develop and establish international public policies" for the Internet. IBSA, as the grouping of three of the world's largest pluralistic, multicultural, and multiracial societies is known, suggested that this new organization would absorb the ITU as well as the IETF and ICANN. Brazil had also signed the ITRs at the WCIT in Dubai, and Washington feared the April 2014 meeting, called the NETmundial Global Multistakeholder Meeting on the Future of Internet Governance, would devolve into one long attack on the Department of Commerce's contract with ICANN and the US position on the Internet. A senior US diplomat in Brazil told me that there was a concern Rousseff was exploiting the espionage and Internet governance issues for domestic political reasons. Standing up to Washington was always a popular position for a Latin American leftist, and it offered a diversion from falling polls and the June protests against standard-of-living issues.

Brazilian diplomats had always insisted that their promotion of multilateral governance approaches differed from that of authoritarian regimes like Russia and China. A Brazilian employee at a major American technology company headquartered in São Paulo explained that this was cultural: "Brazilians tend to believe you need international bureaucracy to solve big challenges." But Brazilian diplomats put a more positive spin on it and seemed weary of the obtuseness of their US counterparts. Yes, the use of the word "multilateral" points to a central role for states but it also recognizes the primary importance of the participation of civil society. In fact, said one high-level Brazilian official, "we discovered that it is very hard to work with China and Russia because there are differences in our values and concepts."

"The problem," the diplomat continued, "is that our intentions are not very well understood by the United States government." Brazil's central focus is increasing the participation of less-developed countries in Internet governance. The multistakeholder process was opaque and exclusive. And there was certainly a great deal to discuss about ICANN. It was, for example, clear to Brasilia that the ownership of the new domain name .amazon should belong to the countries of the Amazon region, not the online shopping giant. In this dispute, "ICANN procedures are not implemented equally. The private sector is favored."[30]

AMERICA'S INTERNET SURRENDER?

Although US policymakers would vociferously deny any connection between their decision to speed the internationalization of ICANN and the Snowden revelations or Brazil's NETmundial meeting, Washington regained some of the initiative on March 14, 2014. On that day, the Department of Commerce announced its "intent to transition key Internet domain name functions to the global multistakeholder community." The IANA function would become truly internationalized, and the contract with ICANN would end. ICANN was given responsibility for designing the transition under four conditions: the process must support the multistakeholder model, maintain the security and stability of the domain name system, meet the needs of users, and maintain the open Internet. The Department of Commerce did not paint a clear picture of what would replace the old system but was explicit about what would not come next: "a government-led or an inter-governmental organization solution" could not replace the Commerce Department's role.[31]

This announcement provoked controversy at home. *Wall Street Journal* columnist Gordon Crovitz, in a piece titled "America's Internet Surrender," argued, "Russia, China, and other authoritarian governments have already been working to redesign the Internet more to their liking, and now they will no doubt leap to fill the power vacuum caused by America's unilateral retreat." Representative John Shimkus (R-IL) echoed these themes: "The proposed transition creates an opportunity for authoritarian governments to supplant ICANN with the United Nation's International Telecommunications Union and expand their ability to censor and restrict access to the Internet around the world."[32]

Despite this reaction, there is little doubt that the decision created room for diplomatic maneuver. US officials rightly argued that instead of energizing authoritarian states in their efforts to influence the Internet, the IANA decision in fact undermined their arguments for government control. Even more importantly, it signaled to Brazil and other rising Internet powers that their concerns about the governance of the domain name system were being taken seriously. Only weeks before the IANA announcement, a senior diplomat told me that Brazil was "concerned by [ICANN's] umbilical relationship with the US government, which does not serve Washington's interests. We are looking for internationalization." At the NETmundial meeting attendees told members of the US delegation that the IANA transition "helped set the stage for a cooperative and collaborative gathering." The important audience for the United States was in Brasilia, not Beijing.[33]

By the time NETmundial commenced in April, Brazil had moved away from its historical promotion of intergovernmental solutions to a position much closer to that of the United States. It had also significantly distanced itself from the argument that the International Telecommunications Union should take over the IANA functions. The meeting opened in front of more than 1,200 participants, including government officials and representatives of nongovernmental organizations and businesses from ninety-seven countries, with President Rousseff signing the Marco Civil da Internet into law onstage. After introducing some basic principles of freedom, privacy, data collection, and universal access in cyberspace, Rousseff noted there would be a continued effort to refine them. "Brazil has its contributions to make, following a broad-ranging discussion, domestic process that has ultimately led to the passing of the Internet Civil Framework Act."

The US delegation must have let out a collective sigh of relief during Rousseff's speech. "Our view," she said, "is that the multisectoral model is the best way to exercise Internet governance." Only later did she add that she attached "a great deal of importance to the multilateral perspective, according to which participation should occur on an equal footing among governments in such a way as to ensure that no country will have or bear greater weight vis-à-vis other countries."[34]

The United States got almost everything it wanted at NETmundial. In a blog post titled "A Major Win for the Open Internet," the heads of the delegation spoke of rising to applaud the final statement, "the ideas it presents, the ideals it embraces, and the multistakeholder process that made it possible." It represented an enthusiastic embrace of the idea that "Internet governance should be built on democratic, multi-stakeholder processes, ensuring the meaningful and accountable participation of all stakeholders." The final statement shied away from directly criticizing the United States on mass surveillance. Rather it stated that the practices of surveillance should be reviewed with a view to upholding the right of privacy.[35]

There is a great deal of uncertainty about the future of the architecture of the Internet. On a practical level, the IANA transition will take longer than the Department of Commerce expected. Technical issues have been addressed, but the governance issue is a Gordian knot, and in August 2015, the Obama administration announced that it was delaying the shift a year, until September 2016. While unpopular with the rest of the world, the contract with the Department of Commerce created accountability. It is more than a little difficult to create a new organization that is free from government interference but answers to all Internet users. Nineteenth- and twentieth-century solutions to accountability—a state agency or corporate board—fail to mesh with the global nature of the web.

ICANN has argued that it can continue the IANA function while becoming more international and responsive to users. Critics question ICANN's role, given the large economic interests involved. Domain name registrars, companies like GoDaddy, pay large fees to ICANN for the privilege of managing (and reselling) top-level domain systems. When ICANN recently opened up new TLDs such as .nyc, .rocks, .photography, .beer, .solutions, and .global, it reaped huge profits. Some of the new domain names have been used almost exclusively by scammers and hackers for spam, malware distribution, botnet operations, and phishing attacks. Civil society activists have suggested making ICANN accountable to a shell company, perhaps registered in Switzerland, or opening the board to more members.[36]

There has also been a notable lessening of the rhetoric surrounding international meetings on Internet governance. The follow-up to the 2012 WCIT, the 2014 ITU Plenipotentiary Conference in Busan, South Korea, ended with no votes and no delegation walkouts. On his return, the head of the US delegation, Ambassador Daniel Sepulveda, praised an environment in which negotiation replaced acrimony. The members, according to Sepulveda, had reached what he called the "Busan Consensus," an agreement that the ITU had a role in promoting connectivity but should leave policy questions to other institutions. Follow-up meetings at the United Nations have been more interested in addressing development and capacity issues than rehashing the debate over the role of state sovereignty in cyberspace.

And yet, the geopolitical rift in cyberspace continues. Take two events separated by a couple of days. On May 4 and 5, 2015, in Ulaanbaatar, Mongolia, the Freedom Online Coalition met for the fifth time. The coalition comprises twenty-six countries, including the United States, most of Europe, and the democracies of Africa, Asia, and Latin America. Members are committed to "the principle that the human rights people have offline are the same online" and to helping individuals access the web, politically and through project aid. At the conference, a working group on transparency and privacy provided guidelines to governments and companies on how to handle government requests for companies to hand over user information or remove content for law enforcement and national security reasons.

On May 8, during President Xi Jinping's visit to Moscow in honor of the seventieth anniversary of the end of World War II, Russia and China announced a cybersecurity pact. The two sides agreed not to conduct cyberattacks on each other as well as to jointly counteract technologies that might "destabilize the internal political and socio-economic atmosphere," "disturb public order," or "interfere with the internal affairs of the state." In effect, while the Freedom Online Coalition pledged to develop new technologies to avoid censorship, Russia and China promised to work harder to counter them and to control the flow of information.

In some ways, the division between two different visions of the Internet—one relatively open, the other advocating for filters, censors, and barriers—is a traditional diplomatic problem. Washington can organize coalitions of like-minded countries, sponsor civil society organizations, and develop new technologies. The State Department, for example, spent approximately $100 million between 2008 and 2012 to fund activities such as training digital activists in hostile environments and building circumvention tools to bypass state-sponsored Internet filters. In September 2015, US Ambassador to the United Nations Samantha Power announced a $10 million venture-capital-like fund for the development of new circumvention technologies, part of an increase of the annual budget for Internet freedom to $33 million. This type of Internet diplomacy is also often beset by the same competing interests and claims of hypocrisy as the support of client states during the Cold War. Bahrain, for example, with some of the highest levels of surveillance and censorship in the world, has been named an "enemy of the Internet" since 2012. Yet it remains one of Washington's most important allies in the Persian Gulf and hosts the US Navy's Fifth Fleet.[37]

In the hacked world order, some of the old diplomatic practices persist, while others lose their utility. Diplomats and policymakers must confront new sources of strategic instability as cyber tools offer new opportunities to disrupt adversaries. The question for US policymakers is whether to continue to fight the battle over competing visions of cyberspace or to design policies that mediate and respond to the splintering of the global Internet into national sovereignties.

Chapter 9

AFTER PAX
DIGITAL AMERICANA

. . . .

For almost fifty years, efforts to construct what Washington viewed as a just and stable international order defined US foreign policy. Washington promoted participation in international organizations such as the United Nations and the International Monetary Fund, respect for territorial sovereignty and national boundaries, and economic interdependence and a liberal trade order. In Asia and Europe, it built alliances to combat and contain the Soviet Union. It advocated for the expansion of participatory democracies, a free press, and the protection of human rights, unless they undermined the interests of client states perceived to be on the front lines in the competition with Moscow.

Even before Year Zero, globalization and the "rise of the rest"—the emergence of Brazil, China, and India as regional and global powers—were already challenging the coherence of this foreign policy strategy and the ideas behind it. Once predominant on the international stage, nation-states had to share power with international organizations, multinational businesses, and civil society groups. The September 11, 2001, attacks on New York and Washington highlighted the dangers of interdependence. The rapid diffusion of information and communication technologies and the falling costs of air and sea transportation not only made building global supply chains possible but also made it far easier for the attackers to travel to Europe and the United States and to communicate with each other. As former president of the

Carnegie Endowment for International Peace Jessica Mathews argued in 1997, the "absolutes of the Westphalian system—territorially fixed states where everything of value lies within some state's borders; a single, secular authority governing each territory and representing it outside its borders; and no authority above states—are all dissolving."[1]

As globalization empowered multinationals, terrorist networks, and nongovernmental organizations, the rising powers questioned the legitimacy of institutions created without their input and began proposing new regional groupings and multilateral organizations like the China-led Asian Infrastructure Investment Bank. There has also been, especially after the great recession of 2008, a backlash against the US vision of capitalism and free trade. China, the Gulf states, Russia, Singapore, and others have developed competing economic models that marry open markets to state-owned enterprises and sovereign investment funds. Moreover, the democratization of societies around the world no longer looks inevitable. Instead there has been notable backsliding in many countries.

The movement of foreign policy into cyberspace has brought many of these trends into much sharper focus. Brazil, China, India, and Russia have their own ideas about the organization of the hacked world order and question the United States' legitimacy in defining the rules of the game. Countries are using the Edward Snowden revelations to reshape their domestic information technology markets, limit the access of US companies, and block the flow of data at their borders. In October 2015, Freedom House, an independent watchdog organization, found that Internet freedom declined for the fifth consecutive year, with negative trends in thirty-two out of sixty-five countries. Governments have passed new laws to criminalize online dissent, pressured independent news websites, and detained and prosecuted individuals for their online activities.[2]

Cyber weapons and digital attacks are being integrated into the full spectrum of military operations. Moreover, now that militaries must defend the virtual world, they are coming into increasing contact with each other. Diplomats and policymakers have struggled to find their footing in a shifting geopolitical terrain, and the demands of the hacked world order—offense advantage, rapid technological change, accelerating pace of communication, blurred boundaries between war and peace, the centrality of the private sector—have compounded and added to their disorientation. No political conflict today lacks a cyber component, and cyber techniques have allowed states to engage in a whole range of actions that fall below the threshold of armed attacks. Policymakers have lost a sense of strategic stability, predictability, and control.

Throughout history, offensive advantage has seesawed with the strengths of the defense. The machine gun and the trench emblematized defense dominance in World War I; the panzer tank, the dive-bomber, and mobile infantry were the tools of blitzkrieg and the ascendance of offense. Cyberattacks present a strong incentive to strike first, to take out an adversary's communications, electric, and transportation grids before one's own are lost. Noting the difficulty of defense, former secretary of defense Leon Panetta argued that the United States may also consider preemptive strikes if it detects "an imminent threat of attack that will cause significant physical destruction in the United States or kill American citizens."[3]

Moreover, a growing black market in malicious software means that more sophisticated cyber weapons could end up in the hands of extremists, lone wolves, and criminal gangs. Imagine a widespread power outage hitting the eastern seaboard. Policymakers might be hard-pressed to know whether to attribute it to Chinese hackers, terrorists, or merely a tree falling on a power line. If this hypothetical blackout occurs during a US-Chinese naval standoff in the South China Sea, US policymakers will feel intense pressure to react quickly, even though they may have only the haziest notion of who (or what) is responsible. The forensics needed to establish responsibility for attacks can take weeks.

That the capacities and skills needed to attack networks are often the same as those for defending against digital assaults complicates the offense-defense balance even further. If you know how to build a defense, you probably also understand how to get into another system. This security dilemma—country A builds what it thinks are better defenses, but they look like potential weapons to country B—undermines strategic stability. Moreover, the growth of the Internet of Things multiplies the range of vulnerabilities. The digital assault on Natanz involved the creative and ambitious use of zero days and new techniques in eye-opening and imagination-expanding ways. With creativity and enough resources, anything looks possible, even if it is not probable. Nation-states are perennially on edge.

The threat of being caught off guard coexists with a fear of falling behind. While pundits and analysts almost always believe they live in an age of incomparable complexity, there is little doubt that the rate of technological change has accelerated. The technologies of nuclear weapons, long-range missiles, and stealth bombers remained steady over decades (and the physics behind their destructiveness and operations for even longer). Facebook, Google, and Twitter did not exist fifteen years ago, and new innovations in computing power, storage, and mobility will create unforeseen opportunities and challenges. The companies and countries that define the next generation of technology standards will exert great influence and power.

Innovation and scientific discovery could overturn many of the current assumptions about cybersecurity. New technologies could make attribution and defense much easier. The use of big data to detect anomalies, automated defenses, and machine-to-machine communication could swing the balance from the offense to the defense. Quantum physics could revolutionize secure communications. In computers today, information is represented in bits, each equaling a one or a zero. Quantum particles exhibit superposition, which allows them to have the value of one and zero at the same time. Using these principles, scientists are trying to build quantum computers that could perform in seconds computations that would take normal computers millions of years. This, theoretically, would enable the decryption of any information.

Quantum physics exhibits another anomaly: two particles can become related and coordinate their properties instantly. Albert Einstein called this "spooky action at a distance," and it is now known as entanglement. Quantum communication exploits this characteristic and promises the ability to share information with absolute security. Both sender and receiver would see any attempt to read an intercepted message and in response could immediately generate a new security key.

There is now a race to achieve quantum computing and communication, and the countries that develop these capabilities first will have significant advantages. The National Security Agency (NSA) is particularly interested in a quantum computer, and a Canadian firm, D-Wave, claims to have built a $15 million version, though other experts are skeptical. Quantum communications is further along. Secure communications using entanglement exist, for example, between bank branches, and China is building a 1,200-mile network between Shanghai and Beijing.

Diplomats and policymakers have also struggled to turn to their advantage the speed with which information spreads and the so-far little-understood process of how ideas go viral. For example, *Kony 2012*, a thirty-minute documentary on a warlord in Uganda known for kidnapping children and turning them into soldiers, went viral over four days in March 2012, racking up more than 50 million views on YouTube and hundreds of thousands of messages on Facebook and Twitter. The video generated as much criticism—for its simplifications of a complex situation and its appeal to the activism of clicking and buying, which some have denigrated as "slacktivism"—as it did positive attention. Its direct political effect was limited; it raised a groundswell of support for the United States "to do something," but few viewers were aware that in October 2011 President Barack Obama had already authorized the deployment of about one hundred American military advisers to help African countries capture Joseph Kony. As of October 2015, while Kony's Lord's Resistance Army was much reduced, to about two hundred fighters, Kony was still at large.

Even if *Kony 2012* did little to change the situation on the ground in East Africa, policymakers are anxious to know when the next information cascade will create demand for action or, in the more extreme cases, help overturn a government. At this point, mass movements energized by communications technology are unknowable and uncontrollable. Big data and the analysis of networks and relationships offer the promise that governments can get out in front of these events. In 2015, the CIA set up a directorate for digital innovation, its first new section since 1963, focused on coming up with "new ways to operate in a much more connected environment," in the words of Andrew Hallman, head of the office. "We have the ability to do more sense-making to provide for analysts a real ability to forecast." But until big data tools deliver, policymakers have little chance to differentiate the viral and ephemeral from the cascading and important.[4]

For almost every action in cyberspace, nation-states have to rely on networks owned by the private sector and used globally for commerce, education, and entertainment. Nation-states have had close relations with companies before—consider, for example, Boeing, Northrop Grumman, Raytheon, and other defense contractors—but the dependence is now prevalent. The private sector innovates and pushes new technologies into global markets. In addition, Apple, Facebook, Google, and others are building "walled gardens" where they set the rules as to how individual users access other parts of the Internet. Nonprofits train online activists and develop technology to circumvent censorship; hackers and cybersecurity companies exploit and sell zero days and uncover state-backed espionage campaigns.

This dependence not only prevents states from acting alone but also pulls them in ever more directions. The private sector has become a central target of cyberattacks, and the attacks are nonstop. This creates a real problem of priorities. If everything is a potential target, what is most important to defend? Such dependence at the same time requires that policymakers have an expansive vision of cyber strategy. It is a cliché that the current generation of diplomats lacks the technological skill and fluency of digital natives—high school students, undergrads, and recent college graduates who grew up in a digitally saturated world. In fact, many digital skills can be learned. The larger problem is developing an understanding of all the facets of digital policy and how they interact.

Professionally, rewards for foreign affairs analysts go to those who specialize in a regional or functional topic. Successful policymaking in cyberspace requires an understanding of technology, economics, anthropology, sociology, and international relations. It also forces policymakers to sit uncomfortably at the seams between government agencies, the public and private sectors, and different nations. Cyber statecraft requires the ability to speak not only to a French official but also to a hacker in Berlin, an entrepreneur in Israel, and a telecom operator in Kenya.

WHAT WE HAVE GAINED

In a description of the emerging conflict in cyberspace, the negative effects on stability and security can overshadow the immense benefits to humanity of a global platform for the sharing of information and knowledge. The spread of the Internet and cell phones has created new economic opportunities for farmers, migrant workers, and urban slum dwellers. A poor fisherman off the coast of the Indian state of Kerala can, for example, use a cell phone to receive constant updates on the weather and market prices. Social and political movements can organize quickly. The web has also connected the isolated and disbursed—aficionados of obscure television shows, speakers of dying languages, sexual minorities. By any measure, the positives of the global Internet outweigh the costs of rising cyber crime, espionage, and data localization.

If states agree to some basic norms of behavior, the hacked world order may also be more humane. So far, the great powers have exercised self-restraint. Cyber war is limited, contained, and discriminate. In the future, well-designed cyberattacks can result in far fewer casualties than traditional, kinetic strikes. Malware can be designed only to damage specific targets for limited periods. The damage may be easily reversed; repairing code and data on computers in the control room of a power grid is simpler than rebuilding and replacing buildings, generators, and towers after they have been blown up.

Stuxnet caused no deaths or injuries. An Israeli or US bombing campaign against Arak, Bushehr, Esfahan, Fordo, Natanz, and other Iranian nuclear facilities would have caused hundreds, if not thousands, of fatalities and possibly provoked a violent reaction across the Middle East. While it is hard (but possible) to find justifications for Operation Olympic Games under international law, the strongest defense may be a humanitarian desire to limit casualties. In the future, the moral expectation may be that states use cyber weapons before kinetic ones.

The radical transparency that has come with digitization, the flash drive, and the cell phone threatens the secret diplomacy often required to reach complex deals. Secret intelligence operations, once expected to remain unknown to the rest of the world for decades, are now often exposed after months or years. Bruce Schneier, the noted cryptologist and cybersecurity expert, wrote in October 2010, "My guess is that Stuxnet's authors, and its target, will forever remain a mystery." Yet barely two years later, because of the work of dedicated teams of researchers at Symantec, Kaspersky, and Langner Group, the mission and workings of the malware had been almost completely unraveled.[5]

Dependence on the private sector complicates and constrains policy. But the participation of the private sector, academics, and activists in the policymaking process should also result in better cyberspace strategy. As we have seen, in numerous instances the NSA appeared willing to risk the security of all technology users and larger economic interests in pursuit of national security goals. No one within the NSA appears to have considered that one of the outcomes of its surveillance programs would be the suspension of the Safe Harbor agreement on digital trade, and in policy deliberations the NSA's perspective dominated (or, perhaps more accurately, ignored) the interests that the Departments of State and Commerce or the National Institute of Standards and Technology, much less Facebook, Google, and Twitter, would have promoted. In some cases the agency made the right decision, but this narrow vision obstructed the pursuit of other diplomatic, political, and economic interests in cyberspace.

The growing centrality of the private sector in cyber policy is an opportunity to counter this trend and rebalance short-term security gains with long-term strategic costs. In effect, just because the United States is capable of doing something in cyberspace does not mean it should be done. The aperture for future decisions needs be opened wider.

THE END OF PAX DIGITAL AMERICANA?

In the hacked world order, the United States is uniquely powerful and vulnerable. It garners power and influence as the originator of the Internet and the home of the leading technology companies. The Pentagon and the NSA invest significant resources into offensive cyber capabilities, and huge amounts of data pass through US territory, collected, processed, and analyzed by government intelligence agencies. Apple, Cisco, Facebook, Google, Intel, LinkedIn, Microsoft, Oracle, Twitter, Yahoo, and others build the software and hardware platforms that the rest of the world uses, and Austin, Boston, Seattle, Silicon Valley, and other innovation hot spots are developing the next generation of information and communications technologies.

Yet the United States is also more exposed than any other country. Smart cities, the Internet of Things, and self-driving cars may open up vast new economic opportunities as well as new targets for destructive attacks. Cyberattacks could disrupt and degrade the American way of war, heavily dependent as it is on sensors, computers, command and control, and information dominance. The Defense Science Board, a committee of civilian experts that advise the Pentagon on science matters, warned in a January 2013 report that the "benefits to an attacker using cyber exploits are potentially spectacular." "US guns, missiles, and bombs may not fire, or may be directed against our own troops," the report stated. "Resupply, including food, water, ammunition, and fuel may not arrive when or where needed. Military Commanders may rapidly lose trust in the information and ability to control US systems and forces. Once lost, that trust is very difficult to regain."[6]

Since Year Zero, US power has eroded steadily. Other cyber powers are working hard to field cyber forces, restructure the global Internet, develop competing technology standards, and champion their own companies. The ideological, cultural, and political differences that shape nation-state behavior in cyberspace will not dissipate, and there will be continued divergence over five fundamental issues: how states interpret a threat, use force, exert influence, spur innovation, and delineate the national good. As a result, the drift toward separate cyberspaces will continue.

Preventing the further attrition of US cyber power and influence requires action. The United States has consistently argued that it is working for a global, open, and secure Internet. A 2013 Council on Foreign Relations Independent Task Force, which I directed and which was cochaired by former IBM chairman Samuel Palmisano and former director of national intelligence and ambassador to the United Nations John Negroponte, argued, "A global Internet increasingly fragmented into national Internets is not in the interest of the United States."[7]

The fundamental challenge of aspiring to a global, open Internet is that Beijing, Moscow, and others see it as a threat to their national security and as inordinately benefiting Washington strategically, economically, and politically. No clever diplomatic pronouncements or easy policy compromises can sway them from their views of their own interests and divert them from their pursuit of cyber sovereignty and greater control over cyberspace. Their cyber strategic cultures are deeply rooted in history, economics, and strategic challenges.

Despite their preference for global markets, the technology companies are already beginning to hedge their strategies, shifting data and manufacturing to countries that have political influence and domestic market power. Brad Smith, Microsoft's top lawyer, caught some of this dynamic when he speculated how the company might respond to British prime minister David Cameron's calling for a law blocking some types of encryption. The *Wall Street Journal* quoted Smith as saying "It's a big market, and it's a country we believe has a fundamental rule of law in place. We still don't like it, but you could imagine one argument that says, 'OK, we're going to do it.'" If the technology companies accommodate the demands of the United Kingdom—a market of almost 45 million—it is even more likely that they will be forced to come to some détente with Brazil, China, the European Union, and India, markets of hundreds of millions.[8]

As a result of these forces, the United States must prepare policies to ameliorate the fallout from a splintered Internet. Here there is an analogy to be drawn with the relative positions of disarmament and arms control in the US foreign policy tool chest. Nuclear disarmament remains the ultimate goal. As President Obama said in a 2009 speech in Prague, "I state clearly and with conviction America's commitment to seek the peace and security of a world without nuclear weapons." But almost everyone who heard these words understood at the time that achieving this lofty objective was a long time off; as the president said, "This goal will not be reached quickly—perhaps not in my lifetime." In the short term, Obama announced that the United States would reduce the importance of nuclear weapons in the national security strategy, negotiate a new Strategic Arms Reduction Treaty with Russia, ratify the Comprehensive Test Ban Treaty, and strengthen the Nuclear Non-Proliferation Treaty—all traditional efforts of arms control.[9]

The same could be said about the goal of keeping cyberspace as an open, global platform. This remains the long term aspiration, but the goal will not be reached quickly, if at all, and the United States must defend its economic and strategic interests in the short term. Arms control measures try to reduce the risks in an anarchic world, and a realistic cyber strategy will do the same. For such a strategy to succeed, it must do three things: improve defense while spurring technological innovation;

build a pragmatic partnership with the private sector; and foster strong international alliances while developing clear countermeasures.

DEFENSE AND INNOVATION

Because the stakes of insecurity in cyberspace are so high and the size and number of breaches are increasing, the challenge is no longer drawing high-level attention to the problem. Cyberattacks first showed up in the director of national intelligence's annual threat assessment in 2008, though they were near the bottom of the list. Since 2013 they have been listed first, and the 2015 report described cyber threats to national and economic security as "increasing in frequency, scale, sophistication, and severity of impact." Almost half (48 percent) of respondents to the 2014 Global Economic Crime Survey said the cyber risks to their organization had increased in the past year, up from 39 percent in 2011.[10]

The clearest evidence of the concern is to follow the money. In 2013, after the Iranian distributed denial-of-service (DDoS) attacks had ended, JPMorgan Chase announced it was increasing cybersecurity spending to $250 million. In 2014, months after discovery of a massive breach, JPMorgan Chase CEO Jamie Dimon announced the financial giant would double its annual spending on cybersecurity to $500 million within five years. During a visit to Silicon Valley in 2010, I had a difficult time finding venture capitalists interested in cybersecurity start-ups. By contrast, cybersecurity companies received over $1.75 billion in venture capital investment in 2014 and $1.2 billion in the first half of 2015. During a July 2015 meeting in San Francisco, a prominent venture capitalist described the situation to me as "almost bubbly," with some companies trading at nearly two hundred times earnings estimates, though very few of the cybsersecurity start-ups were making a profit yet. On the government side, funding for US Cyber Command increased from $120 million in 2010 to $509 million in 2015. A new $1.8 billion, 600,000-square-foot building at Fort Meade will host the NSA, Cyber Command, and marine and navy cyber forces. Worldwide spending on cybersecurity is expected to reach over $75 billion in 2015, according to the research firm Gartner.

Despite all of this money, no one thinks the United States is much safer. As many have noted, there will never be complete security, but policymakers, businesses, and individuals can do much better at building critical infrastructure systems that are resilient, that can operate under attack, and that can recover quickly. In order to achieve these goals, three things need to happen: the division of responsibilities between the public and private sector needs to be clearly mapped; the federal government must support private-sector innovation; and everybody has to get better at the easy stuff.

The White House must map accurately who is responsible, in and out of government, for defending against different types of attacks. Washington must take the confusion surrounding the response to the Sony hack as a warning and fully develop a set of responses linked to specific sets of computer exploitations. The Defense Department, and Cyber Command in particular, should only be used to defend critical infrastructure in extreme cases. The Pentagon's mission is to devise strategies for winning wars—using cyberattacks to degrade opponents' capabilities and ensuring it can "fight through" the inevitable attacks that will disrupt its communication, transportation, intelligence, and other systems.

As the government has failed to protect the private sector, there has been a groundswell of support for active defense, or hacking back, by companies. This is a bad idea. You cannot seize your data back after it has been stolen and copied, and nation-state attackers are unlikely to cease attacks in the face of retaliation from private companies. They are instead going to hit back harder. Moreover, mistakes are bound to happen, and private actors will either damage third parties or cause inadvertent escalation. The end point is a very Hobbesian world, where private actors and nation-states are pursuing selfish interests, and cyberspace is in a never-ending state of war.

The most important thing the United States can do at home is to support and energize research and development and technological innovation. The United States wants to ensure that it can keep pace in the constant race between the attacker and the defender. The strategy so far, as described by Defense Advanced Research Projects Agency (DARPA) director Arati Prabhakar, has been "patch and pray." The defender finds a vulnerability, fixes it, and then moves on to the next one.

For much of the Cold War, the most important military innovations came from the government: technologies like GPS and precision-
guided munitions, stealth technology, and advanced intelligence. The
next wave of innovation is not going to be inside a federal lab, but at
the nexus of public- and private-sector research and development. The
secret of success, in Prabhakar's words, is "going to be to harness that
commercial technology and to turn it into military capabilities much
more powerful than anyone else."[11]

This means that the effort to catalyze cybersecurity research cannot just be more federal funding. Instead, the federal research plan
for cybersecurity, which is now overly broad and lacks details on implementation, should be replaced with a research and development plan
that is a public-private partnership. The plan would have technology
priorities that are justified and jointly set by government agencies,
universities, federal labs, defense contractors, and the technology sector. Within the White House, there would be a small special projects
office, headed by a scientist or engineer and modeled after DARPA,
that would have budget authority to control cyber R&D spending in
other agencies.

The creation of a White House office may attract press attention,
but the majority of work will be quiet, focusing on individual behavior
and elimination of simple mistakes. In fact, some recent hacks show
a widespread failure to do some of the basic work of cybersecurity. A
2015 report from Verizon found that 99.9 percent of vulnerabilities
exploited were compromised more than a year after they were exposed
and a patch was provided. The victims just never got around to installing the patch. The Office of Personnel Management ignored earlier
security warnings and hacks; it did not encrypt its data or use two-
factor authentication—a log-in system that requires a password and
another input, often a randomly generated number sent to your phone
(if you have not set this up on your Facebook, Gmail, Twitter, or other
account, do it now)—and outsourced work to a Chinese company.[12]

This failure to achieve basic security is in part due to a focus on
highly destructive but low-probability outcomes. Politicians and policymakers worry about a "cyber Pearl Harbor" rather than allocating
funds to a little-known government agency to upgrade archaic systems.
As security analyst Adam Elkus put it, "Fantasizing about super-hackers

and visions of cyber-doom are more fun than the boring but necessary drudgery, for example, of modernizing a decrepit and decaying federal information technology base."[13]

A cybersecurity entrepreneur made the same point to me. "The new technologies coming to market are amazing," he said, "but at the end of the day, it still comes down to social awareness and education." The imperfect analog is car safety and seat belts. In 1984 the seat belt use rate was only 14 percent. But after decades of legislation, enforcement, and education, the rates had risen to 86 percent in 2012. Education campaigns are not as attractive to policymakers as information-sharing or breach-notification laws looking to "do something." They are long-term and slow moving. But they are effective, and preventing easy, low-level attacks will free up defenders to focus time and resources on more sophisticated state-backed attacks.

BUILDING NEW BRIDGES

The White House has tried to restore trust with the technology companies and US friends and allies through relatively greater transparency and oversight. IC on the Record is a website where the intelligence agencies post formerly secret documents about surveillance programs. Presidential Policy Directive 28 created rules for protecting the privacy of foreign nationals during intelligence collection. The USA Freedom Act transferred the holding of phone metadata from the NSA to the telecommunication companies. And, most consequentially, the Obama administration dropped its efforts to get legislation requiring technology companies to build in backdoors, though that effort could be picked up by whoever is in the White House in January 2017.

Further reforms of surveillance practices, such as greater declassification of Foreign Intelligence Surveillance Court opinions, and more transparency on the process through which the US government chooses when to disclose vulnerabilities and when to hold onto them for intelligence or offensive purposes, would also narrow the gap with the technology companies. Currently the director of the NSA is also the head of Cyber Command. Proponents of this "dual-hatted" structure argue that to be good at offense you need to understand defense, and vice versa, and that there would be significant costs to reproducing the NSA's capabilities in the relatively newly established Cyber Command. The dual-hatted structure, however, results in the same individual acting in an intelligence and operational role. Splitting the two would add one more voice in the debate over what actions the United States should take in cyberspace, and could signal that intelligence collection would no longer be the default priority over all other objectives in cyberspace.

Bureaucratic structure in the White House should also change. Placed in the National Security Council and the National Economic Council, the National Cyber Coordinator is supposed to harmonize competing interests across the US government. The current coordinator, however, has neither the budget nor the authority to contend with the Departments of Defense and Homeland Security. Giving the next "cyber czar" both will not only improve decisionmaking but also broadcast that the principles of Internet freedom, technological innovation, openness, and connectivity are to be accorded at least equal status with security.

These moves would narrow but not eliminate the trust issue. Policymakers and the tech community must be clear-eyed that distrust is bound to endure for at least two reasons. First, Apple, Facebook, Google, LinkedIn, Twitter, and the others have strong economic incentives to protect the privacy of their global users and few obvious inducements to cooperate more closely with the US government. The lure of foreign markets is going to remain strong. Second, during the Cold War, the NSA directed its efforts at specialized government systems and networks. That's where the secrets were. Today military, government, commercial, and individual users all use the same networks, computers, and devices. Your data is very likely going to travel and be stored next to that of a terrorist, hacker, or arms dealer, and as a result, Silicon Valley platforms and products are always going to be targets.

Since this Gordian knot is not going to be untangled, Washington and Silicon Valley have to find less divisive, more productive areas for cooperation that proceed parallel to surveillance reform, including information sharing; procurement, recruitment, and investment policies; and talent development. The debate over information-sharing legislation has cast an outsize shadow. Companies already manage to share information through organizations like the Financial Services—Information Sharing

and Analysis Center, and private companies now offer threat information as a service. Moreover, no matter how good the system to spread
threat information is, it will not stop the most sophisticated attacks,
since you cannot share information about an attack you have never seen
before. Still, encouraging greater information flow between the private
sector and government as well as among private companies—while preserving user privacy—is an important goal. The government can also
play an important and unique role by extending the secure, classified
network it uses to communicate among different agencies when its normal networks have been compromised to private-sector firms. When
large defense contractors are hacked, they use this network to develop
and implement a plan for ejecting the hackers (if they used their normal
networks, the hackers would see and respond). This classified network
involves Boeing, Northrop Grumman, Raytheon, and others and could
also be expanded to financial, electric, water, and other critical infrastructure providers.[14]

The White House and the Department of Defense have established
official liaisons to Silicon Valley, and both President Obama and Secretary of Defense Ash Carter have made personal visits to technology
conferences, companies, and educational institutions. These gestures
have to be paired with concrete efforts to make the federal government
more agile in its dealing with the technology community. According to
a study by the research firm Standish Group, 94 percent of large federal technology programs were unsuccessful. More than half were over
budget, delayed, or did not meet user expectations.[15]

The byzantine code guiding federal contracts—the more than
1,800-page Federal Acquisition Regulation—ensures that the firms
contracted to do technology work are the ones that can manage the
bureaucratic process. Opening up new avenues for small companies
to supply technology to the government is an important step. Terry
Halvorsen, the chief information officer of the Pentagon, put it bluntly
when he described the power of government contracts: "I spend $36.8
billion a year. That buys a lot of potential trust." In addition to changes
in procurement, establishing a strategic investment unit modeled on
In-Q-Tel, the CIA's venture capital firm; appointing civilian experts to
specific DoD projects; and expanding the US Digital Service, a White
House initiative that brings technologists into the Pentagon to work

on health data, climate change, Ebola, and veteran issues would all be useful measures for building relations between the military and technology communities.[16]

Talent is essential for both offense and defense, and it is not simply a numbers game. As Steve Jobs said, "A small team of A players can run circles round a giant team of B and C players." Demand for skilled coders and hackers in the private sector and government will only grow.

In the recent past, the NSA had the advantage in the competition for the best and the brightest because it offered them the chance to work on some of the hardest problems with some of the coolest tools. That monopoly no longer exists. Technology companies can now offer access to supercomputers, 3-D printing, and other cutting-edge innovations. Engineers and computer scientists at Google can work on artificial intelligence, self-driving cars, contact lenses that monitor glucose levels for diabetics, and an Internet network supported by balloons flying in the stratosphere. The NSA can now offer retention bonuses and bypass the sclerotic federal hiring process, but the money is better in the private sector. "We're throwing the kitchen sink at them from our standpoint," said a director of human resources at the NSA. "And they're writing in to us, as they leave, in their exit interviews, 'I'm leaving to double my salary.'"[17]

DARPA has managed to maneuver around the barriers of security clearance and pay gaps, the NSA has set up centers of excellence for cyber operations on university campuses, and Cyber Command has developed curricula for high school students. Short-term fixes might also include a "Hack for America" program, based on Teach for America, through which coders and hackers spend a year working for the government, and creation of a cyber reserve, which, like Estonia's cyber militia, could tap into the skills of veterans and citizens in times of crisis.

Perennial solutions to the talent shortage include increasing the numbers of women and minorities enrolling as science, technology, engineering, and mathematics majors through focused teaching, mentorship, and networking, and revitalizing the teaching of these subjects at the primary, secondary, and tertiary school levels. The most important move would be reforming immigration laws so doctoral and master's students receive green cards and are not forced to return home, and can eventually apply for citizenship. Researchers from the Kauffman Foundation found that about 25 percent of engineering and technology companies started in the United States between 2005 and 2012 had at least one foreign-born founder. In Silicon Valley, the number was close to half, and the role these immigrant entrepreneurs have played in communication technologies and the Internet could be repeated in cybersecurity technologies.[18]

STRONG ALLIANCES AND A CODE OF CONDUCT

Once policymakers acknowledge that cyberspace will be fragmented and fractured, they can concentrate on sending clear signals to potential adversaries and drawing friends closer. As noted earlier, the hacked world order has so far been one of strategic restraint. While China and Russia have been more than willing to rely on cyber exploits for espionage, influence, disruption, and coercion, they have not launched destructive attacks. The United States (along with Israel) has allegedly "crossed the Rubicon," destroying Iranian centrifuges at Natanz, but the malware was carefully designed to only attack one specific system, and Washington has resisted using destructive digital attacks in a number of other instances.

One of Washington's priorities must be to reinforce this restraint by the great powers. The United States, Russia, and China are unlikely to launch destructive attacks against each other unless they are already engaged in military conflict or perceive core interests as being threatened. The greatest risks are misperception, miscalculation, and escalation. Beijing, Moscow, and Washington have a shared interest in preventing escalatory cyber operations—the attacker might see breaking into a power grid as legitimate surveillance, but the victim could view it as prepping the battlefield. Washington should continue to push for formal discussions on acceptable norms of behavior and possible thresholds for use of force as well as greater transparency on offensive cyber doctrine.

The three great powers also share an interest in preventing extremists and other nonstate actors from developing the capabilities to attack critical infrastructure. Given the high degree of interdependence between the two economies, the United States and China will want to maintain the stability of the international financial system against attacks from third parties. Terrorist groups have so far shown greater dexterity in the use of the web for recruitment, fundraising, and propaganda than in launching destructive attacks, but that will change over time. The Islamic State, for example, wants to develop cyber weapons and has reportedly recruited hackers from Western Europe and attempted to break into power grids. To respond to emerging challenges, the United States should develop with Russia and China joint measures to prevent the proliferation of cyber capabilities.

Washington should also revisit the idea suggested several years ago by Richard Clarke, President George W. Bush's cybersecurity adviser, as well as several other experts, of creating a global Cyber Risks Reduction Center that would improve the transparency of reporting malware and attacks and facilitate cooperation between the public and private sectors. Nations suffering an attack could turn to the center and request assistance. If a country refused, especially if it was the source of the attack, it could be cut off not only from the information supplied by the center, but also, depending on the severity of the attacks, from the global financial system.

Massive espionage campaigns directed at political or military targets, such as the OPM hack, will be extremely damaging to US interests and upsetting to those who know their personal data has been taken. But given how good the United States is at spying, there is little Washington will want to do except make such operations harder for Chinese and Russian spies to conduct by improving defenses and covertly disrupting their efforts through "active defense" cyberattacks.

Just weeks after he visited Washington, President Xi agreed in a meeting with UK prime minister David Cameron that neither side would conduct commercial espionage. A few weeks after that, China and Germany announced that they would stop economic cyber spying. If China fails to abide by the September 2015 agreement to reduce commercial espionage, the United States should pursue sanctions, and it should be ready and willing to expose some intelligence assets in order to bolster support for the action among China's other victims.

Washington will want to respond quickly and decisively to disruptive or coercive attacks. The response should not necessarily be through a counter cyberattack. Sanctions or other tools should be deployed quickly: North Korea and Iran, for example, should not be left to think they can operate with impunity. In addition, Washington should be prepared to be more transparent about attribution to build international condemnation of an attacker's actions.

In effect, the United States will need to develop a code of conduct that draws a clear line between its friends and allies and its potential adversaries. It could then limit cyberattacks to military and narrowly targeted covert operations. These will have to be regulated by the laws of armed conflict and international law. Cyber espionage of potential adversaries for political and military advantage will continue; the norm against economic espionage will be strengthened through sanctions and trade agreements; and cyber spying on friends will still occur, but it will be rare. The default assumption should be that almost all cyber espionage will eventually be discovered. Unless strategic gains clearly outweigh the costs to diplomatic and economic interests as well as the potential threat to the stability of the global Internet, cyber operations should not be conducted. In order to fight terrorists and nonstate actors, the United States and its friends should collect and analyze data from online communications under laws that are clear, precise, and consistent with the principles of necessity and proportionality; that involve a third-party mechanism to ensure accountability; and that provide legal redress in case of unlawful or arbitrary surveillance.

The United States will want to develop this code with the input of and feedback from "like-minded" countries, first those in the European Union and NATO, then Asia-Pacific allies, and eventually emerging powers such as Brazil, India, Indonesia, and South Africa. Washington must also be clear on what it is offering its allies and friends. For allies like Australia, Japan, NATO countries, and South Korea, this will mean a willingness to respond to destructive attacks and to provide diplomatic, economic, political, and technical support in the case of coercive and disruptive attacks. Getting an agreement on privacy and data flows with Europe will also be essential. Berlin, London, Paris, and Washington should forge agreements that allow for law enforcement access to data. These agreements should include explicit protections of individual rights and personal data, requirements that governments regularly disclose when and why they are requesting data, and clear timetables for cooperation and response by governments.

Europe will also want to see surveillance reform. The United States should alter Section 702 of FISA (the program known as PRISM) and adopt the six criteria named in Presidential Policy Directive 28. This will narrow the justification for spying on foreigners from the broader need of "foreign affairs" to the more precise categories of espionage, terrorism, proliferation of weapons of mass destruction, cybersecurity threats, threats to US or allied military forces, and transnational crime. This shift should satisfy Europe's demands that US surveillance be conducted only "based on considerations of national security or the prevention of crime," as framed in the words of the Court of Justice of the European Union in the *Schrems v. Data Protection Commissioner* decision. As European countries expand their own surveillance powers, they will also have to be more transparent about the actions of their intelligence collection agencies and implement some of the same reforms they are calling for from Washington.

With friends such as Brasilia and Delhi, Washington will need to deepen bilateral ties and partner in building capacity in developing economies. While Brasilia and Delhi are unlikely to ever completely adopt US norms or to sanction or isolate Beijing and Moscow, the three multiethnic democracies should be able to identify acceptable rules of behavior in cyberspace. Moreover, Washington will want to reinforce recent moves by Brasilia and Delhi to embrace the multistakeholder model of Internet governance. This effort will require that the IANA transition—the end of the Department of Commerce's contract with the Internet Corporation for Assigned Names and Numbers and the internationalization of the domain name system governance process—proceeds and is not derailed by Congress.

Some of this alliance building will come from the United States providing resources and protection—the traditional instruments of diplomacy. But Washington has another source of leadership. The United States' capacity to bring policymakers, industry leaders, academics, scientists, and civil society representatives together to address issues and generate new ideas remains unmatched in the rest of the world. This capability will be essential as self-driving cars, big data, artificial intelligence, and autonomous weapons increasingly produce political, economic, social, and ethical choices that cannot be made by one set of interests in one type of venue. Months after US hackers turned off a Jeep on a St. Louis highway and an industry group announced new initiatives on security for the Internet of Things, a Chinese company announced that it was organizing a similar industry alliance to address car safety. Even as some forms of power diminish, Washington still exerts influence through agenda setting and the force of new ideas.

The hacked world order is defined by the empowerment of individuals and groups as well as by new expressions of geopolitics. New vulnerabilities arise, but the great powers have the technology, talent, and capital to create novel forms of influence and coercion. The conflict over cyberspace is the strategic imperative of the future, and everyone is struggling to understand what is at stake, who the critical actors are, and how cyber power works. The United States cannot afford to stumble forward blindly; the window of opportunity is closing as others define and pursue their interests in cyberspace. While the United States will continue to strive for an open, secure, and global cyberspace, it must also prepare for the more likely future of a fractured Internet.

ACKNOWLEDGMENTS

· ·

One of the mantras of cybersecurity—both as a field of study and a practice—is that it is a team sport, requiring partnerships and collaboration. This book benefited from the assistance of many people and institutions.

I am extremely proud to work at the Council on Foreign Relations (CFR), and I thank Richard N. Haass, CFR president, for his extremely helpful comments on the book, his support of me as a scholar, and his promotion of the Digital and Cyberspace Policy Program.

James Lindsay, director of studies, provided important feedback on the book and all the work I do at CFR. He has been a real partner in developing the cyber program. I also want to thank Amy Baker, Patricia Dorff, Janine Hill, and Shira Schwartz for making things at CFR go smoothly and efficiently. Michelle Baute and Leigh Gusts constantly e-mailed me reports, articles, and links to data they thought would be useful for my research. Two anonymous reviewers also helped make the book stronger. The camaraderie of Michael Levi, Shannon O'Neil, Jonathan Tepperman, and Micah Zenko in New York, and Steven Cook in Washington, DC, has always made coming to work a pleasure.

I gratefully acknowledge the Starr Foundation for its generous funding of my research and work as the Maurice R. Greenburg Senior Fellow for China Studies at CFR.

I visited nine countries to research this book, and I thank everyone who took the time to meet with me. I especially want to thank the following for introductions, logistics, and intellectual aid along the way: Sérgio Alves Jr., Kamlesh Bajaj, Jacob Olcott, Audrey Plonk, Stewart

Room, Sandro Suffert, Lior Tabansky, and Heli Tiirmaa-Klaar.

I spent a fantastic month at the Hoover Institution at Stanford University finishing the book, and I want to thank Amy Zegart and Herb Lin for inviting me and making me part of the community working on cybersecurity at the Center for International Security and Cooperation. Rawi Abdelal, Benjamin Brake, Elizabeth Economy, and Matthew Waxman read all or parts of the manuscript and gave extremely helpful feedback. All are good friends.

It has been a real pleasure to work with Clive Priddle at PublicAffairs. Since our first meeting, he has had an expansive vision of what this book was about. If I have come anywhere near achieving that vision it is in large part because of his fine editing and insightful comments. I thank Jennifer Kelland for her excellent copyediting and Shena Redmond for shepherding me through the process. Lisa Adams of the Garamond Agency once again ably guided me from raw idea to finished proposal and frequently checked in and offered advice as I wrote the book. I am grateful to her and David Miller.

Two research assistants at CFR, Patrick Browne and Sharone Tobias, conducted early research for the book. Lincoln Davidson updated much of the data, conducted follow-up research, and tracked down bibliographic information. I thank all of them for their help. Alex Grigsby, who works with me as the assistant director of the Digital and Cyberspace Program, made this book possible by doing his work so ably. Without Alex's oversight of the *Net Politics* blog, cyber policy brief series, and a wide array of meetings and workshops, I would never have had time to research or write.

Once I finished my last book, Lily began insisting that the next one be dedicated to her and her brother Noah. I am unsure if their impatience with the speed with which I was writing stemmed from their annoyance at my having to work on the weekends or the desire finally to see their names in print at the front of the book. So here it is: this book is dedicated to you.

I thank my brother and sister-in-law, Jonny and Alison Segal, for their love and cheerleading, and my in-laws, Richard and Cecile Sheramy for the same, as well as their constant interest in my work. Once again, my parents, Freya and Tony Segal, offered love, support at home, picnics at Tanglewood, and the occasional drink out on the deck.

None of the travel, research, and writing would have been possible without the help of my wife, Rona Sheramy. I can never thank her enough for all she does. She is my love and my life.

NOTES

· ·

CHAPTER 1: THE HACKED WORLD ORDER

1. David Sanger, "Obama Order Sped Up Wave of Cyberattacks Against Iran," *New York Times,* June 1, 2012, http://www.nytimes.com/2012/06/01/world/middle east/obama-ordered-wave-of-cyberattacks-against-iran.html.

2. David Sanger, "Iran Fights Malware Attacking Computers," *New York Times,* September 10, 2012, http://www.nytimes.com/2010/09/26/world/middle east/26iran.html. For various estimates of the damage, see David Albright, Paul Brannan, and Christina Walrond, "Did Stuxnet Take Out 1,000 Centrifuges at the Natanz Enrichment Plant? Preliminary Assessment," Institute for Science and International Security, December 22, 2010, http://isis-online.org/isis -reports/detail/did-stuxnet-take-out-1000-centrifuges-at-the-natanz-enrichment -plant; Ivanka Barzashka, "Are Cyber-Weapons Effective? Assessing Stuxnet's Impact on the Iranian Enrichment Programme," *RUSI Journal* 158, no. 2 (April 2013): 48–56.

3. David Sanger, "U.S. Rejected Aid for Israeli Raid on Iranian Nuclear Site," *New York Times,* January 10, 2009, http://www.nytimes.com/2009/01/11 /washington/11iran.html.

4. David Kushner, "The Real Story of Stuxnet," *IEEE Spectrum,* February 26, 2013, http://spectrum.ieee.org/telecom/security/the-real-story-of-stuxnet; Kim Zetter, *Countdown to Zero Day: Stuxnet and the Launch of the World's First Digital Weapon* (New York: Crown, 2014), 29.

5. Hayden quoted in Sanger, "Obama Order Sped Up Wave of Cyberattacks Against Iran"; Rattray quoted in Ellen Nakashima, "Iran Blamed for Cyber-attacks on U.S. Banks and Companies," *Washington Post,* September 21, 2012, http://www.washingtonpost.com/world/national-security/iran-blamed-for -cyberattacks/2012/09/21/afbe2be4-0412-11e2-9b24-ff730c7f6312_print.html.

6. Ashton B. Carter, keynote address by Deputy Secretary of Defense Ashton Carter to the RSA Conference, San Francisco, California, February 28, 2012, http://www.defense.gov/speeches/speech.aspx?speechid=1655; Dugan quoted

in Larry Shaughnessy, "The Internet: Frontline of the Next War?," *CNN*, November 7, 2011, http://www.cnn.com/2011/11/07/us/darpa.

7. Graham Cluley, "Twitter, Facebook and LiveJournal Hit by Massive Denial-of-Service Attack," *Naked Security*, August 6, 2009, http://nakedsecurity.sophos.com/2009/08/06/twitter-hit-massive-denialofservice-attack.

8. Leon Panetta, speech given to Business Executives for National Security, New York, October 12, 2012, http://www.defensenews.com/article/20121012/DEFREG02/310120001/Text-Speech-by-Defense-U-S-Secretary-Leon-Panetta; Jim Finkle, "Insiders Suspected in Saudi Cyber Attack," *Reuters*, September 7, 2012, http://in.reuters.com/article/2012/09/07/net-us-saudi-aramco-hack-idINBRE8860CR20120907.

9. Moussavian quoted in Mark Clayton, "Cyber-War: In Deed and Desire, Iran Emerging as a Major Power," *Christian Science Monitor*, March 16, 2014, http://www.csmonitor.com/World/Passcode/2014/0316/Cyber-war-In-deed-and-desire-Iran-emerging-as-a-major-power.

10. Leon Panetta, speech given to Business Executives for National Security.

11. Kim Zetter, "The NSA Acknowledges What We All Feared: Iran Learns from US Cyberattacks," *Wired*, February 10, 2015, http://www.wired.com/2015/02/nsa-acknowledges-feared-iran-learns-us-cyberattacks.

12. Ellen Nakashima, "Confidential Report Lists U.S. Weapons System Designs Compromised by Chinese Cyberspies," *Washington Post*, May 27, 2013, http://www.washingtonpost.com/world/national-security/confidential-report-lists-us-weapons-system-designs-compromised-by-chinese-cyberspies/2013/05/27/a42c3e1c-c2dd-11e2-8c3b-0b5e9247e8ca_print.html; Josh Rogin, "NSA Chief: Cybercrime Constitutes the 'Greatest Transfer of Wealth in History,'" *Foreign Policy*, July 9, 2012, http://foreignpolicy.com/2012/07/09/nsa-chief-cybercrime-constitutes-the-greatest-transfer-of-wealth-in-history.

13. Nicole Perlroth, "Hackers in China Attacked The Times for Last 4 Months," *New York Times*, January 30, 2013, http://www.nytimes.com/2013/01/31/technology/chinese-hackers-infiltrate-new-york-times-computers.html.

14. President Barack Obama, *Charlie Rose*, June 17, 2013, http://www.charlierose.com/watch/60230424.

15. Dilma Rousseff, statement at the opening of the general debate of the 68th session of the United Nations General Assembly, New York, September 24, 2013, http://gadebate.un.org/sites/default/files/gastatements/68/BR_en.pdf; Daniel Kurtz-Phelan, "The World's Emerging Democracies Don't Like Us Either," *Time*, September 25, 2013, http://ideas.time.com/2013/09/25/the-worlds-emerging-democracies-dont-like-us-either.

16. Pratap Bhanu Mehta, "Snowden's Revelations Highlight the Moral Decline of America," *Financial Times*, July 7, 2013, http://www.ft.com/intl/cms/s/0/04b972d8-e59b-11e2-ad1a-00144feabdc0.html#axzz3cbHxKEWh.

17. Henry Kissinger, *World Order* (New York: Penguin, 2014), 344–345.

18. McGregor quoted in Damian Paletta, Danny Yardon, and Jennifer

Valentino-Devries, "Cyberwar Ignites a New Arms Race," *Wall Street Journal*, October 11, 2015, http://www.wsj.com/articles/cyberwar-ignites-a-new-arms-race-1444611128.

19. "Ongoing Sophisticated Malware Campaign Compromising ICS," ICS-CERT, US Department of Homeland Security, December 10, 2014, https://ics-cert.us-cert.gov/alerts/ICS-ALERT-14-281-01B.

20. Jessica Silver-Greenberg, Matthew Goldstein, and Nicole Perlroth, "JPMorgan Chase Hacking Affects 76 Million Households," *DealB%k* (blog), *New York Times*, October 2, 2014, http://dealbook.nytimes.com/2014/10/02/jpmorgan-discovers-further-cyber-security-issues.

21. Michael Corkery, Jessica Silver-Greenberg, and David E. Sanger, "Obama Had Security Fears on JPMorgan Data Breach," *DealB%k* (blog), *New York Times*, October 8, 2014, http://dealbook.nytimes.com/2014/10/08/cyberattack-on-jpmorgan-raises-alarms-at-white-house-and-on-wall-street.

22. Chris Strohm, "Former NSA Chief Says JPMorgan Hack May Be a Warning from Russia," *Bloomberg*, September 3, 2014, http://www.bloomberg.com/news/articles/2014-09-03/former-nsa-chief-says-jpmorgan-hack-may-be-a-warning; Ellen Nakashima, "FBI: 'No Indication' JPMorgan Was Hacked Because of Sanctions Against Russia," *Washington Post*, October 20, 2014, http://www.washingtonpost.com/business/economy/fbi-no-indication-jpmorgan-was-hacked-because-of-sanctions-against-russia/2014/10/20/66031f16-58af-11e4-b812-38518ae74c67_story.html; Matthew Goldstein and Nicole Perlroth, "Authorities Closing In on Hackers Who Stole Data from JPMorgan Chase," *New York Times*, March 15, 2015, http://www.nytimes.com/2015/03/16/business/dealbook/authorities-closing-in-on-hackers-who-stole-data-from-jpmorgan-chase.html; Michael Riley and Jordan Robertson, "Digital Misfits Link JPMorgan Hack to Pump-and-Dump Fraud," *Bloomberg*, July 21, 2015, http://www.bloomberg.com/news/articles/2015-07-21/fbi-israel-make-securities-fraud-arrests-tied-to-jpmorgan-hack.

23. Max Fisher, "Syrian Hackers Claim AP Hack That Tipped Stock Market by $136 Billion. Is It Terrorism?," *WorldViews* (blog), *Washington Post*, April 23, 2013, http://www.washingtonpost.com/blogs/worldviews/wp/2013/04/23/syrian-hackers-claim-ap-hack-that-tipped-stock-market-by-136-billion-is-it-terrorism; Nicole Perlroth, "No Joke: Syrians Hack The Onion," *Bits* (blog), *New York Times*, May 6, 2013, http://bits.blogs.nytimes.com/2013/05/06/no-joke-syrians-hack-the-onion/?gwh=9073CB1441AACFE96A0FE656B92C9A00&gwt=pay.

24. "Cyberspace Policy Review: Assuring a Trusted and Resilient Information and Communications Infrastructure," White House, http://www.whitehouse.gov/assets/documents/Cyberspace_Policy_Review_final.pdf.

25. Craig Timberg, Ellen Nakashima, and Danielle Douglas-Gabriel, "Cyberattacks Trigger Talk of 'Hacking Back,'" *Washington Post*, October 9, 2014, http://www.washingtonpost.com/business/technology/cyberattacks-trigger-talk-of-hacking-back/2014/10/09/6f0b7a24-4f02-11e4-8c24-487e92bc997b_story.html.

26. "Clinton Calls WikiLeaks Documents 'an Attack on the International

Community,'" *New York Post*, November 29, 2010, http://nypost.com/2010/11/29
/clinton-calls-wikileaks-documents-an-attack-on-the-international-community
/#ixzz16kRfnGL0.

27. Yaakov Lappin, "Netanyahu: Israel Should Be a Global Cyber-Power," *Jerusalem Post*, June 9, 2011, http://www.jpost.com/Diplomacy-and-Politics /Netanyahu-Israel-should-be-a-global-cyber-power.

28. Brian Chen, "IPhone Sales in China Bolster Apple Earnings," *New York Times*, January 27, 2015, http://www.nytimes.com/2015/01/28/technology/apple -quarterly-earnings.html; Matt Krantz, "10 US Companies Take the Most Foreign Money," *USA Today*, July 15, 2015.

29. Matthieu Pélissié du Rausas et al., "Internet Matters: The Net's Sweeping Impact on Growth, Jobs, and Prosperity," McKinsey Global Institute, May 2011, http://www.mckinsey.com/insights/mgi/research/technology_and _innovation/internet_matters.

30. Interview, French Foreign Ministry official, Paris, February 10, 2015.

31. John Villasenor, "Recording Everything: Digital Storage as an Enabler of Authoritarian Governments," Brookings Institution, December 14, 2011, http:// www.brookings.edu/research/papers/2011/12/14-digital-storage-villasenor.

32. Dana Bash and Tom Cohen, "Officials Cite Thwarted Plots, Oversight in Defending Surveillance," *CNN*, June 19, 2013, http://www.cnn.com/2013/06/18/ politics/nsa-leaks.

33. Rogers quoted in Patrick Tucker, "NSA Chief: Yes, We Still Have Friends," *Defense One*, September 16, 2014, http://www.defenseone.com/politics/2014/09 /nsa-chief-yes-we-still-have-friends/94265; Dan Geer, "We Are All Intelligence Officers Now," RSA Conference, San Francisco, California, February 28, 2014, http://www.rsaconference.com/writable/presentations/file_upload/exp-f02-we -are-all-intelligence-officers-now.pdf.

34. Interview, cybersecurity company employee, Palo Alto, California, July 1, 2015.

35. Jennifer Granick, "The End of the Internet Dream," https://medium.com /backchannel/the-end-of-the-internet-dream-ba060b17da61.

36. Ibid.

CHAPTER 2: THE ANATOMY OF CYBER POWER

1. Janna Anderson and Lee Rainie, "Net Threats," Pew Research Center, July 3, 2014, http://www.pewinternet.org/2014/07/03/net-threats; Paul Mozur, "China's Internet Censorship Anthem Is Revealed, Then Deleted," *Sinosphere* (blog), *New York Times*, February 12, 2015, http://sinosphere.blogs.nytimes .com/2015/02/12/chinas-internet-censorship-anthem-is-revealed-then-deleted.

2. Information Office of the State Council of the People's Republic of China, "The Internet in China," China.org.cn, June 8, 2010, http://www.china.org .cn/government/whitepaper/node_7093508.htm; Paul Mozur and Jane Perlez, "Gregarious and Direct: China's Web Doorkeeper," *New York Times*, December 1, 2014, http://www.nytimes.com/2014/12/02/world/asia/gregarious-and-direct -chinas-web-doorkeeper.html.

3. "We Can Absolutely Not Allow the Internet Become a Lost Territory of People's Minds," *PLA Daily*, May 12, 2015, translated by Rogier Creemers, *China Copyright and Media*, May 13, 2015, https://chinacopyrightandmedia.wordpress .com/2015/05/13/army-newspaper-we-can-absolutely-not-allow-the-internet -become-a-list-territory-of-peoples-minds/.

4. Jonathan Kaiman, "China Cracks Down on Social Media with Threat of Jail for 'Online Rumors,'" *Guardian*, September 10, 2013, http://www.theguardian .com/world/2013/sep/10/china-social-media-jail-rumours; "Severe Penalties for Defamatory Retweets in China," *Xinhua*, September 9, 2013, http://news .xinhuanet.com/english/china/2013-09/09/c_132705863.htm; Jaime A. Flor-Cruz, "Online Popularity Can Be Perilous as China Obsesses About Internet Rumors," *CNN*, Friday 13, 2013, http://www.cnn.com/2013/09/13/world/asia /china-online-rumors-crackdown-florcruz.

5. "Xi Jinping Leads Internet Security Group," *Xinhua*, February 27, 2014, http://news.xinhuanet.com/english/china/2014-02/27/c_133148273.htm; "China on Frontlines of Cyber Security Threat," *China Daily*, April 19, 2014, http://www.chinadaily.com.cn/china/2014-04/19/content_17447912.htm; Rogier Creemers, "Cybersecurity and Informatization Leading Group: Names and Documents," *China Copyright and Media*, March 13, 2014, https:// chinacopyrightandmedia.wordpress.com/2014/03/13/cybersecurity-and -informatization-leading-group-names-and-documents.

6. Tania Branigan, "China Accuses US of Online Warfare in Iran," *Guardian*, January 24, 2010, http://www.theguardian.com/world/2010/jan/24/china-us -iran-online-warfare; "New Big Points Buried in the U.S. Cyberwar Strategy [Meiguowangzhan celüe maixia xinde baodian]," *Xinhua*, April 7, 2015, http://news .xinhuanet.com/zgjx/2015-04/07/c_134128303.htm.

7. David Bandurski, "The Internet Must Have Brakes," *China Media Project*, September 11, 2014, http://cmp.hku.hk/2014/09/11/36011; "China's Web Regulator Denies Shutting Foreign Websites," *BBC*, October 30, 2014, http://www.bbc .com/news/world-asia-china-29828982.

8. "China Web Conference Opens amid Internet Freedom Criticism," *BBC*, November 19, 2014, http://www.bbc.com/news/world-asia-china-30110430.

9. James T. Areddy, "China Delivers Midnight Internet Declaration—Offline," *China Real Time* (blog), *Wall Street Journal*, November 21, 2014, http://blogs.wsj .com/chinarealtime/2014/11/21/china-delivers-midnight-internet-declaration -offline.

10. Lu Wei, "Cyber Sovereignty Must Rule Global Internet," *Huffington Post*, December 15, 2015, http://www.huffingtonpost.com/lu-wei/china-cyber -sovereignty_b_6324060.html; Paul Mozur, "Warm West Coast Reception for China's Web Czar (Chillier in Washington)," *Bits* (blog), *New York Times*, December 8, 2014, http://bits.blogs.nytimes.com/2014/12/08/a-trip-to-california -for-chinas-internet-czar.

11. Franklin D. Kramer, Stuart H. Starr, and Larry K. Wentz, *Cyberpower and National Security* (Lincoln, NE: Potomac Books, 2009); William Gibson, *Neuromancer* (New York: Penguin Putnam, 2003), 55.

12. David Meyer, "'Cyberspace' Must Die. Here's Why," *Gigaom*, February 7, 2015, https://gigaom.com/2015/02/07/cyberspace-must-die-heres-why.

13. Timothy B. Lee, Twitter post, August 11, 2011, 6:11 a.m., https://twitter.com/binarybits/statuses/101490932595171328.

14. Henry Farrell, "The Political Science of Cybersecurity II: Why Cryptography Is So Important," *Washington Post*, February 12, 2014, http://www.washingtonpost.com/blogs/monkey-cage/wp/2014/02/12/the-political-science-of-cybersecurity-ii-why-cryptography-is-so-important; Nicole Perlroth, Jeff Larson, and Scott Shane, "N.S.A. Able to Foil Basic Safeguards of Privacy on Web," *New York Times*, September 5, 2013, http://www.nytimes.com/2013/09/06/us/nsa-foils-much-internet-encryption.html; Raul Zibechi, "South American Fiber Optic Ring," *Americas Program*, April 12, 2012, http://www.cipamericas.org/archives/6734; Hayden quoted in Michael Hirsch, "How America's Top Tech Companies Created the Surveillance State," *National Journal*, July 25, 2013, http://www.nationaljournal.com/magazine/how-america-s-top-tech-companies-created-the-surveillance-state-20130725.

15. Office of the Press Secretary, "Remarks by the President at the Cybersecurity and Consumer Protection Summit," White House, February 13, 2015, http://www.whitehouse.gov/the-press-office/2015/02/13/remarks-president-cybersecurity-and-consumer-protection-summit; Tova Dvorin, "Secret Shin Bet Unit at the Front Lines of Israel's Cyber-War," *Arutz Sheva*, April 25, 2014, http://www.israelnationalnews.com/News/News.aspx/179925#.VS5wQPnF_zg.

16. "'Stalker Economy' Here to Stay," *CNN*, November 26, 2013, http://edition.cnn.com/2013/11/20/opinion/schneier-stalker-economy/index.html.

17. Interview, US intelligence official, Washington, DC, February 26, 2015.

18. Ralph Langner, "Defending Cyber Dominance," Brookings Institution, March 19, 2014, http://www.brookings.edu/research/speeches/2014/03/19-defending-cyber-dominance-langner.

19. United Nations Institute for Disarmament Research (UNIDIR), "The Cyber Index: International Security Trends and Realities," UNIDIR, 2013, http://www.unidir.org/files/publications/pdfs/cyber-index-2013-en-463.pdf; Interview, former Shin Bet official, Tel Aviv, April 22, 2014; Andretta Towner, "The Future of Iranian Cyber Threat," Atlantic Council, April 9, 2015, http://www.atlanticcouncil.org/events/past-events/the-future-of-iranian-cyber-threat.

20. The Grugq, Twitter post, April 17, 2015, 9:17 a.m., https://twitter.com/thegrugq/status/588949360823570432.

21. "International Strategy for Cyberspace: Prosperity, Security, and Openness in a Networked World," White House, May 2011, http://www.whitehouse.gov/sites/default/files/rss_viewer/international_strategy_for_cyberspace.pdf.

22. David Bandurski, "Lu Wei on the 'Dream of the Web,'" *China Media Project*, February 17, 2015, http://cmp.hku.hk/2015/02/17/38218.

23. Buttarelli quoted in Tom Fairless and Stephen Fidler, "Europe Wants the World to Embrace Its Internet Rules," *Wall Street Journal*, February 24,

2015, http://www.wsj.com/articles/europe-wants-the-world-to-embrace-its-data -privacy-rules-1424821453.

24. Siobhan Gorman, "Intel Chief: Russia Tops China as Cyber Threat," *Washington Wire* (blog), *Wall Street Journal*, October 17, 2014, http://blogs.wsj.com/wash wire/2014/10/17/intel-chief-russia-tops-china-as-cyber-threat; Sean Lyngaas, "DNI Worries about Cumulative, Not Catastrophic, Cyber Threat," *FCW*, February 26, 2015, http://fcw.com/articles/2015/02/26/cumulative-cyber-threat.aspx.

25. James Appell, "The Short Life and Speedy Death of Russia's Silicon Valley," *Foreign Policy*, May 6, 2015, http://foreignpolicy.com/2015/05/06/the-short -life-and-speedy-death-of-russias-silicon-valley-medvedev-go-russia-skolkovo.

26. The idea of strategic cultures is discussed in Jack L. Snyder, "The Soviet Strategic Culture: Implications for Limited Nuclear Operations," Rand Corporation, September 1977, http://www.rand.org/content/dam/rand/pubs/reports /2005/R2154.pdf.

27. Stephen Sestanovich, "Could It Have Been Otherwise?," *American Interest*, April 14, 2015, http://www.the-american-interest.com/2015/04/14/could -it-have-been-otherwise.

28. Anita Chang, "China Group Says US Uses Facebook to Sow Unrest," *Salon*, July 9, 2010, http://www.salon.com/news/2010/07/09/as_china_social_media; Miriam Elder, "Nervous Kremlin Seeks to Purge Russia's Internet of 'Western' Influences," *Guardian*, April 15, 2012, http://www.theguardian.com/technology /2012/apr/15/kremlin-purge-russia-internet-western-influences; "Russian National Security Concept," Consulate General of the Russian Federation in Mumbai, http://www.russiaconsulmumbai.mid.ru/sec.html.

29. John Markoff and Thom Shanker, "Halted '03 Iraq Plan Illustrates U.S. Fear of Cyberwar Risk," *New York Times*, August 1, 2009, http://www.nytimes.com /2009/08/02/us/politics/02cyber.html.

30. James Blitz, "UK Becomes First State to Admit to Offensive Cyber Attack Capability," *Financial Times*, September 29, 2013, http://www.ft.com/intl/cms /s/0/9ac6ede6-28fd-11e3-ab62-00144feab7de.html#axzz3cbHxKEWh.

31. David J. Betz and Timothy C. Stevens, *Cyberspace and the State: Towards a Strategy for Cyberpower* (New York: Routledge, 2012); "Cyber Leaders: A Discussion with the Honorable Eric Rosenbach," Center for Strategic and International Studies, October 2, 2014, http://csis.org/event/cyber-leaders.

32. Georgi Kantchev, "Diplomats on Twitter: The Good, the Bad, and the Ugly," *Digits* (blog), *Wall Street Journal*, February 24, 2015, http://blogs.wsj.com /digits/2015/02/24/diplomats-on-twitter-the-good-the-bad-and-the-ugly.

33. Fernandez quoted in Simon Cottee, "Why It's So Hard to Stop ISIS Propaganda," *Atlantic*, March 2, 2015, http://www.theatlantic.com/international /archive/2015/03/why-its-so-hard-to-stop-isis-propaganda/386216.

34. "Guidelines on National Medium- and Long-Term Program for Science and Technology Development" (2006–2020), People's Republic of China State Council, February 6, 2009, www.gov.cn/jrzg/2006-02/09/content_183787.htm.

35. "Oettinger Calls for 'Europeanisation' of Digital Policy," *EurActiv*, March 17, 2015, http://www.euractiv.com/sections/infosociety/oettinger-calls-europeanisation-digital-policy-312946.

CHAPTER 3: GUARDIANS OF PEACE, LITTLE GREEN MEN, AND THE ELECTRONIC ARMIES OF THE FUTURE

1. Ben Fritz, Danny Yardon, and Erich Schwartzel, "Behind the Scenes at Sony as Hacking Crisis Unfolded," *Wall Street Journal*, December 30, 2014, http://www.wsj.com/articles/behind-the-scenes-at-sony-as-hacking-crisis-unfolded-1419985719.

2. Choe Sang Hun, "North Korea Warns U.S. Over Film Mocking Its Leader," *New York Times*, June 25, 2014, http://www.nytimes.com/2014/06/26/world/asia/north-korea-warns-us-over-film-parody.html.

3. James R. Clapper, "National Intelligence, North Korea, and the National Cyber Discussion," remarks delivered at the International Conference on Cyber Security, New York, January 8, 2015, http://www.dni.gov/index.php/newsroom/speeches-and-interviews/208-speeches-interviews-2015/1156-remarks-as-delivered-by-dni-james-r-clapper-on-%E2%80%9Cnational-intelligence,-north-korea,-and-the-national-cyber-discussion%E2%80%9D-at-the-international-conference-on-cyber-security.

4. Sangwoon Yoon, "North Korea Recruits Hackers at School," *Al Jazeera*, June 20, 2011, http://www.aljazeera.com/indepth/features/2011/06/201162081543573839.html; Danni Z, "Surprisingly Great Hotel—Clean, Tasteful . . . and North Korean!," TripAdvisor review, June 19, 2013, http://www.tripadvisor.com/ShowUserReviews-g297454-d455525-r164506979-Chilbosan-Shenyang_Liaoning.html#UR164506979.

5. Amanda Holpuch, "Sony Email Hack: What We've Learned About Greed, Racism, and Sexism," *Guardian*, December 15, 2014, http://www.theguardian.com/technology/2014/dec/14/sony-pictures-email-hack-greed-racism-sexism; Christopher Rosen, "Scott Rudin & Amy Pascal Apologize After Racially Insensitive Emails About Obama Leak," *Huffington Post*, December 11, 2014, http://www.huffingtonpost.com/2014/12/11/scott-rudin-amy-pascal-apology_n_6310040.html; "Leaked Sony Emails Exhibit Wealthy Elite's Maneuvering to Get Child into Ivy League School," *Russia Today*, April 24, 2015, http://rt.com/usa/252885-sony-emails-ivy-league.

6. Arik Hesseldahl and Dawn Chmielewski, "Sony Hackers Threaten Violence over 'The Interview,'" *Re/code*, December 16, 2014, http://recode.net/2014/12/16/sony-hackers-threaten-violence-over-the-interview.

7. Office of the Press Secretary, "Remarks by the President in Year-End Press Conference," White House, December 19, 2014, https://www.whitehouse.gov/the-press-office/2014/12/19/remarks-president-year-end-press-conference.

8. Shane Harris, "Did Vigilantes Knock North Korea Offline?," *Daily Beast*, March 24, 2015, http://www.thedailybeast.com/articles/2015/03/24/did-vigilantes-knock-north-korea-offline.html.

9. Hua Chunying, "Foreign Ministry Spokesperson Hua Chunying's Regular

Press Conference on December 22, 2014," Ministry of Foreign Affairs, the People's Republic of China, December 22, 2014, http://www.fmprc.gov.cn/mfa _eng/xwfw_665399/s2510_665401/t1221668.shtml.

10. The Grugq, "Cyber Attribution in Cyber Conflicts. Cyber," *Hacker Tradecraft,* December 29, 2014, http://grugq.tumblr.com/post/106516121088/cyber -attribution-in-cyber-conflicts-cyber.

11. Symantec Security Response, "Four Years of DarkSeoul Cyberattacks Against South Korea Continue on Anniversary of Korean War," *Symantec Official Blog,* June 26, 2013, http://www.symantec.com/connect/blogs/four-years-dark seoul-cyberattacks-against-south-korea-continue-anniversary-korean-war.

12. Marc Rogers, "Why I *Still* Don't Think It's Likely That North Korea Hacked Sony," *Marc's Security Ramblings,* December 21, 2014, http://marcrogers .org/2014/12/21/why-i-still-dont-think-its-likely-that-north-korea-hacked-sony. On the IP addresses, see sardonic security expert Krypt3ia's post titled "FAUX-TRIBUTION?" at Krypt3ia.wordpress.com, December 20, 2014, https://krypt 3ia.wordpress.com/2014/12/20/fauxtribution.

13. James B. Comey, speech at the International C̲   ̶ce on Cyber Security, Fordham University, New York, January ̲ ̲   ̲www.fbi.gov /news/speeches/addressing-the-cyber-securit̲ ̲

14. Nicholas Weaver, "Why It's Possibl̲   the Sony Hack," *Mashable,* December 18, 2014, ht̲   ̲/18/nsa -track-sony-hackers/#zn8u7t.OqSky; Barto̲   ̲hima, "U.S. Spy Agencies Mounted 231 Offensive̲   ̲Doc- uments Show," *Washington Post,* August 30,̲   ̲ton post.com/world/national-security/us-spy-age̲   offensive -cyber-operations-in-2011-documents-show/201̲3̲   ̲a6ae-119e-11e3 -b4cb-fd7ce041d814_story.html.

15. David Sanger and Martin Fackler, "N.S.A. Breached North Korean Networks Before Sony Attack, Officials Say," *New York Times,* January 18, 2015, http://www.nytimes.com/2015/01/19/world/asia/nsa-tapped-into-north-korean -networks-before-sony-attack-officials-say.html.

16. "Advance Questions for Vice Admiral Michael S. Rogers, USN Nominee for Commander, United States Cyber Command," US Senate, Armed Services Committee, http://www.armed-services.senate.gov/imo/media/doc/Rogers _03-11-14.pdf; Jacob Appelbaum et al., "The Digital Arms Race: NSA Preps America for Future Battle," *Spiegel,* January 17, 2015, http://www.spiegel.de /international/world/new-snowden-docs-indicate-scope-of-nsa-preparations -for-cyber-battle-a-1013409.html; Gellman and Nakashima, "U.S. Spy Agencies Mounted 231 Offensive Cyber-Operations in 2011, Documents Show."

17. "International Strategy for Cyberspace," White House, May 2011, http:// www.whitehouse.gov/sites/default/files/rss_viewer/international_strategy_for _cyberspace.pdf; Siobhan Gorman and Julian Barnes, "Cyber Combat: Act of War," *Wall Street Journal,* May 31, 2011, http://www.wsj.com/articles/SB100014240 52702304563104576355623135782718; Barack Obama, "Taking the Cyberattack

Threat Seriously," *Wall Street Journal*, July 19, 2012, http://www.wsj.com/articles /SB10000872396390444330904577535492693044650.

18. "Strategy for Operating in Cyberspace," Department of Defense, July 2011, http://csrc.nist.gov/groups/SMA/ispab/documents/DOD-Strategy-for -Operating-in-Cyberspace.pdf.

19. Painter quoted in Ellen Nakashima, "Why the Sony Hack Drew an Unprecedented U.S. Response Against North Korea," *Washington Post*, January 15, 2015, http://www.washingtonpost.com/world/national-security/why-the-sony -hack-drew-an-unprecedented-us-response-against-north-korea/2015/01/14 /679185d4-9a63-11e4-96cc-e858eba91ced_story.html.

20. Chris Strohm, "Sony Hack Prompts U.S. Review of Public Role in Company Security," *Bloomberg*, January 8, 2015, http://www.bloomberg.com/news/2015 -01-08/sony-hack-prompts-u-s-review-of-public-role-in-company-security.html.

21. Steven Lee Myers, "Russia Rebukes Estonia for Moving Soviet Statue," *New York Times*, April 27, 2007, http://www.nytimes.com/2007/04/27/world /europe/27cnd-estonia.html.

22. "Deadly Riots in Tallinn: Soviet Memorial Causes Rift Between Estonia and Russia," *Spiegel*, April 27, 2007, http://www.spiegel.de/international/europe /deadly-riots-in-tallinn-soviet-memorial-causes-rift-between-estonia-and-russia -a-479809.html; Interview, former official, Ministry of Defense, Tallinn, October 12, 2009.

23. Clay Wilson, *Botnets, Cybercrime, and Cyberterrorism: Vulnerabilities and Policy Issues for Congress*, CRS Report for Congress, Congressional Research Service, January 29, 2008, https://www.fas.org/sgp/crs/terror/RL32114.pdf.

24. Vladimir Putin, "Speech at the Military Parade Celebrating the 62nd Anniversary of Victory in the Great Patriotic War," President of Russia, May 9, 2007, http://archive.kremlin.ru/eng/text/speeches/2007/05/09/1432_type 82912type127286_127675.shtml.

25. A. A. K., "How Did Estonia Become a Leader in Technology?," *Economist*, July 30, 2013, http://www.economist.com/blogs/economist-explains/2013/07 /economist-explains-21.

26. Patrick Kingsley, "How Tiny Estonia Stepped Out of USSR's Shadow to Become an Internet Titan," *Guardian*, April 15, 2012, http://www.theguardian .com/technology/2012/apr/15/estonia-ussr-shadow-internet-titan.

27. "Viewing cable 07TALLINN375, Estonia's Cyber Attacks: Lessons Learned," US Embassy in Tallinn, June 6, 2007, https://wikileaks.org/cable /2007/06/07TALLINN375.html.

28. Interview with Linnar Viik, Tallinn, October 12, 2009; Joshua Davis, "Hackers Take Down the Most Wired Country in Europe," *Wired*, August 21, 2007, http://archive.wired.com/politics/security/magazine/15-09/ff_estonia.

29. Evgeny Morozov, "NATO Hammers Out Strategy for Cyberattack," *Newsweek*, April 17, 2009, http://www.newsweek.com/nato-hammers-out-strategy -cyberattack-77499.

30. Ian Traynor, "Russia Accused of Unleashing Cyberwar to Disable Estonia," *Guardian*, May 16, 2007, http://www.theguardian.com/world/2007/may/17/top stories3.russia; Jason Healey and Karl Grindal, *A Fierce Domain: Conflict in Cyberspace, 1986 to 2012* (Arlington, VA: Cyber Conflict Studies Association, 2013).

31. NSA report mentioned in Nicole Perlroth, "Online Security Experts Link More Breaches to Russian Government," *New York Times*, October 29, 2014, http://www.nytimes.com/2014/10/29/technology/russian-government -linked-to-more-cybersecurity-breaches.html.

32. Interview, bank official, Tallinn, October 13, 2009; Patrick Tucker, "Who Defends the Virtual Countries of Tomorrow?," *Defense One*, September 5, 2014, http://www.defenseone.com/technology/2014/09/who-defends -virtual-countries-tomorrow/93293.

33. Charles King, "Five Day War," *Foreign Affairs*, November/December 2008, http://www.foreignaffairs.com/articles/64602/charles-king/the-five-day-war; Noah Shachtman, "Top Georgian Official: Moscow Cyberattacked Us—We Just Can't Prove It," *Wired*, March 3, 2009, http://www.wired.com/2009/03 /georgia-blames.

34. Jose Nazario, "Georgia on My Mind—Political DDoS," Arbor Networks, July 20, 2008, http://www.arbornetworks.com/asert/2008/07/georgia -on-my-mind-political-ddos; Information Warfare Monitor, "CCDCOE: Cyberattacks Against Georgia: Legal Lessons Identified," *Infowar Monitor*, April 16, 2009, http://www.infowar-monitor.net/2009/04/ccdcoe-cyber-attacks -against-georgia-legal-lessons-identified.

35. Brian Krebs, "Report: Russian Hacker Forums Fueled Georgia Cyberattacks," *Security Fix* (blog), *Washington Post*, October 16, 2008, http://voices.washingtonpost .com/securityfix/2008/10/report_russian_hacker_forums_f.html; Project Grey Goose, "Project Grey Goose Report on Critical Infrastructure: Attacks, Actors, and Emerging Threats," Data Clone Labs, January 21, 2010, http://dataclonelabs.com /security_talkworkshop/papers/25550091-Proj-Grey-Goose-report-on-Critical -Infrastructure-Attacks-Actors-and-Emerging-Threats.pdf.

36. "Overview by the US-CCU of the Cyber Campaign Against Georgia in August 2008," A US-CCU Special Report, *Registran*, August 2009, http://www .registan.net/wp-content/uploads/2009/08/US-CCU-Georgia-Cyber-Campaign -Overview.pdf; Khorishko quoted in John Markoff, "Before the Gunfire, Cyberattacks," *New York Times*, August 12, 2008, http://www.nytimes.com/2008/08/13 /technology/13cyber.html; Evgeny Morozov, "An Army of Ones and Zeroes," *Slate*, August 14, 2008, http://www.slate.com/articles/technology/technology /2008/08/an_army_of_ones_and_zeroes.html.

37. Shachtman, "Top Georgian Official."

38. Siobhan Gorman, "Georgia States Computers Hit by Cyberattack," *Wall Street Journal*, August 12, 2008, http://online.wsj.com/articles/SB121850756472932159; Noah Shachtman, "Estonia, Google Help 'Cyberlocked' Georgia," *Wired*, August 11, 2008, http://www.wired.com/2008/08/civilge-the-geo.

39. Stephen Korns and Joshua Kastenberg, "Georgia's Cyber Left Hook," *Parameters* 38, no. 4 (winter 2008–2009), http://www.army.mil/article/19351/georgias -cyber-left-hook.

40. Healey and Grindal, *Fierce Domain*.

41. "The Military Doctrine of the Russian Federation," Carnegie Endowment for International Peace, February 5, 2010, http://carnegieendowment.org/files /2010russia_military_doctrine.pdf.

42. Keir Giles, "With Russia and Ukraine, Is All Really Quiet on the Cyber Front?," *Ars Technica*, March 11, 2014, http://arstechnica.com/tech-policy /2014/03/with-russia-and-ukraine-is-all-really-quiet-on-the-cyber-front; Sam Jones, "Cyber Snake Plagues Ukraine Networks," *Financial Times*, March 7, 2014, http://www.ft.com/intl/cms/s/0/615c29ba-a614-11e3-8a2a-00144feab7de.html.

43. Jeffery Carr, "Cybersecurity Meets Modern Warfare," *CNN*, March 25, 2014, http://www.cnn.com/2014/03/25/opinion/crimea-cyber-war/index.html.

44. Olga Razumovskaya, "From Twitter with Hack: Russian PM's Account Hijacked," *Digits* (blog), *Wall Street Journal*, August 14, 2014, http://blogs.wsj .com/digits/2014/08/14/from-twitter-with-hack-russian-pms-account-hijacked.

45. Ellen Nakashima, "Hackers Breach Some White House Computers," *Washington Post*, October 28, 2014, http://www.washingtonpost.com/world /national-security/hackers-breach-some-white-house-computers/2014/10 /28/2ddf2fa0-5ef7-11e4-91f7-5d89b5e8c251_story.html; Luke Harding and Shaun Walker, "Crimea Votes to Secede from Ukraine in 'Illegal' Poll," *Guardian*, March 16, 2014, http://www.theguardian.com/world/2014/mar/16/ukraine -russia-truce-crimea-referendum.

46. Leonid Bershidsky, "How Hackers Exposed Ukraine's Vulnerability," *Bloomberg*, May 26, 2014, http://www.bloombergview.com/articles/2014-05-26 /how-hackers-exposed-ukraine-s-vulnerability.

47. Peter Pomerantsev and Michael Weiss, "The Menace of Unreality: How the Kremlin Weaponizes Information, Culture, and Money," *Interpreter*, November 22, 2014, http://www.interpretermag.com/the-menace-of-unreality-how-the -kremlin-weaponizes-information-culture-and-money; "President Putin's Fiction: 10 False Claims About Ukraine," Office of the Spokesperson, US Department of State, March 5, 2014, http://www.state.gov/r/pa/prs/ps/2014/03/222988.htm.

48. Kiselev quoted in Joshua Jaffa, "Dmitry Kiselev Is Redefining the Art of Russian Propaganda," *New Republic*, July 1, 2014, http://www.newrepublic.com/article /118438/dmitry-kiselev-putins-favorite-tv-host-russias-top-propogandist; Ewen MacAskill, "Putin Calls Internet a 'CIA Project' Renewing Fears of Web Breakup," *Guardian*, April 24, 2014, http://www.theguardian.com/world/2014 /apr/24/vladimir-putin-web-breakup-internet-cia.

49. Ben Farmer and Nick Squires, "I Can Take Kiev in Two Weeks, Vladimir Putin Warns European Leaders," *Telegraph*, September 1, 2014, http://www .telegraph.co.uk/news/worldnews/europe/ukraine/11069070/I-can-take-Kiev -in-two-weeks-Vladimir-Putin-warns-European-leaders.html.

50. Anthony Cuthbertson, "Estonia First Country to Offer E-residency Digital Citizenship," *International Business Times*, October 7, 2014, http://www.ibtimes.co .uk/estonia-first-country-offer-e-residency-digital-citizenship-1468766.

51. "Estonia to Establish Digital Embassies," *Postimees in English*, August 27, 2014, http://news.postimees.ee/2900519/estonia-to-establish-digital-embassies.

52. Sam Jones, "Nato Holds Largest Cyber War Games," *Financial Times*, November 20, 2014, http://www.ft.com/intl/cms/s/0/9c46a600-70c5-11e4-8113-00144 feabdc0.html.

53. "NATO 2020: Assured Security, Dynamic Engagement," North Atlantic Treaty Organization, May 17, 2010, http://www.nato.int/strategic-concept /expertsreport.pdf; Richard Norton-Taylor, "Nato Faces Cyberattack Threat, Says Study of Defenses," *Guardian*, May 17, 2010, http://www.theguardian.com /world/2010/may/17/nato-faces-cyber-attacks-study; "Lisbon Summit Declaration," North Atlantic Treaty Organization, November 20, 2010, http://www.nato .int/cps/en/natolive/official_texts_68828.htm.

54. "Wales Summit Declaration," North Atlantic Treaty Organization, September 5, 2014, http://www.nato.int/cps/en/natohq/official_texts_112964.htm.

55. Steve Jordan, "NATO Updates Cyber Defense Policy as Digital Attacks Become a Standard Part of Conflict," *ZDNet*, June 30, 2014, http://www.zdnet .com/article/nato-updates-cyber-defence-policy-as-digital-attacks-become-a -standard-part-of-conflict.

CHAPTER 4: BREAKING THINGS AND THE SEARCH FOR ORDER

1. Andy Greenberg, "The Mac Hacker Strikes Again," *Forbes*, March 25, 2010, http://www.forbes.com/forbes/2010/0412/technology-apple-hackers-charlie -miller.html.

2. Jesse Bogan, "Wildwood Man Is Renowned for Hacking, Cybersecurity Skills," *St. Louis Post-Dispatch*, June 18, 2012, http://www.stltoday.com/news /local/metro/wildwood-man-is-renowned-for-hacking-cybersecurity-skills/article _6483524f-608b-5bcb-b27d-546886698dfb.html.

3. "Digital Carjackers Show Off New Attacks," YouTube video, 4:47, posted by *Forbes*, July 24, 2013, https://www.youtube.com/watch?v=oqe6S6m73Zw; Andy Greenberg, "Hackers Remotely Kill a Jeep on the Highway—With Me in It," *Wired*, July 21, 2015, http://www.wired.com/2015/07/hackers-remotely -kill-jeep-highway/; Andy Greenberg, "After Jeep Hack, Chrysler Recalls 1.4M Vehicles for Bug Fix," *Wired*, July 24, 2015, http://www.wired.com/2015/07/jeep -hack-chrysler-recalls-1-4m-vehicles-bug-fix/; Mike Isaac and Nicole Perlroth, "Uber Hires Two Engineers Who Show Cars Can Be Hacked," *New York Times*, August 28, 2015, http://www.nytimes.com/2015/08/29/technology/uber -hires-two-engineers-who-showed-cars-could-be-hacked.html.

4. Andy Greenberg, "A $60 Gadget That Makes Car Hacking Far Easier," *Wired*, March 25, 2015, http://www.wired.com/2015/03/60-gadget-thatll -make-car-hacking-easier-ever.

5. Karen Tillman, "How Many Internet Connections Are in the World? Right. Now.," *Platform*, July 29, 2013, http://blogs.cisco.com/news/cisco-connections-counter.

6. Dan Geer, "We Are All Intelligence Officers Now."

7. US Department of Defense, "The Department of Defense Cyber Strategy," April 2015, http://www.defense.gov/News/Special-Reports/0415_Cyber-Strategy; William J. Lynn, "Defending a New Domain: The Pentagon's Cyberstrategy," *Foreign Affairs*, September/October 2010, https://www.foreignaffairs.com/articles/united-states/2010-09-01/defending-new-domain.

8. "Russian and Chinese Assertiveness Poses New Foreign Policy Challenges: A Conversation with Robert M. Gates," Council on Foreign Relations, New York, May 21, 2014, http://www.cfr.org/defense-and-security/russian-chinese-assertiveness-poses-new-foreign-policy-challenges/p35645.

9. Michael S. Rogers, "Statement of Admiral Michael S. Rogers, Commander, United States Cyber Command, Before the Senate Committee on Armed Services, 19 March 2015," US Senate Committee on Armed Services, March 19, 2015, http://www.armed-services.senate.gov/imo/media/doc/Rogers_03-19-15.pdf.

10. Jacobs quoted in Bruce Schneier, "Has U.S. Started an Internet War?," *CNN*, June 18, 2013, http://www.cnn.com/2013/06/18/opinion/schneier-cyberwar-policy/index.html.

11. Chris Strohm, "Russian Government Seen Behind White House Computer Hack," *Bloomberg*, April 8, 2015, http://www.bloomberg.com/politics/articles/2015-04-08/russian-government-said-to-be-behind-white-house-computer-hack.

12. David Sanger, "U.S. Tries Candor to Assure China on Cyberattacks," *New York Times*, April 6, 2014, http://www.nytimes.com/2014/04/07/world/us-tries-candor-to-assure-china-on-cyberattacks.html; Chuck Hagel, speech at the retirement ceremony for General Keith Alexander, Fort Meade, Maryland, March 28, 2014, http://archive.defense.gov/Speeches/Speech.aspx?SpeechID=1837.

13. James Lewis, "Reconsidering Deterrence for Space and Cyberspace," in *Anti-satellite Weapons, Deterrence and Sino-American Space Relations*, ed. Michael Krepon and Julia Thompson (Washington, DC: Stimson Center, 2013); Ben Elgin and Michael Riley, "Now at the Sands Casino: An Iranian Hacker in Every Server," *Bloomberg*, December 11, 2014, http://www.bloomberg.com/bw/articles/2014-12-11/iranian-hackers-hit-sheldon-adelsons-sands-casino-in-las-vegas.

14. "Hearing to Receive Testimony on U.S. Strategic Command, U.S. Transportation Command, and U.S. Cyber Command in Review of the Defense Authorization Request for Fiscal Year 2016 and the Future Years Defense Program," US Senate, Armed Services Committee, March 19, 2015, http://www.armed-services.senate.gov/imo/media/doc/15-30%20-%203-19-15.pdf; Ellen Nakashima, "Several Nations Trying to Penetrate U.S. Cyber-Networks, Says Ex-FBI Official," *Washington Post*, April 18, 2012, http://www.washingtonpost.com/world/national-security/several-nations-trying-to-penetrate-us-cyber-networks-says-ex-fbi-official/2012/04/17/gIQAFAGUPT_story.html.

15. Andrea Shalal-Esa, "Ex-U.S. General Urges Frank Talk on Cyber Weapons," *Reuters*, November 6, 2011, http://uk.reuters.com/article/2011/11/06/us-cyber-cartwright-idUKTRE7A514C20111106; Ellen Nakashima, "Cyber Chief: Efforts to Deter Attacks Against the U.S. Are Not Working," *Washington Post*, March 19, 2015, http://www.washingtonpost.com/world/national-security/head-of-cyber-command-us-may-need-to-boost-offensive-cyber-powers/2015/03/19/1ad79a34-ce4e-11e4-a2a7-9517a3a70506_story.html.

16. "U.S. Needs 'Digital Warfare Force,'" *BBC*, May 5, 2009, http://news.bbc.co.uk/2/hi/8033440.stm.

17. Jeremy Kirk, "Irked by Cyberspying, Georgia Outs Russia-Based Hacker—with Photos," *Network World*, October 30, 2012, http://www.networkworld.com/article/2161067/byod/irked-by-cyberspying--georgia-outs-russia-based-hacker----with-photos.html.

18. Barton Gellman and Ellen Nakashima, "U.S. Spy Agencies Mounted 231 Offensive Cyber-Operations in 2011, Documents Show," *Washington Post*, August 30, 2013, http://www.washingtonpost.com/world/national-security/us-spy-agencies-mounted-231-offensive-cyber-operations-in-2011-documents-show/2013/08/30/d090a6ae-119e-11e3-b4cb-fd7ce041d814_story.html.

19. Bryan quoted in Healey and Grindal, *A Fierce Domain*.

20. Aliya Sternstein, "US Cyber Command Has Just Half the Staff It Needs," *Defense One*, February 8, 2015, http://www.defenseone.com/threats/2015/02/us-cyber-command-has-just-half-staff-it-needs/104847.

21. Ellen Nakashima, "Cyberattacks Should Require Presidential Authorization, Official Says," *Washington Post*, March 27, 2012, http://www.washingtonpost.com/world/national-security/cyberattacks-should-require-presidential-authorization-official-says/2012/03/27/gIQA0312eS_story.html; US Department of Defense, "The Department of Defense Cyber Strategy," April 2015, http://www.defense.gov/News/Special-Reports/0415_Cyber-Strategy.

22. Glenn Greenwald and Ewen MacAskill, "Obama Orders US to Draw Up Overseas Target List for Cyber-Attacks," *Guardian*, June 7, 2013, http://www.theguardian.com/world/2013/jun/07/obama-china-targets-cyber-overseas.

23. Michael Gross, "Stuxnet Worm: A Declaration of Cyber-War," *Vanity Fair*, April 2011, http://www.vanityfair.com/news/2011/04/stuxnet-201104.

24. "Conceptual Views Regarding the Activities of the Armed Forces of the Russian Federation in the Information Space," NATO Cooperative Cyber Defence Centre of Excellence, https://ccdcoe.org/strategies/Russian_Federation_unofficial_translation.pdf.

25. Eugene Gerden, "$500 Million for New Russian Cyber Army," *SC Magazine*, November 6, 2014, http://www.scmagazineuk.com/500-million-for-new-russian-cyber-army/article/381720/.

26. Shane Harris, "China Reveals Its Cyberwar Secrets," *Daily Beast*, March 18, 2015, http://www.thedailybeast.com/articles/2015/03/18/china-reveals-its-cyber-war-secrets.html; Joe McReynolds, *China's Evolving Military Strategy* (Washington, DC: Jamestown Foundation, 2015).

27. Keith Bradsher, "Market's Echo of Tiananmen Date Sets Off Censors," *New York Times*, June 4, 2012, http://www.nytimes.com/2012/06/05/world/asia /anniversary-of-tiananmen-crackdown-echos-through-shanghai-market.html.

28. Office of the Press Secretary, "Executive Order—'Blocking the Property of Certain Persons Engaging in Significant Malicious Cyber-Enabled Activities,'" White House, April 1, 2015, https://www.whitehouse.gov/the-press-office/2015 /04/01/executive-order-blocking-property-certain-persons-engaging-significant-m.

29. John Markoff and Andrew Kramer, "U.S. and Russia Differ on Treaty for Cyberspace," *New York Times*, June 28, 2009, http://www.nytimes.com/2009 /06/28/world/28cyber.html.

30. Harold Koh, "International Law in Cyberspace" (speech given at the USCYBERCOM Inter-agency Legal Conference, Fort Meade, Maryland, September 18, 2012), http://opiniojuris.org/2012/09/19/harold-koh-on -international-law-in-cyberspace.

31. Interview, former government official, Tel Aviv, April 24, 2014.

32. Dmitry Rogozin, "The Price of the Issue," *Kommersant*, February 16, 2011, cited in Keir Giles, "'Information Troops'—a Russian Cyber Command?," in *2011 3rd International Conference on Cyber Conflict*, ed. C. Czosseck, E. Tyugu, and T. Wingfield (Tallinn, Estonia: CCD COE Publications, 2011), 45–60, https:// ccdcoe.org/ICCC/materials/proceedings/giles.pdf.

33. Henry Farrell, "Promoting Norms for Cyberspace," CFR Cyber Brief, Council on Foreign Relations, April 2015, http://www.cfr.org/cybersecurity /promoting-norms-cyberspace/p36358.

34. Interview, Foreign Ministry official, Jerusalem, April 23, 2014.

35. Ms. Smith, "Sony Hacked in February, Knew About Security Flaws Before Data Leak," *Network World*, December 14, 2014, http://www.network world.com/article/2859473/microsoft-subnet/sony-hacked-in-feb-knew-about -huge-security-flaws-before-cybersecurity-train-wreck.html; Ashley Feinberg, "Sony Execs Knew About Extensive IT Flaws Two Months Before Leaks," *Gizmodo*, December 12, 2014, http://gizmodo.com/sony-execs-knew-about-extensive -it-flaws-two-months-bef-1670203774.

36. Green quoted in Feinberg, "Sony Execs Knew About Extensive IT Flaws."

37. "Comprehensive National Cybersecurity Initiative," White House, https:// www.whitehouse.gov/issues/foreign-policy/cybersecurity/national-initiative.

38. "Remarks by the President on Securing Our Nation's Cyber Infrastructure," White House, May 30, 2009, https://www.whitehouse.gov/the_press_office /Remarks-by-the-President-on-Securing-Our-Nations-Cyber-Infrastructure.

39. Siobhan Gorman, "Security Cyber Czar Steps Down," *Wall Street Journal*, August 4, 2009, http://www.wsj.com/articles/SB124932480886002237; Ellen Nakashima, "Cybersecurity Official Resigns over Delays in Appointment," *Washington Post*, August 4, 2009, http://www.washingtonpost.com/wp-dyn /content/article/2009/08/03/AR2009080302697.html.

40. Dan Verton, "Ten Years On, Tough Questions Remain About DHS,"

Homeland Security Today, September 12, 2013, http://www.hstoday.us/channels /dhs/single-article-page/ten-years-on-tough-questions-remain-about-dhs-cyber security/6a5d46c6c1157a46dae6edd630a58f20.html; Blair quoted in Kim Zetter, "NSA Should Oversee Cybersecurity, Intel Chief Says," *Wired*, February 26, 2009, http://www.wired.com/2009/02/nsa-should-over.

41. Rod Beckstrom, resignation letter as director of the National Cybersecurity Center, *Wall Street Journal*, March 5, 2009, http://online.wsj.com/public /resources/documents/BeckstromResignation.pdf; Andy Greenberg, "Top Cyber Official Sounds Off," *Forbes*, March 9, 2009, http://www.forbes .com/2009/03/09/rod-beckstrom-security-technology-security-beckstrom.html.

42. Schmidt quoted in Ryan Singel, "White House Cyber Czar: 'There Is No Cyberwar,'" *Wired*, March 4, 2010, http://www.wired.com/2010/03/schmidt -cyberwar.

43. Ellen Nakashima, "White House, NSA Weigh Cybersecurity, Personal Privacy," *Washington Post*, February 27, 2012, http://www.washingtonpost.com /world/national-security/white-house-nsa-weigh-cyber-security-personal-privacy /2012/02/07/gIQA8HmKeR_story.html.

44. "007 or DDoS: What Is Real World Cyber?," White House, February 28, 2013, https://www.whitehouse.gov/sites/default/files/docs/2013-02-28_final_rsa _speech.pdf.

45. Healey quoted in Zachary Fryer-Biggs, "Report: U.S. Tied for 4th Among 23 Countries in Cyber Defense," *Defense News*, January 31, 2012, http:// archive.defensenews.com/article/20120131/DEFREG02/301310002/Report -U-S-Tied-4th-Among-23-Countries-Cyber-Defense.

46. Office of the Press Secretary, "Executive Order—Improving Critical Infrastructure Cybersecurity," White House, February 12, 2013, https://www .whitehouse.gov/the-press-office/2013/02/12/executive-order-improving -critical-infrastructure-cybersecurity; Office of the Press Secretary, "Presidential Memorandum—Establishment of the Cyber Threat Intelligence Integration Center," White House, February 25, 2013, https://www.whitehouse .gov/the-press-office/2015/02/25/presidential-memorandum-establishment -cyber-threat-intelligence-integrat.

47. Sara Sorcher, "Obama's Info-Sharing Plan Won't Significantly Reduce Security Breaches," *Christian Science Monitor Passcode*, http://passcode.csmonitor .com/influencers-infosharing.

48. Benjamin Dean, "Why Companies Have Little Incentive to Invest in Cybersecurity," *Conversation*, March 4, 2015, http://theconversation.com/why -companies-have-little-incentive-to-invest-in-cybersecurity-37570.

49. Siobhan Gorman, "China Hackers Hit U.S. Chamber," *Wall Street Journal*, December 21, 2011, http://www.wsj.com/articles/SB10001424052970204058404 577110541568535300; Ken Dilanian, "U.S. Chamber of Commerce Leads Defeat of Cyber-Security Bill," *Los Angeles Times*, August 3, 2012, http://articles.latimes .com/2012/aug/03/nation/la-na-cyber-security-20120803.

50. Jonathan Zittrain and Molly Sauter, "Will the U.S. Get an Internet 'Kill Switch'?," *Technology Review*, March 4, 2011, http://www.technologyreview.com /news/423196/will-the-us-get-an-internet-kill-switch.

51. Sara Sorcher, "U.S. Government Not Invited to Facebook's ThreatExchange Party," *Passcode*, August 20, 2015, http://www.csmonitor.com/World /Passcode/2015/0820/US-government-not-invited-to-Facebook-s-Threat Exchange-party.

CHAPTER 5: EVERYBODY SPIES

1. Joey Cheng, "US Arrests Chinese Aerospace Exec in Hacking Conspiracy," *Defense Systems*, July 14, 2014, http://defensesystems.com/articles/2014/07/14 /doj-arrests-chinese-aerospace-exec-hacking.aspx.

2. John Reed, "Now the Chinese Are Hacking Us Through Our Limos," *Foreign Policy*, October 14, 2013, http://foreignpolicy.com/2013/10/14/now-the -chinese-are-hacking-us-through-our-limos.

3. Indictment, Criminal Case No. 14-00131, US District Court for Central District of California, US Department of Justice, June 2014, https://www.document cloud.org/documents/1276138-su-bin-indictment.html.

4. Indictment, Criminal Case No. 14-118, US District Court for the Western District of Pennsylvania, US Department of Justice, May 1, 2014, http://www .justice.gov/iso/opa/resources/5122014519132358461949.pdf; "Attorney General Eric Holder Speaks at the Press Conference Announcing U.S. Charges Against Five Chinese Military Hackers for Cyber Espionage," US Department of Justice, May 19, 2014, http://www.justice.gov/iso/opa/ag/speeches/2014 /ag-speech-140519.html.

5. Interview, Chinese official, Washington, DC, February 3, 2015.

6. Sam Frizell, "How to Hunt a Chinese Hacker," *Time*, July 3, 2014, http:// time.com/2918689/how-to-hunt-a-chinese-hacker; "Putter Panda," CrowdStrike Intelligence Report, CrowdStrike, http://cdn0.vox-cdn.com/assets/4589853 /crowdstrike-intelligence-report-putter-panda.original.pdf.

7. Ellen Nakashima, "Confidential Report Lists U.S. Weapons System Designs Compromised by Chinese Cyberspies," *Washington Post*, May 27, 2013, http://www .washingtonpost.com/world/national-security/confidential-report-lists-us -weapons-system-designs-compromised-by-chinese-cyberspies/2013/05/27/a42 c3e1c-c2dd-11e2-8c3b-0b5e9247e8ca_story.html; Matthew Pennington, "Intel Chief Warns U.S. Tech Threatened by China Cyber Theft," *Military Times*, February 3, 2015, http://www.militarytimes.com/story/military/tech/2015/02/03 /intel-chief-warns-us-tech-threatened-by-china-cyber-theft/22810269.

8. David Fulghum, Bill Sweetman, and Amy Butler, "China's Role in Spiraling JSF Costs," *Aviation Week*, February 3, 2012, http://www.defense -aerospace.com/article-view/release/132486/chinese-hacking-forced-costly -redesign-of-f_35-parts%3A-report.html; Adam Ashton, "I Corps Troops to Turn Focus on Pacific," *Olympian*, February 23, 2013, http://www.theolympian .com/2013/02/23/2433964/i-corps-troops-to-turn-focus-on.html.

9. "Cybersecurity, Terrorism, and Beyond: Addressing Evolving Threats to the Homeland," US Senate Committee on Homeland Security and Governmental Affairs, September 10, 2014, http://www.hsgac.senate.gov/hearings/cyber security-terrorism-and-beyond-addressing-evolving-threats-to-the-homeland.

10. Michael Riley and Jordan Robertson, "Chinese State-Sponsored Hackers Suspected in Anthem Attack," *Bloomberg*, February 2, 2015, http://www .bloomberg.com/news/articles/2015-02-05/signs-of-china-sponsored-hackers -seen-in-anthem-attack; David Perera and Joseph Marks, "Newly Disclosed Hacks Got 'Crown Jewels,'" *Politico*, June 12, 2015, http://www.politico.com/story /2015/06/hackers-federal-employees-security-background-checks-118954.html; Brian Bennet and W. J. Hennigan, "China and Russia Are Using Hacked Data to Target U.S. Spies, Officials Say," *Los Angeles Times*, August 31, 2015, http://www .latimes.com/nation/la-na-cyber-spy-20150831-story.html; Ellen Nakashima and Adam Goldman, "CIA Pulled Officers from Beijing After Breach of Federal Personnel Records," *Washington Post*, September 30, 2015, https://www .washingtonpost.com/world/national-security/cia-pulled-officers-from-beijing -after-breach-of-federal-personnel-records/2015/09/29/1f78943c-66d1-11e5 -9ef3-fde182507eac_story.html.

11. Nakashima, "Confidential Report Lists U.S. Weapons System Designs Compromised by Chinese Cyberspies"; Brian Krebs, "Hackers Plundered Israeli Defense Firms That Built 'Iron Dome' Missile Defense System," *Krebs on Security*, July 28, 2014, http://krebsonsecurity.com/2014/07/hackers-plundered-israeli -defense-firms-that-built-iron-dome-missile-defense-system.

12. "John Kerry: It's 'Very Likely' Russia and China Are Reading My Email," *CBS News*, August 11, 2015, http://www.cbsnews.com/news/john-kerry -its-very-likely-russia-and-china-are-reading-my-emails/.

13. Geoffrey A. Fowler and Jason Dean, "Skype's China Practices Draw Ire," *Wall Street Journal*, October 3, 2008, http://www.wsj.com/articles/SB 122291621892397279; Citizen Lab, "Communities @ Risk: Targeted Digital Threats Against Civil Society," TargetedThreats.net, November 11, 2011, https:// targetedthreats.net/media/1-ExecutiveSummary.pdf.

14. Andrea Peterson, "Chinese Cyberspies Have Hacked Middle East Experts at Major U.S. Think Tanks," *Washington Post*, July 7, 2014, http://www.washington post.com/blogs/the-switch/wp/2014/07/07/chinese-cyberspies-have-hacked -middle-east-experts-at-major-u-s-think-tanks; Siobhan Gorman, Devlin Barrett, and Danny Yadron, "Chinese Hackers Hit U.S. Media," *Wall Street Journal*, January 30, 2013, http://online.wsj.com/news/articles/SB10001424127887323926104 578276202952260718?mg=reno64-wsj.

15. Adam Elkus, "Moonlight Maze," in Healey and Grindal, *A Fierce Domain*.

16. Ellen Nakashima, "Defense Official Discloses Cyberattack," *Washington Post*, August 24, 2010, http://www.washingtonpost.com/wp-dyn/content/article /2010/08/24/AR2010082406154.html.

17. Loucif Kharouni et al., "Operation Pawn Storm," *Trend Micro*, 2014, http://www.trendmicro.com/cloud-content/us/pdfs/security-intelligence/white

-papers/wp-operation-pawn-storm.pdf; FireEye, "APT28: A Window into Russia's Cyber Espionage Operations?," FireEye, 2014, https://www.fireeye.com/resources/pdfs/apt28.pdf.

18. Michael Riley, "How the U.S. Government Hacks the World," *Bloomberg*, May 23, 2013, http://www.businessweek.com/articles/2013-05-23/how-the-u-dot-s-dot-government-hacks-the-world.

19. Electronic Privacy Information Center, "Foreign Intelligence Surveillance Act Court Orders 1979–2014," Epic.org, https://www.epic.org/privacy/wiretap/stats/fisa_stats.html.

20. Kim Zetter, "Feds Threatened to Fine Yahoo $250K Daily for Not Complying with PRISM," *Wired*, September 11, 2014, http://www.wired.com/2014/09/feds-yahoo-fine-prism.

21. Barton Gellman and Ashkan Soltani, "NSA Infiltrates Links to Yahoo, Google Data Centers Worldwide, Snowden Documents Say," *Washington Post*, October 30, 2013, http://www.washingtonpost.com/world/national-security/nsa-infiltrates-links-to-yahoo-google-data-centers-worldwide-snowden-documents-say/2013/10/30/e51d661e-4166-11e3-8b74-d89d714ca4dd_story.html.

22. Joseph Menn, "Exclusive: Secret Contract Tied NSA and Security Industry Pioneer," *Reuters*, December 20, 2013, http://www.reuters.com/article/2013/12/20/us-usa-security-rsa-idUSBRE9BJ1C220131220.

23. James Ball, Julian Borger, and Glenn Greenwald, "Revealed: How US and UK Spy Agencies Defeat Internet Privacy and Security," *Guardian*, September 6, 2013, http://www.theguardian.com/world/2013/sep/05/nsa-gchq-encryption-codes-security.

24. Office of the Press Secretary, "President Obama's Meeting with the Review Group on Intelligence and Communications Technologies," White House, December 18, 2013, https://www.whitehouse.gov/the-press-office/2013/12/18/president-obama-s-meeting-review-group-intelligence-and-communications-t.

25. David Sanger, "Obama Lets N.S.A. Exploit Some Internet Flaws, Officials Say," *New York Times*, April 12, 2014, http://www.nytimes.com/2014/04/13/us/politics/obama-lets-nsa-exploit-some-internet-flaws-officials-say.html; Michael Daniel, "Heartbleed: Understanding When We Disclose Cyber Vulnerabilities," White House, April 24, 2014, http://www.whitehouse.gov/blog/2014/04/28/heartbleed-understanding-when-we-disclose-cyber-vulnerabilities.

26. Mathew Schwartz, "NSA Contracted with Zero-Day Vendor Vupen," *Dark Reading*, September 17, 2013, http://www.darkreading.com/risk-management/nsa-contracted-with-zero-day-vendor-vupen/d/d-id/1111564?; Shane Harris, *@War: The Rise of the Military-Internet Complex* (Boston, MA: Houghton Mifflin Harcourt, 2014), 90; Kim Zetter, "U.S. Gov Insists It Doesn't Stockpile Zero-Day Exploits to Hack Enemies," *Wired*, November 17, 2014, http://www.wired.com/2014/11/michael-daniel-no-zero-day-stockpile.

27. Barton Gellman and Ellen Nakashima, "U.S. Spy Agencies Mounted 231 Offensive Cyber-Operations in 2011, Documents Show," *Washington Post*, August 30, 2013, http://www.washingtonpost.com/world/national-security/us-spy-agencies-mounted-231-offensive-cyber-operations-in-2011-documents

-show/2013/08/30/d090a6ae-119e-11e3-b4cb-fd7ce041d814_story.html; Riley, "How the U.S. Government Hacks the World"; Spiegel Staff, "Inside TAO: Documents Reveal Top NSA Hacking Unit," *Der Spiegel*, December 29, 2013, http://www.spiegel.de/international/world/the-nsa-uses-powerful-toolbox-in-effort-to-spy-on-global-networks-a-940969.html.

28. Ellen Nakashima, Greg Miller, and Julie Tate, "U.S., Israel Developed Flame Computer Virus to Slow Iranian Nuclear Efforts, Officials Say," *Washington Post*, June 19, 2012, http://www.washingtonpost.com/world/national-security/us-israel-developed-computer-virus-to-slow-iranian-nuclear-efforts-officials-say/2012/06/19/gJQA6xBPoV_story.html.

29. Joseph Menn, "Russian Researchers Expose Breakthrough U.S. Spying Program," *Reuters*, February 16, 2015, http://www.reuters.com/article/2015/02/16/us-usa-cyberspying-idUSKBN0LK1QV20150216; Dan Goodin, "How 'Omnipotent' Hackers Tied to NSA Hid for 14 Years—and Were Found at Last," *Ars Technica*, February 16, 2015, http://arstechnica.com/security/2015/02/16/how-omnipotent-hackers-tied-to-the-nsa-hid-for-14-years-and-were-found-at-last.

30. Sherry Sontag, Christopher Drew, and Annette Lawrence Drew, *Blind Man's Bluff: The Untold Story of American Submarine Espionage* (New York: Public-Affairs, 2008).

31. A conversation with Alex Karp, CEO Palantir Technologies, *Charlie Rose*, PBS, August 11, 2009, http://www.charlierose.com/view/interview/10549; Jim Finkle, "Iran Hackers Target Airlines, Energy, Defense Companies—Researchers," *Reuters*, December 2, 2014, http://www.reuters.com/article/2014/12/02/cybersecurity-iran-idUSL2N0TL0SZ20141202; Joe Gould, "Report: Iran Hacked Airlines, Energy, Defense Firms," *Military Times*, December 2, 2014, http://www.militarytimes.com/story/military/tech/2014/12/02/report-iran-hacked-airlines-energy-defense-firms/19784087; Julian B. Barnes and Siobhan Gorman, "U.S. Says Iran Hacked Navy Computers," *Wall Street Journal*, September 27, 2013, http://www.wsj.com/articles/SB10001424052702304526204579101602356751772.

32. Elias Groll, "Economic Spying Not New, and China Is Not Alone," *Charlotte Observer*, May 26, 2014, http://www.charlotteobserver.com/opinion/op-ed/article9124721.html.

33. Office of the National Counterintelligence Executive, "Foreign Spies Stealing U.S. Economic Secrets in Cyberspace," Office of the Director of National Intelligence, October 11, 2011, http://www.dni.gov/reports/20111103_report_fecie.pdf.

34. Carl Sears and Michael Isikoff, "Chinese Firm Paid Insider 'to Kill My Company,' American CEO Says," *NBC News*, August 6, 2013, http://www.nbcnews.com/news/other/chinese-firm-paid-insider-kill-my-company-american-ceo-says-f6C10858966; Ashlee Vance and Michael Riley, "China Corporate Espionage Boom Knocks Wind Out of US Companies," *Bloomberg*, March 15, 2012, http://www.bloomberg.com/news/articles/2012-03-15/china-corporate-espionage-boom-knocks-wind-out-of-u-s-companies; Ellen Nakashima, "U.S. Indicts 6 Chinese Citizens on Charges of Stealing Trade Secrets," *Washington Post*, May 19, 2015, http://www.washingtonpost.com/world/national-security/us-indicts-6

-chinese-on-charges-of-stealing-trade-secrets/2015/05/19/f11fd35e-fdd8-11e4
-805c-c3f407e5a9e9_story.html.

35. "2015 Data Breach Investigations Report," Verizon, http://www.verizon
enterprise.com/DBIR/2014; Mandiant, "M-Trends 2015: A View from the Front
Lines," FireEye, https://www2.fireeye.com/rs/fireye/images/rpt-m-trends
-2015.pdf; Richard Bejtlich, testimony before US Senate Committee on
Homeland Security and Governmental Affairs, Washington, DC, January 28,
2015, http://www.hsgac.senate.gov/hearings/protecting-america-from-cyber
-attacks-the-importance-of-information-sharing.

36. Benjamin Elgin, Dune Lawrence, and Michael A. Riley, "Coke Gets
Hacked and Doesn't Tell Anyone," *Bloomberg*, November 4, 2012, http://www
.bloomberg.com/news/articles/2012-11-04/coke-hacked-and-doesn-t-tell.

37. Joseph Menn, "Exclusive: Hacked Companies Still Not Telling Inves-
tors," *Reuters*, February 2, 2012, http://www.reuters.com/article/2012/02/02
/us-hacking-disclosures-idUSTRE8110YW20120202.

38. Spiegel Staff, "Cyber Menace: Digital Spying Burdens German-Chinese
Relations," *Spiegel*, February 25, 2013, http://www.spiegel.de/international
/world/digital-spying-burdens-german-relations-with-beijing-a-885444.html;
John F. Burns, "Britain Warned Businesses of Threat of Chinese Spying,"
New York Times, January 31, 2010, http://www.nytimes.com/2010/02/01/world
/europe/01spy.html.

39. Josh Rogin, "NSA Chief: Cybercrime Constitutes the 'Greatest
Transfer of Wealth in History,'" *Foreign Policy*, July 9, 2012, http://foreign
policy.com/2012/07/09/nsa-chief-cybercrime-constitutes-the-greatest-transfer
-of-wealth-in-history; Commission on the Theft of American Intellectual Property, "The IP Commission Report," National Bureau of Asian Research, May
2013, http://www.ipcommission.org/report/IP_Commission_Report_052213
.pdf; Center for Strategic and International Studies and McAfee, "Net Losses:
Estimating the Global Cost of Cybercrime," McAfee, June 2014, http://www
.mcafee.com/us/resources/reports/rp-economic-impact-cybercrime2.pdf;
National Counterintelligence and Security Center, "Foreign Spies Stealing U.S.
Economic Secrets in Cyberspace," Office of the National Counterintelligence
Executive, October 2011, http://www.ncsc.gov/publications/reports/fecie_all
/Foreign_Economic_Collection_2011.pdf.

40. Erica Naone, "Cybercrime Surveys Aren't Telling Us What We Need to
Know," *MIT Technology Review*, June 28, 2011, http://www.technologyreview
.com/news/424492/cybercrime-surveys-arent-telling-us-what-we-need-to-know;
Ross Anderson and Tyler Moore, "The Economics of Information Security," *Science* 314, no. 5799 (2006): 610–613.

41. "Nortel Collapse Linked to Chinese Hackers," *CBC News*, February 15,
2012, http://www.cbc.ca/news/business/nortel-collapse-linked-to-chinese
-hackers-1.1260591.

42. Spiegel Staff, "Cyber Menace"; Burns, "Britain Warned Businesses of Threat
of Chinese Spying"; Rosemary Barton, "Chinese Cyberattack Hits Canada's

National Research Council," *CBC News*, July 29, 2014, http://www.cbc.ca/news/politics/chinese-cyberattack-hits-canada-s-national-research-council-1.2721241.

43. Jacob Appelbaum et al., "The Digital Arms Race: NSA Preps America for Future Battle," *Spiegel*, January 17, 2015, http://www.spiegel.de/international/world/new-snowden-docs-indicate-scope-of-nsa-preparations-for-cyber-battle-a-1013409.html.

44. Office of the Press Secretary, "Remarks by Tom Donilon, National Security Advisor to the President: 'The United States and the Asia-Pacific in 2013,'" White House, March 11, 2013, http://www.whitehouse.gov/the-press-office/2013/03/11/remarks-tom-donilon-national-security-advisory-president-united-states-a; Office of the Secretary of Defense, "Military and Security Developments Involving the People's Republic of China 2013," Annual Report to Congress, US Department of Defense, http://www.defense.gov/pubs/2013_China_Report_FINAL.pdf.

45. Barack Obama, interview with Charlie Rose, *Charlie Rose*, New York, June 16, 2013, http://www.charlierose.com/watch/60230424; Office of the Press Secretary, "Remarks by President Obama and President Xi Jinping of the People's Republic of China After Bilateral Meeting," White House, June 8, 2013, http://www.whitehouse.gov/the-press-office/2013/06/08/remarks-president-obama-and-president-xi-jinping-peoples-republic-china-.

46. "Indicting China's Hackers," *Wall Street Journal*, May 20, 2014, http://online.wsj.com/news/articles/SB10001424052702304652804579572320276145640?mg=reno64-wsj&url=http%3A%2F%2Fonline.wsj.com%2Farticle%2FSB10001424052702304652804579572320276145640.html.

47. Obama, interview with Charlie Rose; Riley, "How the U.S. Government Hacks the World."

48. "Statement by Director of National Intelligence James R. Clapper on Allegations of Economic Espionage," IC on the Record, September 8, 2013, http://icontherecord.tumblr.com/post/60712026846/statement-by-director-of-national-intelligence.

49. Tang Lan, "Let Us Join Hands to Make Internet Safe," *China Daily*, February 7, 2012, http://www.chinadaily.com.cn/opinion/2012-02/07/content_14548725.htm.

50. "Expert Analyzes U.S. Military's Cyber Deterrence Strategy, Says Practical Results Difficult to Achieve [Zhuanjia jiexi meijun wangluo weishe zhanlüe cheng shiji xiaoguo nan yi dacheng]," *China News Service*, January 9, 2012, http://www.chinanews.com/gj/2012/01-09/3590771.shtml.

51. Carlos Tejada, "Microsoft, the 'Guardian Warriors,' and China's Cybersecurity Fears," *Wall Street Journal*, July 29, 2014, http://blogs.wsj.com/digits/2014/07/29/microsoft-the-guardian-warriors-and-chinas-cybersecurity-fears.

52. Zhang Ye, "Microsoft 'Surprised' at Move to Change Systems," *Global Times*, May 21, 2014, http://www.globaltimes.cn/content/861408.shtml; Chris Luo, "'Nubia,' Not iPhone, Is Chinese First Lady Peng Liyuan's Latest Choice of Smart Phone," *South China Morning Post*, March 30, 2014, http://www.scmp.com

/news/china-insider/article/1461006/nubia-not-iphone-chinese-first-lady-peng
-liyuans-latest-choice; Gao Yuan, "Foreign Phones Set to 'Disconnect,'" *China
Daily*, September 23, 2014, http://usa.chinadaily.com.cn/epaper/2014-09/23
/content_18647433.htm; Steven Yang, Keith Zhai, and Tim Culpan, "China
Said to Plan Sweeping Shift from Foreign Technology to Own," *Bloomberg*,
December 17, 2014, http://www.bloomberg.com/news/articles/2014-12-17
/china-said-to-plan-sweeping-shift-from-foreign-technology-to-own.

53. Paul Carsten and Michael Martina, "China Regulator Determines Qualcomm Has Monopoly: State-Run Newspaper," *Reuters*, July 24, 2014, http://
www.reuters.com/article/2014/07/24/us-qualcomm-china-idUSKBN0FT0
AU20140724; Tim Culpan, Ian King, and Dina Bass, "China Raids Microsoft Offices in Anti-monopoly Probe," *Bloomberg*, July 29, 2014, http://www
.bloomberg.com/news/articles/2014-07-29/microsoft-probed-by-regulators-in
-china-amid-u-s-tension; Paul Carsten, "China Anti-trust Regulator Conducts
New Raids on Microsoft, Accenture," *Reuters*, August 6, 2014, http://www.reuters
.com/article/2014/08/06/us-microsoft-china-idUSKBN0G60GR20140806.

54. Jim Finkle, Gerry Shih, and Ben Blanchard, "China-Backed Hackers Target Apple's iCloud Users: Blog," *Reuters*, October 21, 2014, http://www.reuters
.com/article/2014/10/21/us-apple-china-security-idUSKCN0I92H020141021.

55. Bill Bishop, "In China, a Push for Cleaner Air," *DealB%k*, June 17, 2013,
http://dealbook.nytimes.com/2013/06/17/in-china-a-push-for-cleaner-air.

56. Nathaniel Ahrens, "China's Competitiveness: Myth, Reality, and Lessons
for the United States and Japan," Hills Program in Governance Report, Center for Strategic and International Studies, February 2013, http://csis.org/files
/publication/130215_competitiveness_Huawei_casestudy_Web.pdf; "Mile-
stones," Huawei, http://huawei.com/en/about-huawei/corporate-info/milestone
/index.htm.

57. Christopher Rhoads, "Motorola Claims Huawei Plot," *Wall Street Journal*, July 22, 2010, http://www.wsj.com/articles/SB10001424052748704684604
4575381362665259760; Scott Thurm, "Cisco Sues Huawei of China, Alleging
It Violated Patents," *Wall Street Journal*, January 24, 2003, http://www.wsj.com/
articles/SB1043337053732688864; Plummer quoted in Joseph Menn, "White
House–ordered Review Found No Evidence of Huawei Spying: Sources," *Reuters*, October 18, 2012, http://www.reuters.com/article/2012/10/18/us-huawei
-spying-idUSBRE89G1Q920121018; Peter Goodman, "Huawei Founder Ren
Zhengfei Dismisses Chinese Military Connections," *International Business
Times*, January 22, 2015, http://www.ibtimes.com/huawei-founder-ren-zhengfei
-dismisses-chinese-military-connections-1791228; Michael Kan, "Huawei's Elusive Founder Tries to Dispel Spying Concerns and Air of Mystery," *Computer World*,
January 22, 2015, http://www.computerworld.com/article/2873967/huaweis
-elusive-founder-tries-to-dispel-spying-concerns-and-air-of-mystery.html.

58. Evan S. Medeiros et al., *A New Direction for China's Defense Industry* (Santa
Monica, CA: RAND Corporation, 2005); Bryan Krekel, Patton Adams, and
George Bakos, *Occupying the Information High Ground: Chinese Capabilities for*

Computer Network Operations and Cyber Espionage (Washington, DC: US-China Economic and Security Review Commission, 2012).

59. Steven R. Weisman, "Sale of 3Com to Huawei Is Derailed by U.S. Security Concerns," *New York Times*, February 21, 2008, http://www.nytimes.com/2008/02/21/business/worldbusiness/21iht-3com.1.10258216.html; Shayndi Raice, "Small Deal Brings Scrutiny to Huawei," *Wall Street Journal*, November 18, 2010, http://www.wsj.com/articles/SB10001424052748703374304575622884122938068; Todd Shields, "Locke Says Sprint's Chief Was Called About Huawei Bid Concerns," *Bloomberg*, December 7, 2010, http://www.bloomberg.com/news/articles/2010-12-07/commerce-s-locke-says-sprint-s-chief-was-called-about-huawei-bid-concerns.

60. David E. Sanger and Nicole Perlroth, "N.S.A. Breached Chinese Servers Seen as Security Threat," *New York Times*, March 22, 2014, http://www.nytimes.com/2014/03/23/world/asia/nsa-breached-chinese-servers-seen-as-spy-peril.html; "Targeting Huawei: NSA Spied on Chinese Government and Networking Firm," *Spiegel*, March 22, 2014, http://www.spiegel.de/international/world/nsa-spied-on-chinese-government-and-networking-firm-huawei-a-960199.html.

61. Ellyne Phneah, "Huawei, ZTE Under Probe by Indian Government," *ZDNet*, May 10, 2013, http://www.zdnet.com/article/huawei-zte-under-probe-by-indian-government; Maggie Lu Yueyang, "Australia Bars Huawei from Broadband Project," *New York Times*, March 26, 2012, http://www.nytimes.com/2012/03/27/technology/australia-bars-huawei-from-broadband-project.html; "Huawei to Come Under Increased Scrutiny from GCHQ," *BBC*, December 17, 2013, http://www.bbc.com/news/technology-25417332; Steve Ranger, "Huawei Equipment Not a Risk to National Security Says Report," *ZDNet*, March 25, 2015, http://www.zdnet.com/article/huawei-equipment-not-a-risk-to-national-security-says-report; Huawei Cyber Security Evaluation Center (HCSEC) Oversight Board, "Annual Report to the National Security Adviser of the United Kingdom," Gov.uk, March 2015, https://www.gov.uk/government/uploads/system/uploads/attachment_data/file/416878/HCSEC_Report.pdf.

62. Eric Engleman, "Huawei, ZTE Face Scrutiny from U.S. House Intelligence Panel," *Bloomberg*, November 18, 2011, http://www.bloomberg.com/news/articles/2011-11-17/house-intelligence-panel-probing-chinese-phone-companies-in-u-s-.

63. Office of the Press Secretary, "Fact Sheet: President Xi Jinping's State Visit to the United States," White House, September 25, 2015, https://www.whitehouse.gov/the-press-office/2015/09/25/fact-sheet-president-xi-jinpings-state-visit-united-states; Aaron Mehta, "Clapper Skeptical of US-China Cyber Deal," *Defense News*, September 29, 2015.

CHAPTER 6: THE BATTLE OVER DATA: SECURITY, PRIVACY, AND TRADE POWER

1. Markus Beckedahl, "Yes, We Scan! Salvaging Public Trust in a Post-Snowden Germany," in *Stakes Are High: Essays on Brazil and the Future of the Global Internet*, ed. Ellery Roberts Biddle, Ronaldo Lemos, and Monroe Price, April 2014, http://

globalnetpolicy.org/wp-content/uploads/2014/04/StakesAreHigh_Brazil
NETmundial_final.pdf.

2. Quentin Peel, "Merkel Cornered over US Surveillance Claims," *Financial Times*, July 8, 2013, http://www.ft.com/intl/cms/s/0/d235c3e2-e7e9-11e2-babb-00144feabdc0.html#axzz3duqw2BP7.

3. Chris Bryant, "Merkel's Mobile Habit," *Financial Times*, October 24, 2013, http://blogs.ft.com/the-world/2013/10/merkels-mobile-habit.

4. "The Right to Privacy in the Digital Age," Resolution 68/167, United Nations General Assembly, December 18, 2013, http://www.un.org/ga/search/view_doc.asp?symbol=A/RES/68/167.

5. "'Privacy Essential to Democracy': Germany, Brazil Introduce Anti-spying UN Resolution," *RT*, November 7, 2013, http://rt.com/news/germany-brazil-un-spying-resolution-394.

6. "Right to Privacy in the Digital Age—U.S. Redlines," Turtle Bay, http://columlynch.tumblr.com/post/67588682409/right-to-privacy-in-the-digital-age-u-s.

7. Philip Oltermann, "Germany 'Should Offer Edward Snowden Asylum After NSA Revelations,'" *Guardian*, November 3, 2013, http://www.theguardian.com/world/2013/nov/03/germany-edward-snowden-asylum.

8. Alison Smale and David Sanger, "Spying Scandal Alters U.S. Ties with Allies and Raises Talk of Policy Shift," *New York Times*, November 11, 2013, http://www.nytimes.com/2013/11/12/world/spying-scandal-alters-us-ties-with-allies-and-raises-talk-of-policy-shift.html; Susanne Koelbl and Marcel Rosenbach, "Obama Advisor John Podesta: 'Every Country Has a History of Going over the Line,'" *Spiegel*, June 30, 2014, http://www.spiegel.de/international/germany/interview-with-obama-advisor-john-podesta-on-nsa-and-cyber-security-a-978297.html; David Sanger, "U.S. and Germany Fail to Reach a Deal on Spying," *New York Times*, May 1, 2014, http://www.nytimes.com/2014/05/02/world/europe/us-and-germany-fail-to-reach-a-deal-on-spying.html.

9. Marcel Furstenau, "German Parliament to Inquire into NSA," *Deutsche Welle*, March 20, 2014, http://www.dw.com/en/german-parliament-to-inquire-into-nsa/a-17510640.

10. Constanze Stelzenmüller and Josh Raisher, "Transatlantic Majorities Oppose Domestic Surveillance," Trends Brief, German Marshall Fund, November 2013, http://trends.gmfus.org/files/2013/11/TTBrief_Domestic Surveillance_Nov13.pdf.

11. "'Key Partners': Secret Links Between Germany and the NSA," *Spiegel*, July 22, 2013, http://www.spiegel.de/international/world/german-intelligence-worked-closely-with-nsa-on-data-surveillance-a-912355.html.

12. Interview with senior German official, Berlin, March 2014; Henry Farrell, "Senseless Spying," *Foreign Affairs*, July 9, 2013, https://www.foreignaffairs.com/articles/europe/2013-07-09/senseless-spying.

13. Rolf Mowatt-Larssen, "Beyond the US-German Case: Understanding the Espionage 'Rules of the Game,'" *Just Security*, July 15, 2014, http://justsecurity.org/12888/germany-spy-espionage-rules-of-the-game-mowatt-larssen.

14. Sanger, "U.S. and Germany Fail to Reach a Deal on Spying."

15. Katy Connolly, "Court Rejects Attempt to Allow Edward Snowden into Germany," *Guardian*, December 12, 2014, http://www.theguardian.com/us-news /2014/dec/12/court-edward-snowden-germany-nsa.

16. Julia Edwards, "Obama Acknowledges Damage from NSA Eavesdropping on Merkel," *Reuters*, February 9, 2015, http://uk.mobile.reuters.com/article/id UKKBN0LD22D20150209?irpc=932.

17. "New NSA Revelations: Inside Snowden's Germany File," *Spiegel*, June 18, 2014, http://www.spiegel.de/international/germany/new-snowden -revelations-on-nsa-spying-in-germany-a-975441.html; Greg Miller, "Back-lash in Berlin over NSA Spying Recedes as Threat from Islamic State Rises," *Washington Post*, December 29, 2014, http://www.washingtonpost.com/world /national-security/backlash-in-berlin-over-nsa-recedes-as-islamic-state-rises /2014/12/29/c738af28-8aad-11e4-a085-34e9b9f09a58_story.html; Erik Kirschbaum, "Merkel Defends German Intelligence Cooperation with NSA," *Reuters*, May 4, 2015, http://www.reuters.com/article/2015/05/04/us-germany -spying-merkel-idUSKBN0NP13620150504.

18. Kara Swisher, "White House. Red Chair. Obama Meets Swisher," Re/code, February 15, 2015, http://recode.net/2015/02/15/white-house-red-chair-obama -meets-swisher.

19. Robert W. Holleyman II, "Remarks by Deputy U.S. Trade Representative Robert Holleyman to the New Democrat Network," Office of the US Trade Rep-resentative, May 1, 2015, https://ustr.gov/about-us/policy-offices/press-office /speechestranscripts/2015/may/remarks-deputy-us-trade.

20. Matthieu Pélissié du Rausas et al., "Internet Matters: The Net's Sweeping Impact on Growth, Jobs, and Prosperity," McKinsey Global Institute, May 2011, http://www.mckinsey.com/insights/mgi/research/technology_and_innovation /internet_matters; "Value of Connectivity: Economic and Social Benefits of Expanding Internet Access," Deloitte, February 2014, http://www.denetimnet .net/UserFiles/Documents/TMT_value-of-connectivity.pdf.

21. Organization for Economic Cooperation and Development, "The Eco-nomic Impact of Shutting Down Internet and Mobile Phone Services in Egypt," February 4, 2011, http://www.oecd.org/countries/egypt/theeconomicimpactof shuttingdowninternetandmobilephoneservicesinegypt.htm.

22. Paul Zwillenberg, Dominic Field, and David Dean, "The Connected World: Greasing the Wheels of the Internet Economy," Boston Consulting Group, January 2014, https://www.icann.org/en/system/files/files/bcg-internet -economy-27jan14-en.pdfklm; World Economic Forum, "Enabling Trade Valu-ing Growth Opportunities," 2013, http://www3.weforum.org/docs/WEF_SCT _EnablingTrade_Report_2013.pdf.

23. Erik van der Marel, Hosuk Lee-Makiyama, and Matthias Bauer, "The Costs of Data Localisation: A Friendly Fire on Economic Recovery," ECIPE Occasional Paper, European Centre for International Political Economy, March 2014, http://www.ecipe.org/publications/dataloc.

24. Edward Wong, "China's Internet Restrictions Are Hampering Business, Foreign Companies Say," *Bits* (blog), *New York Times*, February 15, 2015, http://

bits.blogs.nytimes.com/2015/02/13/chinas-internet-restrictions-are-hampering
-business-foreign-companies-say.

25. Jane Qiu, "A Land Without Google?," *Nature*, February 24, 2010, http://
www.nature.com/news/2010/100224/full/4631012a.html.

26. Guy Faulconbridge, "Father of Web Says China Will Dismantle 'Great
Firewall,'" *Reuters*, http://www.reuters.com/article/2013/11/22/china-internet
-berners-lee-idINDEE9AL00R20131122?irpc=932.

27. "German Minister: Drop Google if You Fear US Spying," *Yahoo! News*, July
3, 2013, http://news.yahoo.com/german-minister-drop-google-fear-us-spying
-105524847.html; Friedrich quoted in Mirko Hohmann et al., "Technological
Sovereignty: Missing the Point? An Analysis of European Proposals After June 5,
2013," *New America*, November 24, 2014, https://www.newamerica.org/downloads
/Technological_Sovereignty_Report.pdf; German Government, "Digitale
Agenda 2014–2017," Die Bundesregierung, 2014, http://www.bmwi.deBMWi
/Redaktion/PDF/Publikationen/digitale-agenda-2014-2017,property=pdf
,bereich=bmwi,sprache=de,rwb=true.pdf, 4.

28. Cornelius Rahn, Marie Mawad, and Claudia Rach, "NSA Fallout in Europe
Boosts Alternatives to Google Boom," *Bloomberg*, December 23, 2013, http://
www.bloomberg.com/news/2013-12-19/nsa-fallout-in-europe-boosts-alternatives
-to-google.html; "Boom Triggered by NSA: German Email Services Report
Surge in Demand," *Spiegel*, August 26, 2013, http://www.spiegel.de/international
/germany/growing-demand-for-german-email-providers-after-nsa-scandal
-a-918651.html.

29. Anton Troianovski and Danny Yadron, "German Government Ends Verizon Contract," *Wall Street Journal,* June 26, 2014, http://www.wsj.com/articles
/berlin-weighs-possible-hit-to-u-s-tech-firms-1414967090.

30. Susan Crawford, "NSA Scandal May Help Build Cyber-Barriers," *Bloomberg*,
December 27, 2013, http://www.bloombergview.com/articles/2013-12-27/nsa
-scandal-may-help-build-cyber-barriers.

31. Kalev Aasme, "After PRISM, Europe Has to Move to Its Own Clouds, Says
Estonia's President," *ZDnet*, July 15, 2013, http://www.zdnet.com/article/after
-prism-europe-has-to-move-to-its-own-clouds-says-estonias-president; Directorate General for Internal Policies, "The US Surveillance Programmes and
Their Impact on EU Citizens' Fundamental Rights," European Parliament,
2013 http://www.europarl.europa.eu/meetdocs/2009_2014/documents/libe/dv
/briefingnote_/briefingnote_en.pdf.

32. Murad Ahmed, "Amazon to Open German Data Centres to Soothe European Concerns," *Financial Times*, October 23, 2013, http://www.ft.com/intl
/cms/s/0/56181a6e-5a96-11e4-b449-00144feab7de.html.

33. Brief quoted in Nick Wingfield, "Tech and Media Companies Back
Microsoft in Privacy Case," *Bits* (blog), *New York Times*, December 15, 2015,
http://bits.blogs.nytimes.com/2014/12/15/tech-and-media-companies-back
-microsoft-in-privacy-case.

34. William Long, Geraldine Scali, and Alan Charles Raul, "European Union Overview," *Privacy, Data Protection and Cybersecurity Law Review*, 2014, http://www .sidley.com/~/media/Files/Publications/2014/11/The%20Privacy%20Data%20 Protection%20and%20Cybersecurity%20La__/Files/European%20Union%20 Overview/FileAttachment/European%20Union.

35. "Informal Justice Council in Vilnius," European Commission, July 19, 2013, http://europa.eu/rapid/press-release_MEMO-13-710_en.htm.

36. "Plan to Restore Trust in U.S.-EU Data Flows amid Growing Anger over U.S. Surveillance," Wiley Rein LLP, December 2013, http://www.wileyrein.com /newsroom-newsletters-item-4819.html.

37. Mark Scott, "Data Transfer Pact Between U.S. and Europe Is Ruled Invalid," *New York Times*, October 6, 2015, http://www.nytimes.com/2015/10/07 /technology/european-union-us-data-collection.html?ref=technology; Natalia Drozdiak and Sam Schechner, "EU Court Says Data-Transfer Pact with U.S. Violates Privacy," *Wall Street Journal*, October 6, 2015, http://www.wsj.com/articles /eu-court-strikes-down-trans-atlantic-safe-harbor-data-transfer-pact-1444121361.

38. Timothy Edgar, "Schrems v. Data Protection Commissioner: Some Inconvenient Truths The European Court of Justice Ignores," *Lawfare*, October 6, 2015, https://www.lawfareblog.com/schrems-v-data-protection-commissioner -some-inconvenient-truths-european-court-justice-ignores.

39. Gideon Rachman, "The Political Storm over the Googleplex," *Financial Times*, April 27, 2015; Richard Pells, *Not Like Us: How Europeans Have Loved, Hated, and Transformed American Culture* (New York: Basic Books, 1998).

40. Matt Rosoff, "Here's How Dominant Google Is in Europe," *Business Insider*, November 29, 2014, http://www.businessinsider.com/heres-how-dominant -google-is-in-europe-2014-11; "Statement of VP Almunia on the Google Antitrust Investigation," European Commission, May 21, 2012, http://europa.eu/rapid /press-release_SPEECH-12-372_en.htm.

41. Danny Hakim, "Google Is Target of European Backlash on U.S. Tech Dominance," *New York Times*, September 8, 2014, http://www.nytimes.com /2014/09/09/technology/google-is-target-of-european-backlash-on-us-tech -dominance.html; Sam Schechner and Vanessa Mock, "Group Calls for EU to Revisit Google Antitrust Deal," *Wall Street Journal*, May 15, 2014, http://www.wsj .com/articles/SB10001424052702304908304579564143860828978.

42. Eric Schmidt, "The New Gründergeist," *Google Europe Blog*, October 13, 2014, http://googlepolicyeurope.blogspot.com/2014/10/the-new-grundergeist .html.

43. "Should Digital Monopolies Be Broken Up?," *Economist*, November 29, 2014, http://www.economist.com/news/leaders/21635000-european -moves-against-google-are-about-protecting-companies-not-consumers-should -digital.

44. E. B. Boyd, "What the Google Buzz–FTC Settlement Means for the 'Apology Approach' to Innovation," *Fast Company*, April 4, 2011, http://

www.fastcompany.com/1744163/what-google-buzz-ftc-settlement-means
-apology-approach-innovation.

45. Jeffery Rosen, "The Right to Be Forgotten," *Stanford Law Review Online*,
February 13, 2012, http://www.stanfordlawreview.org/online/privacy-paradox
/right-to-be-forgotten; James Q. Whitman, "The Two Western Cultures of Privacy: Dignity Versus Liberty," *Yale Law Journal*, http://digitalcommons.law.yale
.edu/cgi/viewcontent.cgi?article=1647&context=fss_papers; Samuel Warren
and Louis Brandeis, "The Right to Privacy," *Harvard Law Review* 4, no. 5 (1890),
http://groups.csail.mit.edu/mac/classes/6.805/articles/privacy/Privacy_brand
_warr2.html.

46. Advisory Council, "How Should One Person's Right to Be Forgotten Be
Balanced with the Public's Right to Information?," Google, https://www.google
.com/advisorycouncil.

47. "European Privacy Requests for Search Removals," Google, https://
www.google.com/transparencyreport/removals/europeprivacy (accessed June
24, 2015); Lisa Fleisher and Sam Schechner, "How Google's Top Minds Decide
What to Forget," *Wall Street Journal*, May 12, 2015, http://www.wsj.com/articles
/how-googles-top-minds-decide-what-to-forget-1431462018.

48. Mark Scott, "French Official Campaigns to Make 'Right to Be Forgotten' Global," *Bits* (blog), *New York Times*, December 3, 2014, http://bits
.blogs.nytimes.com/2014/12/03/french-official-campaigns-to-make-right
-to-be-forgotten-global; Sam Schechner and Frances Robinson, "EU Says Google
Should Extend 'Right to Be Forgotten' to '.com' Websites," *Wall Street Journal*,
November 26, 2014, http://www.wsj.com/articles/eu-says-google-should-extend
-right-to-be-forgotten-to-com-websites-1417006254.

49. Peter Fleischer, "We Need a Better, Simpler Narrative of US Privacy Laws,"
Privacy . . . ?, March 12, 2013, http://peterfleischer.blogspot.com/2013/03/
we-need-better-simpler-narrative-of-us.html.

50. Office of the Press Secretary, "Remarks by President Obama and German Chancellor Merkel in Joint Press Conference," White House, June 19,
2013, https://www.whitehouse.gov/the-press-office/2013/06/19/remarks
-president-obama-and-german-chancellor-merkel-joint-press-confere.

51. Office of the Press Secretary, "President Obama's Meeting with the Review
Group on Intelligence and Communications Technologies," White House,
December 18, 2013, https://www.whitehouse.gov/the-press-office/2013/12/18
/president-obama-s-meeting-review-group-intelligence-and-communications-t;
Peter Swire, "The USA FREEDOM Act, the President's Review Group and the
Biggest Intelligence Reform in 40 Years," International Association of Privacy
Professionals, June 8, 2015, https://privacyassociation.org/news/a/the-usa
-freedom-act-the-presidents-review-group-and-the-biggest-intelligence-reform
-in-40-years.

52. Obama quoted in Amy Davidson, "Obama and Charlie Rose: The N.S.A.'s
Road to Nowhere," *New Yorker*, June 18, 2013, http://www.newyorker.com/news/
amy-davidson/obama-and-charlie-rose-the-n-s-a-s-road-to-nowhere.

53. Richard A. Clarke et al., "Protecting Citizens, and Their Privacy," *New York Times,* December 19, 2013, http://www.nytimes.com/2013/12/20/opinion /protecting-citizens-and-their-privacy.html.

54. Office of the Press Secretary, "Presidential Policy Directive—Signals Intelligence Activities," White House, January 17, 2014, https://www.white house.gov/the-press-office/2014/01/17/presidential-policy-directive-signals -intelligence-activities; Rainey Reitman, "Obama Announces New Privacy Rules for the World. World Not Impressed," Electronic Frontier Foundation, February 10, 2015, https://www.eff.org/deeplinks/2015/02/obama-announces-new -privacy-rules-world-world-not-impressed.

55. Dominic Rushe, "Zuckerberg: US Government 'Blew It' on NSA Surveillance," *Guardian,* September 11, 2013, http://www.theguardian.com/technology /2013/sep/11/yahoo-ceo-mayer-jail-nsa-surveillance.

56. Office of the Press Secretary, "Remarks by the President on Review of Signals Intelligence," White House, January 17, 2104, https://www.whitehouse.gov /the-press-office/2014/01/17/remarks-president-review-signals-intelligence.

57. "Global Government Surveillance Reform," Reform Government Surveillance, May 19, 2015, https://www.reformgovernmentsurveillance.com.

58. Brad Smith, "Protecting Customer Data from Government Snooping," *Microsoft Blog,* December 4, 2013, http://blogs.microsoft.com/blog/2013/12/04 /protecting-customer-data-from-government-snooping.

59. Glenn Greenwald, "Edward Snowden: NSA Whistleblower Answers Reader Questions," *Guardian,* June 17, 2013, http://www.theguardian.com/world/2013 /jun/17/edward-snowden-nsa-files-whistleblower.

60. Remarks by James B. Comey at the Brookings Institution, Washington, DC, FBI, October 16, 2014, http://www.fbi.gov/news/speeches/going-dark-are -technology-privacy-and-public-safety-on-a-collision-course.

61. Cindy Cohn, "Nine Epic Failures of Regulating Cryptography," Electronic Frontier Foundation, September 26, 2014, https://www.eff.org/deeplinks /2014/09/nine-epic-failures-regulating-cryptography.

62. Peter Swire, "The FBI Doesn't Need More Access: We're Already in the Golden Age of Surveillance," *Just Security,* November 17, 2014, https://www.just security.org/17496/fbi-access-golden-age-surveillance/.

63. John Reed, "Transcript: NSA Director Mike Rogers vs. Yahoo! on Encryption Back Doors," *Just Security,* February 23, 2015, http://justsecurity.org/20304 /transcript-nsa-director-mike-rogers-vs-yahoo-encryption-doors.

64. "China Justifies Counterterrorism Law, Slams U.S. Accusation," *Xinhua,* March 4, 2015, http://news.xinhuanet.com/english/2015-03/04/c_134036882 .htm.

65. Joseph Menn, "White House Seeks Silicon Valley Help on Strong Yet Breakable Encryption," *Reuters,* April 21, 2015, http://www.reuters.com/article /2015/04/21/us-cybersecurity-rsa-encryption-idUSKBN0NC2LT20150421; Nicole Perlroth, "Code Specialists Oppose U.S. and British Government Access to Encrypted Communication," *New York Times,* July 7, 2015, http://www.nytimes

.com/2015/07/08/technology/code-specialists-oppose-us-and-british-government
-access-to-encrypted-communication.html.

66. NSC spokesman quoted in Nicole Perlroth and David Sanger, "Obama Won't Seek Access to Encrypted User Data," *New York Times*, October 10, 2015, http://www.nytimes.com/2015/10/11/us/politics/obama-wont-seek-access-to -encrypted-user-data.html?hp&action=click&pgtype=Homepage&module=first -column-region&region=top-news&WT.nav=top-news; Ellen Nakashima and Andrea Peterson, "Obama Faces Growing Momentum to Support Widespread Encryption," *Washington Post*, September 16, 2015, https://www.washington post.com/world/national-security/tech-trade-agencies-push-to-disavow -law-requiring-decryption-of-phones/2015/09/16/1fca5f72-5adf-11e5-b38e -06883aacba64_story.html.

67. Philip Ewing, "Ash Carter's Appeal to Silicon Valley: We're 'Cool' Too," *Politico*, April 23, 2015, http://www.politico.com/story/2015/04/ash-carter -silicon-valley-appeal-117293.html; Committee on Appropriations, "Defense Subcommittee Hearing: FY16 Budget Request for the Department of Defense," US Senate, May 6, 2015, http://www.appropriations.senate.gov/webcast /defense-subcommittee-hearing-fy16-budget-request-department-defense.

68. David Gauthier-Villars and Sam Schechner, "Tech Companies Are Caught in the Middle of Terror Fight," *Wall Street Journal*, February 17, 2015, http://www.wsj.com/articles/tech-companies-are-caught-in-the-middle -of-terror-fight-1424211060.

CHAPTER 7: LET SLIP THE TWITTER FOLLOWERS OF WAR: INFORMATION, IDEAS, AND LEGITIMACY

1. Rory McCarthy, "Gaza Truce Broken as Israeli Raid Kills Six Hamas Gunmen," *Guardian*, November 5, 2008, http://www.theguardian.com/world/2008 /nov/05/israelandthepalestinians.

2. Jenny Percival, "Israel Launches Deadly Gaza Attacks," *Guardian*, December 27, 2008, http://www.theguardian.com/world/2008/dec/27/israelandthe palestinians.

3. Jaron Gilinsky, "How Social Media War Was Waged in Gaza-Israel Conflict," *PBS*, February 13, 2009, http://www.pbs.org/mediashift/2009/02/how -social-media-war-was-waged-in-gaza-israel-conflict044.

4. Noah Shachtman, "Israel's Accidental YouTube War," *Wired*, January 21, 2009, http://www.wired.com/2009/01/israels-acciden; Daniel Bennett, "How the IDF Fell Off the Social Media Bandwagon," *Frontline Club*, February 25, 2009, http://www.frontlineclub.com/the_problems_with_the_israeli _defence_forces_social_media_campaign.

5. United Nations Fact-Finding Mission on the Gaza Conflict, "Human Rights in Palestine and Other Occupied Arab Territories," United Nations, September 25, 2009, http://www2.ohchr.org/english/bodies/hrcouncil/docs/12session /A-HRC-12-48.pdf.

6. Gili Izikovich and Anshel Pfeffer, "New IDF Unit to Fight Enemies on Facebook, Twitter," *Haaretz*, December 1, 2009, http://www.haaretz.com/print-edition

/news/new-idf-unit-to-fight-enemies-on-facebook-twitter-1.3088; Senior member quoted in Rebecca Stein, "Inside Israel's Twitter War Room," Middle East Research and Information Project, November 24, 2012, http://www.merip .org/mero/mero112412.

7. Robert Booth, "Israeli Attack on Gaza Flotilla Sparks International Outrage," *Guardian*, May 31, 2010, http://www.theguardian.com/world/2010/may /31/israeli-attacks-gaza-flotilla-activists.

8. Noah Shachtman, "Israel Turns to YouTube, Twitter After Flotilla Fiasco," *CNN*, June 2, 2010, http://www.cnn.com/2010/TECH/web/06/02/israel.twitter .youtube.

9. Mary Fitzgerald, "'It Is Murder Conducted by a State,'" *Irish Times*, June 1, 2010, http://www.irishtimes.com/news/it-is-murder-conducted-by-a-state-1.672488.

10. Amir Mizroch, "How Free Explains Israel's Flotilla FAIL," *Wired*, June 2, 2010, http://www.wired.com/2010/06/how-free-explains-israels-flotilla-fiasco.

11. Diana Allan and Curtis Brown, "The Mavi Marmara at the Frontlines of Web 2.0," *Journal of Palestine Studies* 40, no. 1 (autumn 2010): 63–77.

12. Brian Fung, "Inside Israel's Social Media Command Center," *Atlantic*, November 20, 2012, http://www.theatlantic.com/international/archive /2012/11/inside-israels-social-media-command-center/265471; David Banks, "State-Sponsored 'Slacktivism': The Social Media Campaigns of the IDF and Hamas," *Cyborgology* (community page), *Society Pages*, December 4, 2012, http:// thesocietypages.org/cyborgology/2012/12/04/state-sponsored-slacktivism -the-social-media-campaigns-of-the-idf-and-hamas.

13. Chris Moody, "Building Sentiment Analysis on the Right Social Data," Gnip presentation, October 30, 2012, video posted by Chris Grimes to Vimeo, https://vimeo.com/53916150.

14. Hussein Ibish, Twitter post, November 15, 2012, 5:40 a.m., https://twitter .com/ibishblog/status/269072426132967425.

15. Michael Koplow, "How Not to Wage War on the Internet," *Foreign Policy*, November 16, 2012, http://www.foreignpolicy.com/articles/2012/11/15 /how_not_to_wage_war_on_the_internet; Anshel Pfeffer, "The Limits of Israel's Online Hasbara," *Haaretz*, November 20, 2012, http://www.haaretz.com/news /diplomacy-defense/the-limits-of-israel-s-online-hasbara.premium-1.479298.

16. Stuart Winer, "Netanyahu: Hamas Wants 'Telegenically Dead Palestinians,'" *Times of Israel*, July 20, 2014, http://www.timesofisrael.com/netanyahu -hamas-wants-telegenically-dead-palestinians.

17. Anne Barnard, Twitter post, July 20, 2014, 3:13 a.m., https://twitter.com /abarnardnyt/status/490801562302676992; Gal Beckerman, "Israel Has a New Worst Enemy—Twitter," *Forward*, August 1, 2014, http://forward.com/opinion /israel/202714/israel-has-a-new-worst-enemy-twitter.

18. Adam Segal, "China's Twitter-Spam War Against Pro-Tibet Activists," *Atlantic*, March 23, 2012, http://www.theatlantic.com/international/archive /2012/03/chinas-twitter-spam-war-against-pro-tibet-activists/254975.

19. Andrew Jacobs, "It's Another Perfect Day in Tibet!," *New York Times*, July 21, 2014, http://www.nytimes.com/2014/07/22/world/asia/trending

-attractive-people-sharing-upbeat-news-about-tibet-.html; Tom Phillips, "China's Communist Party Takes Online War to Twitter," *Telegraph*, September 8, 2014, http://www.telegraph.co.uk/news/worldnews/asia/china/11080909/Chinas -Communist-Party-takes-online-war-to-Twitter.html.

20. Gary King, Jennifer Pan, and Margaret Roberts, "How Censorship in China Allows Government Criticism but Silences Collective Expression," *American Political Science Review* 107, no. 2 (May 2013): 1–18; Xiao Qiang, "Leaked Propaganda Directives and Banned 'Future,'" *China Digital Times*, June 24, 2011, http://chinadigitaltimes.net/2011/06/future-banned-on-sina-weibo -search; Ai Weiwei, "China's Paid Trolls: Meet the 50-Cent Party," *New Statesman*, October 17, 2012, http://www.newstatesman.com/politics/politics/2012/10 /china%E2%80%99s-paid-trolls-meet-50-cent-party.

21. *Beijing Daily* article quoted in Murong Xuecun, "Beijing's Rising Smear Power," *New York Times*, September 22, 2014, http://www.nytimes .com/2014/09/22/opinion/beijings-rising-smear-power.html; Ben Blanchard, "China Cracks Down on Tibetan Burnings, Detains 70," *Reuters*, February 7, 2013, http://www.reuters.com/article/2013/02/07/us-china -tibet-idUSBRE9160CT20130207.

22. Peter Pomerantsev, "Inside the Kremlin's Hall of Mirrors," *Guardian*, April 9, 2015, http://www.theguardian.com/news/2015/apr/09/kremlin -hall-of-mirrors-military-information-psychology.

23. Chris Elliott, "The Readers' Editor on . . . Pro-Russia Trolling Below the Line on Ukraine Stories," *Guardian*, May 4, 2014, http://www.theguardian .com/commentisfree/2014/may/04/pro-russia-trolls-guardian-online.

24. Miriam Elder, "Emails Give Insight into Kremlin Youth Group's Priorities, Means and Concerns," *Guardian*, February 7, 2012, http://www.the guardian.com/world/2012/feb/07/nashi-emails-insight-kremlin-groups -priorities; Max Seddon, "Documents Show How Russia's Troll Army Hit America," *BuzzFeed*, June 2, 2014, http://www.buzzfeed.com/maxseddon/documents -show-how-russias-troll-army-hit-america.

25. Dmitry Rogozin, Twitter post, July 31, 2014, 12:13 p.m., https://twitter.com /drogozin/status/494923729714302976.

26. Alice Speri, "ISIS Fighters and Their Friends Are Total Social Media Pros," *Vice*, June 17, 2014, https://news.vice.com/article/isis-fighters-and-their-friends -are-total-social-media-pros; J. M. Berger, "How ISIS Games Twitter," *Atlantic*, June 16, 2014, http://www.theatlantic.com/international/archive/2014/06/isis -iraq-twitter-social-media-strategy/372856; Alexander Trowbridge, "Jihadists on the Move in Iraq with Weapons, Hashtags," *CBS News*, June 16, 2014, http://www .cbsnews.com/news/isis-jihadists-on-move-in-iraq-using-weapons-and-twitter -hashtags; Jacob Silverman, "The State Department's Twitter Jihad: Can a Bureaucracy Out-Tweet the Terrorists?," *Politico*, July 22, 2014, http://www .politico.com/magazine/story/2014/07/the-state-departments-twitter-jihad -109234.html#ixzz3BmIGM6FU.

27. Speri, "ISIS Fighters and Their Friends Are Total Social Media Pros."

28. Bin Laden quoted in Steven R. Corman and Jill S. Schiefelbein, "Communication and Media Strategy in the Jihadi War of Ideas," Report #0601, Consortium for Strategic Communication, Arizona State University, April 20, 2006, http://csc.asu.edu/wp-content/uploads/2012/06/119.pdf, 3.

29. Gabriel Weimann, "New Terrorism and New Media," Commons Lab, Woodrow Wilson International Center for Scholars, 2014, http://www.wilson center.org/publication/new-terrorism-and-new-media.

30. Richard Norton-Taylor, "British Intelligence Used Cupcake Recipes to Ruin al-Qaida Website," *Guardian*, June 2, 2011, http://www.theguardian.com /uk/2011/jun/02/british-intelligence-ruins-al-qaida-website.

31. Harriet Alexander, "Tweeting Terrorism: How al Shabaab Live Blogged the Nairobi Attacks," *Telegraph*, September 22, 2013, http://www.telegraph .co.uk/news/worldnews/africaandindianocean/kenya/10326863/Tweeting -terrorism-How-al-Shabaab-live-blogged-the-Nairobi-attacks.html; Christopher Anzalone, "The Nairobi Attack and Al-Shabab's Media Strategy," *CTC Sentinel*, October 24, 2013, https://www.ctc.usma.edu/posts/the-nairobi-attack-and-al -shababs-media-strategy.

32. Hayes Brown, "The Social Media Strategy Behind the Brutal Beheading of an American Journalist," *ThinkProgress*, August 20, 2014, http://thinkprogress .org/world/2014/08/20/3473447/isis-foley-syria; Lina Khatib, "What Is the Logic Behind Islamic State's Media Strategy?," *Hurst*, September 3, 2014, http:// www.hurstpublishers.com/islamic-state-media-strategy; Barak Mendelsohn, "Collateral Damage in Iraq," *Foreign Affairs*, June 15, 2014, https://www.foreign affairs.com/articles/iraq/2014-06-15/collateral-damage-iraq.

33. Brian Resnick, "The ISIS Conflict Has Saturated the American Mind," *National Journal*, October 2, 2014, http://www.nationaljournal.com/defense /the-isis-conflict-has-saturated-the-american-mind-20141002; Graeme Wood, "What ISIS Really Wants," *Atlantic*, March 2015, http://www.theatlantic.com /features/archive/2015/02/what-isis-really-wants/384980.

34. Michael Schmidt and Eric Schmitt, "U.S. Identifies Citizens Joining Rebels in Syria, Including ISIS," *New York Times*, August 28, 2014, http://www .nytimes.com/2014/08/29/world/middleeast/us-identifies-citizens-joining -rebels-in-syria.html; Richard Barrett, "Foreign Fighters in Syria," Soufan Group, June 2014, http://soufangroup.com/wp-content/uploads/2014/06 /TSG-Foreign-Fighters-in-Syria.pdf; Daniel Byman and Jeremy Shapiro, "Homeward Bound: Don't Hype the Threat of Returning Jihadists," *Foreign Affairs*, September/October 2014, http://www.foreignaffairs.com/articles/142025 /daniel-byman-and-jeremy-shapiro/homeward-bound; Eric Schmitt and Somini Sengupta, "Thousands Enter Syria to Join ISIS Despite Global Efforts," *New York Times*, September 26, 2015, http://www.nytimes.com/2015/09/27/world/middle east/thousands-enter-syria-to-join-isis-despite-global-efforts.html.

35. Sam Jones, "EU Proposes Terror Unit to Tackle Online Jihadis," *Financial Times*, March 11, 2015, http://www.ft.com/intl/cms/s/0/4d93b7f0-c804-11e4 -9226-00144feab7de.html#axzz3U9tILGE.

36. J. M. Berger, "Resistible Force Meets Movable Object," *Intelwire*, October 2, 2014, http://news.intelwire.com/2014/10/resistable-force-meets-movable-object.html; J. M. Berger and Jonathan Morgan, "The ISIS Twitter Census," Brookings Project on US Relations with the Islamic World, Brookings Institution, March 2015, http://www.brookings.edu/~/media/research/files/papers/2015/03/isis-twitter-census-berger-morgan/isis_twitter_census_berger_morgan.pdf.

37. Rick Noack, "How Twitter's Geolocation Settings Embarrassed the Taliban," *Washington Post*, October 6, 2014, http://www.washingtonpost.com/blogs/worldviews/wp/2014/10/06/how-twitters-geolocation-settings-embarrassed-the-taliban; Colin Daileda and Lorenzo Franceschi-Bicchierai, "U.S. Intelligence Officials Want ISIL Fighters to Keep Tweeting," *Mashable*, July 11, 2014, http://mashable.com/2014/07/11/us-wants-iraq-radicals-to-tweet.

38. Ellen Nakashima, "Dismantling of Saudi-CIA Web Site Illustrates Need for Clearer Cyberwar Policies," *Washington Post*, March 19, 2010, http://www.washingtonpost.com/wp-dyn/content/article/2010/03/18/AR2010031805464_pf.html.

39. Carl Bildt, Twitter post, November 19, 2014, 3:17 a.m., https://twitter.com/carlbildt/status/535029210918977536.

40. Mohammed El-Nawawy, "US Public Diplomacy in the Arab World: The News Credibility of Radio Sawa and Television Alhurra in Five Countries," *Global Media and Communication* 2, no. 2 (2006): 183–203, quoted in Lina Khatib, William H. Dutton, and Michael Thelwall, "Public Diplomacy 2.0: An Exploratory Case Study of the US Digital Outreach Team," *Middle East Journal* 66, no. 3 (summer 2012): 1–20.

41. Judith A. McHale, "Testimony as Nominee for Under Secretary for Public Diplomacy and Public Affairs," US Department of State, May 13, 2009, http://www.state.gov/r/remarks/2009/124155.htm.

42. Colleen Graffy, "The Rise of Public Diplomacy 2.0," *Journal of International Security Affairs*, no. 17 (fall 2009).

43. James K. Glassman, Under Secretary for Public Diplomacy and Public Affairs, "Public Diplomacy 2.0: A New Approach to Global Engagement," New America Foundation, December 1, 2008, http://2001-2009.state.gov/r/us/2008/112605.htm.

44. Jesse Lichtenstein, "Digital Diplomacy," *New York Times*, July 16, 2010, http://www.nytimes.com/2010/07/18/magazine/18web2-0-t.html.

45. "What They Said, Before and After the Attack in Libya," *New York Times*, September 12, 2012, http://www.nytimes.com/interactive/2012/09/12/us/politics/libya-statements.html.

46. Alexis Wichowski, "Social Diplomacy," *Foreign Affairs*, April 5, 2013, https://www.foreignaffairs.com/articles/2013-04-05/social-diplomacy.

47. Asawin Suebsaeng, "The State Department Is Actively Trolling Terrorists on Twitter," *Mother Jones*, March 5, 2014, http://www.motherjones.com/politics/2014/02/state-department-cscc-troll-terrorists-twitter-think-again-turn-away.

48. Office of the President, "National Strategy for Counterterrorism," White House, June 2011, https://www.whitehouse.gov/sites/default/files/counter terrorism_strategy.pdf.

49. "U.S. Launches Media Campaign to Counter ISIS Videos," *NPR*, September 21, 2014, http://www.npr.org/2014/09/21/350316009/u-s-launches-media -campaign-to-counter-isis-videos.

50. Silverman, "The State Department's Twitter Jihad."

51. Greg Miller and Scott Higham, "In a Propaganda War Against ISIS, the US Tried to Play by the Enemy's Rules," *Washington Post*, May 8, 2015, http://www .washingtonpost.com/world/national-security/in-a-propaganda-war-us-tried-to -play-by-the-enemys-rules/2015/05/08/6eb6b732-e52f-11e4-81ea-0649268f729e _story.html.

52. Salma Abdelaziz and Atika Shubert, "Syrian Activists Are Heckling ISIS Online," *CNN*, February 19, 2015, http://www.cnn.com/2015/02/18/middleeast /syria-isis-heckling; Alanna Petroff, "Hundreds of ISIS Social Media Accounts Shut Down," *CNN*, February 10, 2015, http://money.cnn.com/2015/02/10 /technology/anonymous-isis-hack-twitter.

53. Suebsaeng, "The State Department Is Actively Trolling Terrorists on Twitter."

54. Christian Rudder, "We Experiment on Human Beings!," *OkTrends*, July 28, 2014, http://blog.okcupid.com/index.php/we-experiment-on-human-beings; Adam D. I. Kramer, Jamie E. Guillory, and Jeffrey T. Hancock, "Experimental Evidence of Massive-Scale Emotional Contagion Through Social Networks," *PNAS* 111, no. 29 (July 2014): 8777–8790; Vindu Goel, "Facebook Tinkers with Users' Emotions in News Feed Experiment, Stirring Outcry," *New York Times*, June 29, 2014, http://www.nytimes.com/2014/06/30/technology/facebook -tinkers-with-users-emotions-in-news-feed-experiment-stirring-outcry.html; Josie Ensor, "Dating Site OKCupid Admits to Facebook-Style Psychological Testing on Users," *Telegraph*, July 29, 2014, http://www.telegraph.co.uk/news /worldnews/northamerica/usa/10996866/Dating-site-OKCupid-admits-to -Facebook-style-psychological-testing-on-users.html.

55. Zeynep Tufekci, "What Happens to #Ferguson Affects Ferguson: Net Neutrality, Algorithmic Filtering and Ferguson," *Medium*, August 14, 2014, https://medium.com/message/ferguson-is-also-a-net-neutrality -issue-6d2f3db51eb0; Gail Sullivan, "How Facebook and Twitter Control What You See About Ferguson," *Washington Post*, August 19, 2014, http://www .washingtonpost.com/news/morning-mix/wp/2014/08/19/how-facebook -and-twitter-control-what-you-see-about-ferguson.

56. Zeynep Tufekci, "Engineering the Public: Big Data, Surveillance and Computational Politics," *First Monday* 19, no. 7 (July 7, 2014), http://firstmonday.org /ojs/index.php/fm/article/view/4901/4097; Sascha Issenberg, "The Definitive Story of How President Obama Mined Voter Data to Win a Second Term," *MIT Technology Review*, December 19, 2012, http://www.technologyreview .com/featuredstory/509026/how-obamas-team-used-big-data-to-rally-voters.

57. Aram Roston, "Unwitting Sensors: How DoD Is Exploiting Social Media," *Defense News*, November 13, 2012, http://archive.defensenews.com/article /20121113/DEFREG02/311130003/Unwitting-Sensors-How-DoD-Exploiting -Social-Media; Kerry Davis, "Can the US Military Fight a War with Twitter?," *Computerworld*, November 8, 2012, http://www.computerworld.com/article /2493445/social-media/can-the-us-military-fight-a-war-with-twitter-.html.

58. "State Department Faces Criticism in Uphill Social Media War Against Islamic State Group," *Newshour*, PBS, October 22, 2014, http://www.pbs.org /newshour/bb/islamic-state-lures-teens-social-media.

CHAPTER 8: GEOPOLITICS STRIKES BACK: NATION-STATES
AND THE POLITICS OF INTERNET GOVERNANCE

1. Harold Trinkunas and Ian Wallace, *Converging on the Future of Global Internet Governance: The United States and Brazil*, Brookings Institution, July 2015, http:// www.brookings.edu/research/reports/2015/07/internet-governance-brazil -us-trinkunas-wallace.

2. Alberto Chong and Eliana La Ferrara, "Television and Divorce: Evidence from Brazilian Novelas," Inter-American Development Bank, January 2009, http://www.iadb.org/en/research-and-data/publication-details,3169.html?pub _id=WP-651; Cynthia Gorney, "Brazil's Girl Power," *National Geographic*, September 2011, http://ngm.nationalgeographic.com/2011/09/girl-power/gorney-text.

3. Jonathan Watts, "Avenida Brasil Clash Forces President to Cancel Rally," *Guardian*, October 18, 2012, http://www.theguardian.com/world/2012/oct/18 /avenida-brasil-clash-president-cancel-rally.

4. Barlow quoted in Julie Ruvolo, "Why Brazil Is Actually Winning the Internet," *BuzzFeed*, June 29, 2014, http://www.buzzfeed.com/jruv/why-brazil-is -actually-winning-the-internet.

5. "Rene Silva, Scribe of the Slums," *Christian Science Monitor*, January 9, 2012, http://www.csmonitor.com/World/2012/0109/Thirty-ideas-from-people -under-30-The-Social-Media-Stars/Rene-Silva-Scribe-of-the-slums; Flora Charner, "Community Media Makes Waves in Brazil Favelas," *Al Jazeera*, June 8, 2014, http://www.aljazeera.com/indepth/features/2014/06/community-media -makes-waves-brazil-favelas-201467114934619488.html.

6. CGI.br, "Principles for the Governance and Use of the Internet," NETmundial, 2009, http://content.netmundial.br/contribution/principles-for-the -governance-and-use-of-the-internet/266.

7. Joe Karaganis, *Media Piracy in Emerging Economies* (New York: Social Science Research Council, 2011), http://piracy.americanassembly.org/wp-content /uploads/2011/06/MPEE-PDF-1.0.4.pdf.

8. Ronaldo Lemos, "Brazilian Internet Needs Civil Regulatory Framework [Internet brasileira precisa de Marco Regulatório Civil]," *UOL*, May 22, 2007, http://tecnologia.uol.com.br/ultnot/2007/05/22/ult4213u98.jhtm; Juliana Nolasco Ferreira, "Building the Marco Civil: A Brief Review of Brazil's Internet Regulation History," in *Stakes Are High: Essays on Brazil and the Future of the*

Global Internet, ed. Ellery Roberts Biddle, Ronaldo Lemos, and Monroe Price, ITS Rio, April 2014, http://www.itsrio.org/wp-content/uploads/2014/04/Stakes AreHigh_BrazilNETmundial.pdf.

9. Ferreira, "Building the Marco Civil."

10. Vinton Cerf, interview, Reston, Virginia, Smithsonian Institution, April 24, 1990, http://americanhistory.si.edu/comphist/vc1.html.

11. Wolfgang Kleinwächter, "The History of Internet Governance," in *Governing the Internet: Freedom and Regulation in the OSCE Region*, ed. Christian Möller and Arnaud Amouroux (Vienna, Austria: Organization for Security and Cooperation in Europe, 2007), http://www.osce.org/fom/26169?download=true.

12. Abu-Ghazaleh quoted in Jennifer Schenker, "Nations Chafe at U.S. Influence over the Internet," *New York Times*, December 8, 2003, http://www.nytimes.com/2003/12/08/business/nations-chafe-at-us-influence-over-the-internet.html; Milton Mueller, *Networks and States: The Global Politics of Internet Governance* (Cambridge, MA: MIT Press, 2010), 59.

13. Lennard Kruger, "Internet Governance and the Domain Name System: Issues for Congress, " Congressional Research Service, June 24, 2015, http://www.fas.org/sgp/crs/misc/R42351.pdf; Frederick Kempe, "How the Web Was Run," *Wall Street Journal*, October 25, 2005, http://www.wsj.com/articles/SB113016040615477507.

14. Kieren McCarthy, "Read the Letter That Won the Internet Governance Battle," *Register*, December 2, 2005, http://www.theregister.co.uk/2005/12/02/rice_eu_letter; Miller quoted in "Who Should Control the Internet?," *Fox News*, November 10, 2005, http://www.foxnews.com/story/2005/11/10/who-should-control-internet.

15. Jo Twist, "Controversy Blights UN Net Summit," *BBC*, November 18, 2005, http://news.bbc.co.uk/2/hi/technology/4450474.stm.

16. Elliot Noss, "Perspective: A Battle for the Soul of the Internet," *CNET News*, June 8, 2005, quoted in Mueller, *Networks and States: The Global Politics of Internet Governance*, 10.

17. "World Conference on International Telecommunications: Remarks, Terry Kramer," US Department of State, December 13, 2012, http://www.state.gov/e/eb/rls/rm/2012/202040.htm.

18. Interview with Brazilian diplomat, Brasilia, May 13, 2013.

19. Kramer quoted in Eli Dourado, "Behind Closed Doors at the UN's Attempted 'Takeover of the Internet,'" *Ars Technica*, December 20, 2012, http://arstechnica.com/tech-policy/2012/12/behind-closed-doors-at-the-uns-attempted-takeover-of-the-internet.

20. Milton Mueller, "Greatest Threat to Internet: Governments," *SFGate*, July 20, 2012, http://www.sfgate.com/opinion/article/Greatest-threat-to-Internet-governments-3723621.php.

21. Glenn Greenwald, "The NSA's Mass and Indiscriminate Spying on Brazilians," *Guardian*, July 6, 2013, http://www.theguardian.com/commentisfree/2013/jul/07/nsa-brazilians-globo-spying; Larry Rohter, "Brazil Voices 'Deep

Concern' over Gathering of Data by U.S.," *New York Times*, July 7, 2013, http://www.nytimes.com/2013/07/08/world/americas/brazil-voices-deep-concern-over-gathering-of-data-by-us.html.

22. Daniel Trotta, "At U.N., Brazil's Rousseff Blasts U.S. Spying as Breach of Law," *Reuters*, September 24, 2013, http://www.reuters.com/article/2013/09/24/us-un-assembly-brazil-idUSBRE98N0OJ20130924.

23. "Statement by Dilma Rousseff, President of the Federative Republic of Brazil, at the Opening of the General Debate of the 68th Session of the United Nations General Assembly," United Nations, September 24, 2013, http://gadebate.un.org/sites/default/files/gastatements/68/BR_en.pdf.

24. Rousseff quoted in Daniel Kurtz-Phelan, "The World's Emerging Democracies Don't Like Us Either," *Time*, September 25, 2013, http://ideas.time.com/2013/09/25/the-worlds-emerging-democracies-dont-like-us-either.

25. Angelica Mari, "High Expectations for Brazil Undersea Cable to Europe," *ZDNet*, February 12, 2014, http://www.zdnet.com/article/high-expectations-for-brazil-undersea-cable-to-europe.

26. Interview with representative of the Brazilian tech industry, São Paulo, May 15, 2013; Interview, lawyer, São Paulo, February 4, 2014.

27. Lauren McCauley, "Brazil's 'Internet Bill of Rights' a Victory for Web Freedom," *Common Dreams*, April 23, 2014, http://www.commondreams.org/news/2014/04/23/brazils-internet-bill-rights-victory-web-freedom.

28. Interview with senior Itamaraty official, Brasilia, February 5, 2014.

29. Rousseff quoted in Vasudevan Sridharan, "Edward Snowden Fallout: Brazil to Host Global Anti-NSA Summit over Internet Surveillance," *International Business Times*, October 11, 2013, http://www.ibtimes.co.uk/nsa-edward-snowden-brazil-dilma-rousseff-summit-513085.

30. Interview with senior Itamaraty official, Brasilia, May 13, 2013.

31. National Telecommunications and Information Administration, "NTIA Announces Intent to Transition Key Internet Domain Name Functions," US Department of Commerce, March 14, 2014, http://www.ntia.doc.gov/press-release/2014/ntia-announces-intent-transition-key-internet-domain-name-functions.

32. L. Gordon Crovitz, "America's Internet Surrender," *Wall Street Journal*, March 18, 2014, http://www.wsj.com/news/articles/SB10001424052702303563304579447362610955656; John Shimkus, "Keeping the Internet Open and Free," US House of Representatives, http://shimkus.house.gov/media-center/opeds/keeping-the-internet-open-and-free.

33. Interview with senior Itamaraty official, Brasilia, March 5, 2014; Michael Daniel et al., "A Major Win for the Open Internet," *DIPNOTE*, April 29, 2014, https://blogs.state.gov/stories/2014/04/29/major-win-open-internet.

34. Dilma Rousseff, "NETmundial—Dilma Rousseff's Opening Speech," NETmundial, April 23, 2014, http://netmundial.br/wp-content/uploads/2014/04/NETMundial-23April2014-Dilma-Rousseff-Opening-Speech-en.pdf.

35. It was a high-level delegation, involving all the principals of US cyber policy: Michael Daniel, special assistant to the president and the cybersecurity

coordinator for the National Security Council; Larry Strickling, assistant secretary of commerce for communications and information; Chris Painter, coordinator for cyber issues in the State Department; Daniel Sepulveda, deputy assistant secretary of state and US coordinator for international communications and information policy; and Scott Busby, deputy assistant secretary of state in the Bureau of Democracy, Human Rights, and Labor. See Michael Daniel et al., "A Major Win for the Open Internet," *DIPNOTE*, April 29, 2014, https://blogs.state.gov/stories/2014/04/29/major-win-open-internet; "NETmundial Multistakeholder Statement," NETmundial, April 24, 2014, http://netmundial.br/wp-content/uploads/2014/04/NETmundial-Multistakeholder-Document.pdf.

36. Sean Gallagher, "Many New Top-Level Domains Have Become Internet's 'Bad Neighborhoods,'" *Ars Technica*, September 3, 2105, http://arstechnica.com/security/2015/09/many-new-top-level-domains-have-become-internets-bad-neighborhoods.

37. Samantha Power, "Remarks at the Internet Freedom Technology Showcase: The Future of Human Rights Online," City University of New York Graduate Center, New York, September 26, 2015, http://usun.state.gov/remarks/6836.

CHAPTER 9: AFTER PAX DIGITAL AMERICANA

1. Jessica Mathews, "Power Shift," *Foreign Affairs*, January/February 1997, https://www.foreignaffairs.com/articles/1997-01-01/power-shift.

2. "Freedom on the Net 2015," Freedom House, October 2015, https://freedomhouse.org/sites/default/files/FOTN%202015%20Full%20Report.pdf.

3. Leon Panetta, speech to Business Executives for National Security, New York, October 12, 2012, http://www.defensenews.com/article/20121012/DEFREG02/310120001/Text-Speech-by-Defense-U-S-Secretary-Leon-Panetta.

4. Hallman quoted in Patrick Tucker, "Meet the Man Reinventing for the Big Data Era," *Defense One*, October 1, 2015, http://www.defenseone.com/technology/2015/10/meet-man-reinventing-cia-big-data-era/122453.

5. Peter Swire, "The Declining Half Life of Secrets and the Future of Signals Intelligence," New America, July 23, 2015, https://www.newamerica.org/cybersecurity-initiative/the-declining-half-life-of-secrets; Bruce Schneier, "The Story Behind the Stuxnet Virus," *Forbes*, October 7, 2010, http://www.forbes.com/2010/10/06/iran-nuclear-computer-technology-security-stuxnet-worm.html; Kim Zetter, *Countdown to Zero Day: Stuxnet and the Launch of the World's First Digital Weapon* (New York: Crown, 2014).

6. Defense Science Board, "Task Force Report: Resilient Military Systems and the Advanced Cyber Threat," Office of the Under Secretary of Defense for Acquisition, Technology and Logistics, January 2013, http://www.acq.osd.mil/dsb/reports/ResilientMilitarySystems.CyberThreat.pdf.

7. John D. Negroponte, Samuel J. Palmisano, and Adam Segal, "Defending an Open, Global, Secure, and Resilient Internet," Council on Foreign Relations, June 2013, http://i.cfr.org/content/publications/attachments/TFR70_cyber_policy.pdf.pdf.

8. Danny Yardon, "Microsoft's Top Lawyer Says Company Must Weigh Encryption Limits," *Digits* (blog), *Wall Street Journal,* May 27, 2015, http://blogs .wsj.com/digits/2015/05/27/brad-smith-suggests-microsoft-might-obey-law -that-limits-encryption.

9. Office of the Press Secretary, "Remarks by President Barack Obama in Prague, White House, Prague, Czech Republic," April 5, 2009, https://www.white house.gov/the-press-office/remarks-president-barack-obama-prague-delivered.

10. James Clapper, "Worldwide Threat Assessment of the US Intelligence Community, Senate Armed Services Committee," February 26, 2015, http:// www.dni.gov/files/documents/Unclassified_2015_ATA_SFR_-_SASC_FINAL .pdf; Pricewaterhouse Coopers, 2015 US CEO Survey, http://www.pwc.com/us /en/ceo-survey/img/secure-assets-finding.pdf.

11. Mohana Ravindranath, "DOD's Current InfoSec Strategy Is 'Patch and Pray,'" Nextgov, October 1, 2015, http://www.defenseone.com/ideas/2015/10 /dods-current-infosec-strategy-patch-and-pray/122457/?oref=d-river.

12. "Verizon 2015 Data Breach Investigations Report," April 13, 2015, http:// news.verizonenterprise.com/2015/04/2015-data-breach-report-info/#report.

13. Adam Elkus, "The Devastating Breach of US Government Data Highlights an Illusory Cybersecurity Paradox," *Business Insider,* June 18, 2015, http://www.businessinsider.com/the-opm-breachs-cybersecurity-paradox -2015-6#ixzz3fsgCbLBT.

14. Rob Knake, "On Cyber Information Sharing, It's the Medium Not the Message," *Net Politics,* September 2, 2015, http://blogs.cfr.org/cyber/2015/09/02 /on-cyber-information-sharing-its-the-medium-not-the-message.

15. Clay Johnson and Harper Reed, "Why the Government Never Gets Tech Right," *New York Times,* October 24, 2013, http://www.nytimes.com/2013/10/25 /opinion/getting-to-the-bottom-of-healthcaregovs-flop.html.

16. Halvorsen quote from Sara Sorcher, "Pentagon's Top IT Official: My Money Buys Silicon Valley's Trust," *Christian Science Monitor,* October 29, 2015, http://www.csmonitor.com/World/Passcode/2015/1029/Pentagon -s-top-IT-official-My-money-buys-Silicon-Valley-s-trust.

17. Jack Moore, "The NSA's Fight to Keep Its Best Hackers," *Defense One,* April 16, 2015, http://www.defenseone.com/management/2015/04 /nsas-fight-keep-its-best-hackers/110401.

18. Catherine Rampill, "Immigration and Entrepreneurship," *Economix* (blog), *New York Times,* July 1, 2013, http://economix.blogs.nytimes.com/2013/07/01 /immigration-and-entrepreneurship.

INDEX

· ·

Adam Segal is the Maurice R. Greenberg Senior Fellow for China Studies and director of the Program on Digital and Cyberspace Policy at the Council on Foreign Relations (CFR). Before coming to the CFR, Dr. Segal was an arms-control analyst for the China Project at the Union of Concerned Scientists. There, he wrote about missile defense, nuclear weapons, and Asian security issues. He has been a visiting scholar at the Hoover Institution at Stanford University, Massachusetts Institute of Technology's Center for International Studies, the Shanghai Academy of Social Sciences, and the Tsinghua University in Beijing. He has taught at Vassar College and Columbia University. Dr. Segal is the author of *Digital Dragon: High-Technology Enterprises in China* (2003) and *Advantage: How American Innovation Can Overcome the Asian Challenge* (2011). His work has appeared in the *Economist*, the *Financial Times, Foreign Affairs, Foreign Policy*, and the *Wall Street Journal*, among other publications. He currently writes for the blog *Net Politics*. Dr. Segal has a BA and a PhD in government from Cornell University and an MA in international relations from the Fletcher School of Law and Diplomacy, Tufts University.